The Ambivalent Internet

The Ambivalent Internet

Mischief, Oddity, and
Antagonism Online

WHITNEY PHILLIPS and
RYAN M. MILNER

polity

First published in 2017 by Polity Press
Reprinted 2017, 2018, 2019, 2020

Polity Press
65 Bridge Street
Cambridge CB2 1UR, UK

Polity Press
350 Main Street
Malden, MA 02148, USA

ISBN-13: 978-1-5095-0126-7
ISBN-13: 978-1-5095-0127-4 (pb)

A catalog record for this book is available from the British Library.

Library of Congress Cataloging-in-Publication Data

Names: Phillips, Whitney, 1983- author. | Milner, Ryan M., author.
Title: The ambivalent Internet : mischief, oddity, and antagonism online / Whitney Phillips, Ryan M. Milner.
Description: Cambridge, UK ; Malden, MA : Polity Press, 2017. | Includes bibliographical references and index.
Identifiers: LCCN 2016047503 (print) | LCCN 2017004549 (ebook) | ISBN 9781509501267 (hardback) | ISBN 9781509501274 (pbk.) | ISBN 9781509501298 (Mobi) | ISBN 9781509501304 (Epub)
Subjects: LCSH: Internet–Social aspects.
Classification: LCC HM851 .P52 2017 (print) | LCC HM851 (ebook) | DDC 302.23/1–dc23
LC record available at https://lccn.loc.gov/2016047503

Typeset in 10.25 on 13 pt Scala
by Toppan Best-set Premedia Limited
Printed and bound in the United States by LSC Communications

For further information on Polity, visit our website:
politybooks.com

To Mulder & Scully

Contents

Acknowledgments

Our warmest thanks to Abby, Adrienne, Alice, April, Ashley, Bea, Becky, Biella, Brooke, Carl, Caroline, Cullen, Dave, Dave, David, David, Dennis, Elen, Ellen, Eric, Gabriel, Henry, Hilary, Jacob, Janet, Jason, Jean, John, Kaitlin, Kate, Kathy, Katie, Kevin, Keith, Leigh, Limor, Lisa, Lisa, Liza, Lynnika, Maple, Max, Michelle, Mike, Nancy, Pappaw, Patrick, Paul, Pearl, Sami, Sarah, Shira, Sophia, Stacy, Steve, Tim, TL, Wendy, and Wesley.

Introduction

Some initial oddities to set the scene

In the mid-aughts, a t-shirt company called The Mountain added a new item to their Amazon.com product page. Listed as Three Wolf Moon, this 100 percent cotton offering featured a mystical moon, glowing star nebula, and three vertically stacked wolf heads howling into the night. In November 2008, an Amazon reviewer using the handle Amazon Customer posted a review of the shirt. Review, however, doesn't quite capture it. Amazon Customer's assessment, entitled "Dual Function Design," was more like magical realist short fiction. First, he checked to see whether the shirt would properly cover his "girth." He then wandered from his trailer to the neighborhood Wal-Mart, where he was promptly flocked by women looking for love and, as he put it, "mehth." Once inside the Wal-Mart, he mounted a courtesy scooter "side saddle" to show off his wolves and was approached by a woman wearing sweatpants and flip-flops. She told him she liked his shirt and offered him a swig of her Mountain Dew. Amazon Customer attributed these exciting felicities to his wolf shirt, and concluded that, although the shirt was pretty sweet already, it would be better if the wolves glowed in the dark.

After being posted to Amazon, "Dual Function Design" was linked by an amused onlooker to the forums on BodyBuilding.com (a site devoted to exactly that, and, perhaps unexpectedly, a longstanding hotbed of various online shenanigans), and eventually to Facebook. As the Three Wolf Moon legend grew, more and more people began penning

their own *odes de wolf*, many of which lauded the shirt's aphrodisiacal, spiritual, and overall magical powers, including
the power of flight and reversing vasectomies. Countless
photoshopped versions of the shirt began to circulate – cataloging an exotic bestiary of sloths, sharks, camels, hippopotamuses, unicorns, hippopotamus unicorns, *Star Trek* captains,
Charlie Sheens, and Rowlf Muppets (Figure 1) – with a few
up for sale on Amazon as actual shirts. The Mountain itself
even got in on the joke, crafting and selling a parody shirt
featuring the popular internet meme "Grumpy Cat." Three
Wolf Moon reviews and parodies drew so much attention to
the shirt that in May 2009 it topped Amazon's top-selling
apparel list (Applebome 2009).

Figure 1. The Three Wolf Moon t-shirt alongside parody designs.
Left: the original sold on Amazon.com by t-shirt company The
Mountain. Top right: a design featuring hippopotamus unicorns.
Center right: a design featuring Rowlf from the Muppets franchise.
Bottom right: a design featuring Captain Jean-Luc Picard and
Commander William T. Riker from the television series *Star Trek:
The Next Generation*. Collected in 2015.

The person posting as Amazon Customer – who in 2009 outed himself to Peter Applebome of the *New York Times* as a 32-year-old law student from New Jersey – wasn't alone in his desire to bizarrely review a commercial product for laughs. Beyond Three Wolf Moon, there exists an entire genre of what the online reference site *Know Your Meme* calls "fake customer reviews," with Amazon serving as the nexus of such activities ("Fake Customer Reviews" 2015). The premise is simple: head to Amazon (or any other site that supports public-facing customer reviews), choose a strange product (or at least a product that can serve as a conduit for strangeness), and then post something that will highlight, criticize, or poke fun at said product. For instance, reviewing the Hutzler 571 Banana Slicer, reviewer IWonder offered "I would rate this product as just ok. It's kind of cheaply made. But it works better than the hammer I've been using to slice my bananas" ("Banana Slicer Reviews" 2015). Assessing a gallon of "Tuscan Whole Milk" up for sale on Amazon, reviewer Prof PD Rivers commented "I give this Tuscan Milk four stars simply because I found the consistency a little too 'milk-like' for my tastes" (Zeller 2006). And when the consumer plastics company BIC released a line of "Cristal For Her" ballpoint pens – i.e. pens for some reason designed specifically for women – reviewer E. Bradley gushed "I love BIC Cristal for Her! The delicate shape and pretty pastel colors make it perfect for writing recipe cards, checks to my psychologist (I'm seeing him for a case of the hysterics), and tracking my monthly cycle" (Zafar 2012). In these and other cases, the point is to harness customer review capabilities for a wholly unintended collective purpose: to make strangers laugh on the internet, or at least furrow their brow in consternation.

2013 was a big year for R&B artist Robin Thicke. That summer, the 36-year-old warbler took the music world by storm with his jaunty, sexually assaultive hit "Blurred Lines," in which Thicke croons about knowing his paramour "wants it" even though she has already indicated that she does not. Then came his infamous 2013 MTV Video Music Awards (VMAs) performance with then-20-year-old pop singer Miley Cyrus. During this performance, a scantily clad Cyrus rubbed herself all over Thicke, who grinded right back, smirking and sunglassed in a striped black-and-white zoot suit. Facing backlash for their performance, Thicke said he hadn't even noticed what Cyrus was doing. "That's all on her," he shrugged in an interview with talk show host Oprah Winfrey (Jefferson 2013).

In the year following the VMAs, Thicke navigated a very messy separation from his wife Paula Patton, whom he attempted to win back in a series of public reconciliation attempts. Thicke's efforts culminated in 2014's highly confessional (and accusatory, and salacious) *Paula*, a record that critic Sophie Gilbert (2014) described as "one of the creepiest albums ever made." In the run-up to the album's release, Thicke teamed up with music television channel VH1 for some interactive promotion via Twitter. Fans were encouraged to use the hashtag #AskThicke to do exactly that: ask Thicke questions about his upcoming album. Instead, Thicke hecklers, feminist critics, and other amused onlookers inundated Thicke with antagonistic messages decrying everything from his seemingly permissive attitude toward sexual assault to what was deemed "stalkerish" behavior towards his estranged wife. Nestled alongside pointed cultural critiques were more (apparently) tongue-in-cheek assessments of Thicke's VMA wardrobe; many participants tweeted, retweeted, and giddily commented on comparison photos of Thicke and Beetlejuice, the iconic stripy-suited film character who is, by his own insistence, "the ghost with the most" (Parkinson 2014).

#AskThicke was, in other words, a disaster for Thicke and VH1. But it wasn't the first or the last time a celebrity, company, or organization would court public participation and walk away with a wounded brand. In the wake of his ever-lengthening list of rape accusations, for example, disgraced comedian Bill

Cosby invited his followers to "meme him" on Twitter, and included a link to a meme generator featuring a photo series ready for captioning. The response was swift; participants began flooding the #CosbyMeme hashtag with images designed to humiliate Cosby one punchline at a time (Arthur 2014). In similarly ill-advised fashion, McDonald's encouraged patrons to share feel-good dining experiences with the hashtag #McDStories, but instead were inundated with increasingly outrageous tales of fast food grotesquerie (Sherman 2012). The New York Police Department's #myNYPD (Jackson and Foucault Welles 2015), Donald Trump's #AskTrump (Lapowsky 2015a), and Fox News' #OverIt2014 (Harrison 2014) all experienced a similar fate, yielding an overwhelming percentage of caustic, comedic, and at times outright bizarre responses. These and other cases suggest that if you want to extend an olive branch on the internet, don't slap a hashtag to the front.

In May 2015, the Facebook fan page of an infamous American cultural figure was graced with yet another swooning tribute image. Edited in Blingee, a now-defunct online platform that allowed users to add sparkly animations and graphics to uploaded photos, the image features a grinning white teenager tagged with stamps reading "perfection," "my love," and "sexy," as well as animated kisses and hearts. The teenager in the photo is Columbine High School shooter Eric Harris; the Facebook fan page was dedicated to him. In another image posted to microblogging platform Tumblr, the yearbook pictures of Eric Harris and second gunman Dylan Klebold are decorated with hearts and captions. Dylan's images are captioned with the inscriptions "cute but psycho" and "3000%," while Harris' images are captioned with "now real life has no appeal" and another "psycho" (this one inscribed in cartoon hearts). Harris and Klebold are both wearing photoshopped princess flower crowns.

Andrew Ryan Rico (2015) analyzes these and other apparently laudatory images in his exploration of the online fandom surrounding the Columbine High School shooters. As Rico explains, he is interested in the "dark side" of fandom, and foregrounds how these and other images allow fans to express sympathy for and sexual attraction to Harris and Klebold, and provide an outlet to explore complex feelings about death. If that's what these fans are actually doing, of course; Rico concedes that some of these images may also be works of irony, hyperbole, and mischief.

Just looking at the images themselves, it's difficult to know what the posters were hoping to accomplish. What is clear is that spree killers, particularly in the post-Columbine, social networking age, have elicited a great deal of ambiguous online participation. Following the 2012 Aurora, Colorado, movie theatre shootings, for example, *BuzzFeed*'s Ryan Broderick (2012) discovered a tumblog (an individual blog on Tumblr) featuring fan art dedicated to the shooter James Holmes. These images – created by a very small group of self-described "Holmies" – were similar in tone and content to the Columbine shooter adoration described above. They also made celebratory reference to the plaid jacket James Holmes had been wearing at the time of his arrest, as well as his apparent love of slurpees. Disgusted, Broderick published an article featuring the best (that is to say, the worst) examples he could find. This, in turn, resulted in an explosion of media interest and attention, which in turn resulted in a great deal of antagonistic play with the emergent Holmies phenomenon (Phillips 2012). A similar narrative unfolded following the arrests of Boston Bomber Dzhokhar Tsarnaev (Read 2013) and the Norwegian right-wing extremist mass shooter Anders Behring Breivik (Flavia 2012). In these and other cases, the question of "is this a joke or are these people serious?" is a common refrain amongst journalists and citizens alike.

Ambivalence and the internet

For those familiar with the, let's say, *unique* contours of collective online spaces like Twitter, YouTube, Tumblr, Reddit, and 4chan – and before that, subversive alt.* Usenet bulletin boards, LiveJournal blogs, various shock forums, and other early sites rife with playful participation – the above examples probably won't seem all that shocking or unusual. The question is – and this was the question that initially piqued our research interests – exactly how might one assess these sorts of behaviors? Or more basically, how might one describe them? What words should one even use?

Before we zero in on our chosen explanatory lens for this book (spoiler: it's ambivalence), we want to address two descriptors that are commonly used to label cases like those above: that they are examples of *online trolling* or that they are artifacts from the *weird internet*. On the surface, both options seem like intuitive choices, particularly because both of us (Phillips and Milner, nice to meet you) have written quite a bit about both. But neither framing adequately subsumes the examples or arguments presented in this book.

First, as many readers likely know, online behaviors with even the slightest whiff of mischief, oddity, or antagonism are often lumped under the category of *trolling*. Though specific definitions of the term can vary, its use tends to imply deliberate, playful subterfuge, and the infliction of emotional distress on unwitting or unwilling audiences. Each of the cases that opened this book could be read through this lens; in fact, in popular press and academic coverage, all were explicitly described as "trolling," and often in the story lede. Based on these framings, it would appear that trolls are everywhere, doing everything – even when the behaviors are only loosely related, or even outright incompatible. Like writing a satirical Amazon review and tweeting deadly serious, firsthand accounts of police brutality. Or posting thoughtful feminist critiques of rape culture and mocking someone's sunglasses. Or photoshopping one of the Muppets and photoshopping a mass murderer. All, apparently, trolling, at least if the headlines are to be believed.

As illustrated by the above examples, "trolling" as a behavioral catch-all is imprecise and, in terms of classification, ultimately unhelpful. Further, as it often posits a playful or at least performative intent ("I'm not a *real* racist, I just play one on the internet"), the term also tends to minimize the negative effects of the worst kinds of online behaviors. Hence our decision to minimize its use throughout this book.[1] Other vague linguistic framings akin to trolling – like "hating/haters" (slang implying that someone on the internet dislikes something and says so with varying degrees of virulence) or, even more nebulously, "just joking around" – are similarly imprecise and similarly unhelpful, and therefore similarly sidestepped in this analysis.

What is needed, instead, is a framing that addresses the underlying tonal, behavioral, and aesthetic characteristics of these kinds of cases. The most obvious option is that they are, well, pretty weird. Or at least are the sort of things that inspire a brow furrow, confused chuckle, or maybe both. The presumption of the weirdness of digital content ("…what did I just see?") is common in some online circles, and the "weird internet" is foregrounded as a discursive space with its own absurd logics and twisted norms. Journalist Eric Limer (2013) exemplifies this assumption when he casually notes that "weird" online content outnumbers "normal" content at a 2:1 ratio. Limer's point, uncontested by his article's commenters, is seemingly evidenced by phenomena like "rule 34," a common online axiom asserting only somewhat jokingly that if something exists online, there is porn of it. Limer's "weirdness" framing is also underscored by the assertion (again only somewhat joking) that the internet is, in fact, "made of cats," given their predominance in images and videos shared on various forums and social networks.

Researchers have also explored the apparent weirdness of online spaces. In his discussion of the spread of global internet memes, for example, internet activist and media scholar Ethan Zuckerman (2013) takes for granted – and in fact celebrates – the transglobal weirdness of memetic content. Similarly, media critic Nick Douglas (2014) traces the rise of what he loosely describes as "Internet Ugly" on the English-speaking web, an aesthetic privileging absurdist, ambiguous, and poorly made content, which he argues is pervasive online. Even scholars who don't use *weird* specifically often point to the prevalence of silliness, satire, and mischief in online spaces, as participatory media scholar Tim Highfield does in his study of what he calls "the irreverent internet" (2016, 42), and as we both have done in our respective studies of subcultural trolling and memetic media (Phillips 2015; Milner 2016). The topic of online weirdness is so resonant amongst academics that it inspired a "Weird Internet" panel at the 2015 Association of Internet Researchers meeting in Phoenix, Arizona. We presented on that panel alongside digital media scholars Adrienne Massanari, Shira Chess, and Eric Newsom; as we crafted our submission proposal, the deceptively straightforward question of what "weird" even means online precipitated a 51-email thread hashing out the issue.

But as with trolling, the reality of the "weird internet" is more complicated than a singular descriptor. Regardless of how weird or irreverent certain corners of the internet might seem to some, weirdness is a relative term; what might be indescribably weird to one person is just a Tuesday afternoon for another. The three cases that opened this book may be "weird" in that they subvert some audience members' expectations (i.e. that customer reviews, celebrity Q&As, and fannish fawning should be earnest expressions of sincere intentions), but are sensical to those who regard this subversion as entirely the point. *Normal* by their own standards, if not always laudable by the standards of others. Even participants who concede that their behavior is indeed weird (whatever that term might mean to them) may embrace this weirdness as a point of amusement or pride, perhaps echoing the kinds of responses proffered by confused bystanders. Something punctuated with a quick "lol," which someone might mean literally (they actually laughed), metaphorically (they're referring to the platonic ideal of laughter), or ironically (they didn't laugh). Or some silly emoji combination, including, perhaps, an upside down smiley face coupled with cartoon pile of poo. Or even a "shruggie," the emoticon gracing the cover of this book, which functions, variously, as a way to signal "I don't know," "I don't care," or, as *The Awl* writer Kyle Chayka notes (2014), as "a Zen-like tool to accept the chaos of the universe." The variety of reactions to (presumed) weirdness is endless, and often inscrutable – even to those producing that presumed weirdness.

The fact that such expression can inspire divergent responses in divergent audiences – just as behaviors described as trolling can erroneously subsume divergent practices with divergent ends – highlights a more fundamental characteristic of our leading examples, and in fact of all the cases present in this book: they are *ambivalent*. Simultaneously antagonistic and social, creative and disruptive, humorous and barbed, the satirization of products, antagonization of celebrities, and creation of questionable fan art, along with countless other examples that permeate contemporary online participation, are too unwieldy, too variable across specific cases, to be essentialized as *this* as opposed to *that*. Nor can they be pinned to one singular purpose. Because they are not singular; they inhabit, instead, a full spectrum of purposes – all depending on who is participating, who is observing, and what set of assumptions each person brings to a given interaction.

This polysemous framing directly reflects the Latinate prefix of *ambivalent* (*ambi-*), which means "both, on both sides," implying tension, and often fraught tension, between opposites – despite the fact that in everyday usage, the word *ambivalent* is often used as a stand-in for "I don't have an opinion either way," sometimes stylized as the blasé "meh." It should be emphasized – neon-flashing-lights emphasized – that our usage of the term reflects the "both, on both sides" use, not the blasé sense of indifference. This book is full of cases that could go either way, in fact could go any way simultaneously, immediately complicating any easy assessment of authorial intent, social consequence, and cultural worth.

Satirical play with the Three Wolf Moon t-shirt, for example, could be read as simple collective fun. But as evidenced by Amazon Customer's initial review – and the dozens of similarly framed reviews that followed – this fun hinged on ridiculing the shirt and its buyers' presumed "white trash" lifestyle and aesthetic. Some of these participants may have set out to sincerely mock the lives of low income white individuals. Some may have set out to celebrate these lives, or to signal what they regard as "white trash solidarity." In other cases of fake customer reviews, participants, observers, or even targets might regard the behaviors as harmless fun, even as the behaviors meet the criteria of what media scholar Ian Bogost (2016) calls "weaponized subversion" directed at independent businesspersons just trying to sell their banana slicers.

Some of these reviews, including those apparently undertaken in the spirit of mere silliness, may even serve valuable public ends. Feminist satirizations of BIC's "Cristal For Her" pens, for example, call attention to sexist delineations between the things women do and the (ahem, presumably) "real" work done by men – an especially notable point to make when those things are *exactly* the same, like using a damn BIC pen. Similarly, one could distill meaningful feminist critiques of rape culture from the #AskThicke Q&A, though maybe not so easily from comments making fun of Thicke's Beetlejuice wardrobe or Ken doll hair or how he stands like a mannequin or his musical talent more generally (then again, maybe so). Even playful fawning over mass shooters could be seen from several co-occurring vantage points, from excessive attachment to excessive dissociation to a pointed satire of the idolatrous 24-hour news coverage that invariably follows American mass shootings. Maybe the people who post Columbine sweetheart photos are just assholes. Maybe all of the above.

The purpose of this book is to explore these layers of polysemy, a "both, on both sides" that becomes "all, on all sides" thanks to the vast constellations of participants and perspectives constituting digital media. Its contribution lies in this explicit focus on the fundamental ambivalence of digitally mediated expression. Previous studies have, of course, explored ambivalent behaviors; anthropologist Gabriella Coleman's (2014) analysis of the loose hacker and trolling collective Anonymous, feminist media scholar Adrienne Massanari's (2015) study of participatory play on the massive content aggregation site Reddit, Highfield's (2016) previously mentioned exploration of political participation online, and many others, all critically engage with behaviors that could, and do, go either way. Here, we seek to explore the underlying thread of ambivalence that weaves together so many of these and other online communities, interactions, and practices.

Dirt work and the "so what?" question

So the internet is ambivalent. Who cares? What's so important about ambivalence, and why have we chosen to write a book about the subject? More importantly, why would you, our esteemed readers, bother reading a book about it?

The short answer is that, as a mode of being and engaging, ambivalence is every bit as revealing as it is opaque. Most notably, ambivalent behaviors call attention to socially constructed distinctions between "normal" and "aberrant." Mary Douglas (1966) explores a similar notion in her analysis of dirt and taboo. As Douglas argues, the concept of dirt – which she famously describes as "matter out of place" (44) – only makes sense in relation to the concept of cleanliness. Clean comes first; dirt comes second, and is what sullies the clean. Based on this reasoning, one surefire way to reconstruct a specific culture's value system is to unpack what that particular culture regards as dirty, i.e. strange, abnormal, or taboo. Similarly, weirdness can only exist in relation to existing norms. Close analyses of (what are regarded as) non-normative, liminal, or otherwise just plain weird cultural elements can therefore reveal, and in many cases complicate, exactly the opposite – elements that are taken as a given. Preferred elements, normal elements. At least, what that particular culture or community deems normal, allowing for the possibility that one group's normal is another group's weird.

Or the possibility that the norms are themselves quite weird, as Phillips (2015) argues in her exploration of subcultural trolls. As she notes, although these self-identifying trolls' antagonistic behaviors are often framed as aberrational, in reality they replicate many cultural motifs and logics – the privileging of rationality over sentimentality, media sensationalism, and chest-thumping American exceptionalism, to name a few – that are regarded as commonplace and even desirable in ostensibly non-trolling contexts. Similarly, as matter out of place (at least for confused bystanders), the cases that opened this book illustrate as much about common expectations surrounding earnest communication, proper interaction, and sincere emotion online as they do about the form and function of irony, subversion, and play.

In this way, ambivalence collapses and complicates binaries within a given tradition. Not just between normal and abnormal, but, as we'll see in the chapters to follow, between then and now, online and offline, and constitutive and destructive. Studies of ambivalence, in turn, can shine a light on the tangled, messy binary breakdown both precipitating and resulting from everyday expression.

Building on the "dirt work" afforded by ambivalence, these expressive behaviors also butt up against – and therefore help to call attention to – issues related to power, voice, and access, for better or for worse. Or perhaps more accurately, for better *and* for worse. On the one hand, communication that is social *and* antagonistic can silence or otherwise minimize diverse public participation by alienating, marginalizing, or mocking those outside the knowing ingroup. On the other hand – as the *ambi* in *ambivalent* might predict – that same alienating, marginalizing, and mocking communication can also provide an outlet for historically underrepresented populations to speak truth to power. Women, queer people, trans people, people of color, people with disabilities, and members of economically disenfranchised populations – whose voices have historically been undervalued or muted – can thus push back against regressive hegemonic forces, and engage in assertive, confrontational, and empowering expression.

In short, the same behaviors that can wound can be harnessed for social justice. By embracing this ambivalence, essentially by saying yes to each fractured binary, one is better able to track who is pushing back against whom, and to thoughtfully consider the political and ethical stakes on a case-by-case basis. For example, who is speaking, who is listening, and who is refusing to engage? Are members of the dominant group targeting members of historically underrepresented groups ("punching down"), perpetuating even greater marginalization? Are members of historically underrepresented groups targeting members of the dominant group ("punching up"), in the process challenging structural inequalities between races, genders, and classes? What precipitated the behaviors, and what is at stake for whom? Perhaps most importantly, who might be empowered to speak more freely as a result, and who might be alienated, silenced, or shamed? There can be no justice without these answers, and there can be no answers without the right questions. By not filling in any of the relevant blanks, ambivalent behavior forces us to consider each situation on its own terms – in the process providing the necessary building blocks for critical, ethical thinking.

Situating the study

In order to contextualize ambivalent online participation, this book engages with an overlapping spectrum of social sciences, humanities, and cultural studies approaches. It's especially steeped in folklore, Phillips' specialization, and communication, Milner's specialization. This is a natural combination, as both disciplines are concerned, first and foremost, with human expression, whether creative, interpersonal, or political. And both disciplines investigate this expression through complementary lenses: folklore through the lens of tradition, and communication through the lens of interaction. Even as we consider technologies, platforms, and infrastructures, the social and cultural dimensions of mediated interaction will therefore be our principal emphases.

These lenses are also broader and older than the internet, and we will draw from that lineage even as we explore emergent digital media. To that point, some readers might be surprised by the number of embodied and mass media examples (i.e. "offline" examples, though the online/offline binary is one we will complicate) in a book titled *The Ambivalent Internet*. But these examples are critical to understanding why and how the contemporary internet is so overrun with ambivalent expression. In fact, without considering the through line between then and now, embodied and digitally mediated, it is impossible to assess the extent to which these behaviors are, in fact, "new," and, further, what difference that distinction might make. As we will see time and again in the chapters that follow, these lines are often quite fuzzy.

Our opening case studies point to this blur. Amazon Customer's Three Wolf Moon review, for example, may depend on digital communication platforms and tools, but the underlying stereotypes he draws from have a long history in embodied spaces. Likewise, the issues foregrounded in much of the antagonistic commentary directed to the #AskThicke hashtag speak to very embodied and very persistent issues of sexual violence and rape culture. And regardless of what the underlying motivations of (professed) online fans of spree killers might be, their behaviors are highly precedented; as we'll see in the following chapter, ambivalent play with death and disaster has been so pervasive for so long that it is almost expected following mass mediated tragedy. As these and other examples illustrate, established traditions precede and contextualize even the strangest, most absurd, and most apparently emergent online behavior. The older, embodied world outside the networks, protocols, and platforms colloquially framed as "the internet" is therefore essential to understanding emergent online ambivalence.

At the same time, the affordances of digital media change the ethical stakes and even some basic behavioral and aesthetic dimensions of everyday expression. Specifically, they throw already-existing ambivalence into hyperdrive. Certain ambivalent behaviors – satirizing brands, mocking celebrities, joking about tragedy – are certainly possible in embodied spaces, and may have ample precedent. But they can't be amplified as quickly to as many people, with as many possible repercussions, as behavior online – even when these behaviors are directly analogous or outright identical to pre-internet behaviors. The following chapters will focus on the hyperdrive ushered in by the tools of digital mediation, and will consider the ethical and political stakes of the ambivalence specific to online spaces. And yet we will continue to consider old alongside new, then alongside now, analog alongside digital. It's a brave new world, we will argue, and there is nothing new under the sun; and only by embracing this ambivalence can any of us hope to successfully navigate the contemporary digital media landscape.

Our focus on the social and cultural significance of online ambivalence also guides our selection of case studies. By and large, we have confined our analysis to examples embedded within North American cultural contexts, particularly the United States. This does not guarantee, of course, that these examples – and their various iterations – were created by US citizens, nor that they circulated exclusively within US borders. It does mean, however, that the examples spread in English, and are reflective of an American, or at least a broadly Western, perspective.

We populate this book with examples hailing from our own cultural tradition not because we feel that the American tradition is the pinnacle of human culture (lest anyone forget, we are the great nation that brought the world President Donald J. Trump), or because we have forgotten that there's a little place called "the rest of the planet." But rather because participatory content is so densely referential, so tethered to dominant ideology and social mores, that to step outside our own tradition – particularly when the whole purpose of our analysis is to illuminate collapsed binaries within mainstream discourse – would be to risk misrepresentation at best and colonialist appropriation at worst. We are not, in other words, the right people to assess the overall coherence of value systems and cultural traditions with which we are not intimately familiar (Trump, though – we're on it).

A great deal of this work is being done by those who are, however; there is a growing corpus of work focused on ambivalent – often humorous – behavior in non-Western contexts, just as there are a number of studies focused on specific instances of ambivalence in the US and other points West. Mohamed M. Helmy and Sabine Frerichs (2013), for example, describe protest humor during the 2011 Egyptian Revolution as both shield and sword, a point Katy Pearce and Adnan Hajizada (2014) echo in their analysis of the subversive and oppressive potential of internet memes deployed by citizens and co-opted by authorities in Azerbaijan. Similarly, speaking about Turkey's 2013 Gezi Park protests, Mahiye Seçil Dağtas argues that political humor can be both "emancipatory and disciplinary, unifying as well as exclusive and divisive" (2016, 13). But like their Western-focused counterparts, these studies focus on specific bounded events and communities, not ambivalence *as such*. Ultimately, this is our theoretical contribution to the conversation, one that, ideally, future researchers will be able to apply to the vast number of cultures and communities we have not directly engaged.

Chapter overview and a note on tone

Each of the following five chapters explores a prominent category of online participation: folkloric expression, identity play, constitutive humor, collective storytelling, and public debate. Anchoring ambivalent online behaviors to lineages of everyday folk expression, the chapter order moves from the intimately individual (vernacular and identity expression) to the collectively social (shared jokes and stories) to the massively public (wide-scale debate). So while each chapter focuses on its own slice of online ambivalence, each works in concert to paint an increasingly comprehensive picture of the ambivalent internet.

Each chapter opens by situating the chapter topic historically, introducing key concepts and arguments. This overview is followed by a discussion of the fundamental ambivalence of the chapter's focus. The second half of the chapter focuses specifically on the digitally mediated landscape, beginning with a discussion of the continuities between eras and degrees of mediation. It is, after all – and as noted above – impossible to fully understand or appreciate what's *new* without having a solid foundation in what *was*. The chapter then considers digital divergences, i.e. how the affordances of digital media change the ethics, politics, and even basic logistics of these highly precedented behaviors. Ambivalence "dirt work" is woven throughout each section, revealing the binaries that are collapsed and the norms that are complicated when ambivalence is placed in full context. The conclusion applies each chapter's dirt work to a final case study, providing a guide for future digging.

As this chapter overview and overall introduction indicates, the basic ethos of this book is itself ambivalent; it embraces liminality, is peppered with caveats, and generally refuses to fully commit to *this* versus *that*. Not from lack of conviction – our feminist and critical orientations, for example, will be unabashedly forwarded in the pages to follow – but because the behaviors, communities, and content we're describing exist in a constant state of flux. And there's no point in trying to build a wall around a verb, which is precisely how we've approached each of our body chapters: as verbs to be played with and explored.

We are also playing with tone. This is an academic book, and we are both scholars. There will be endnotes and theory and various outcroppings of requisite nerdery. But beyond our titles, we are, first and foremost, people: two separate people with two sets of experiences, senses of humor, and aesthetics. Simultaneously, our identities – both US citizens, both white, both Millennials in our early thirties, both cis-gendered, and both weaned on similar slices of American popular culture – situate our respective experiences within a much broader cultural context. These experiences inform the way we speak, the jokes we make, the media texts we enjoy, and, much more basically, the way we see the world. And of course, directly influence our relationship to and interest in the subject of this book.

Reflecting the tension between the individual and the collective – which we'll continue discussing throughout each chapter – we, singular and plural, will be present in the argument throughout; our collaborative voice is the intertwine of two different voices. Which we use, fairly frequently, to break the academic fourth wall. Sometimes to affirm a theoretical concept, perhaps by presenting a personal experience or first-person exemplar. Sometimes to complicate a theoretical concept, perhaps by illustrating how, actually, that's not how we've seen things done, that's not how we ourselves have done things. Sometimes to indicate that we, as scholars, feel ambivalently about the ambivalent texts and traditions that we, as people, have personally engaged with and enjoyed. Making the book a kind of autoethnographic remix; a study that coolly stands apart from and defiantly inhabits the worlds it describes.

And with that we begin our exploration of the ambivalent internet, of the weird and mean and in-between that characterizes so much of what media scholar Jean Burgess (2007) calls "vernacular creativity," the everyday creative expressions of everyday cultural participants. The result, we hope, is a fuller and more holistic understanding of the vast spectrum of ambivalent texts, traditions, and behaviors that defy even the most thoughtful attempts to declare *"this is what that means."* As we will show, there are no simple answers to forward. There are only ambivalent answers; ever-shifting, self-canceling truths. But that's fine. In fact, it serves as a reminder that here be monsters – so watch your step, and whatever you do, don't get too comfortable.

1

Folkloric Expression

Long before either of us were internet scholars, long before either of us even knew what a scholar was, we were students of everyday folk expression. We wouldn't be the people we are today, and certainly not the scholars we are today, if folkloric expression hadn't so fundamentally shaped our humor, our values, and our basic understanding of the world. Similarly, online ambivalence would be a pale shadow of itself without folklore to blur so many normative boundaries.

This chapter will chronicle these blurred boundaries, emphasizing the overlap between then and now, formal and folk, and commercial and populist. It will focus most intently on then and now, connecting dirty limericks, high school hijinks, saucy photocopier art, Facebook antagonisms, laughter at tragedy, and a fun fellow named Uncle Dolan. As we'll see, every shared meme, every dark joke, every photoshopped image sexually corrupting a beloved children's icon, is a bridge between past and present, pre- and post-internet. Understanding the newest of the new necessitates tracing these connections; new dirt from old soil.

In addition to emphasizing continuity, the chapter will also emphasize divergence. This divergence can be attributed, first and foremost, to the affordances of digital mediation: modularity, modifiability, archivability, and accessibility in particular. These affordances accelerate familiar embodied ambivalence, immediately complicating ethical assessment and even basic classification of digitally mediated content. Irony can be especially difficult to parse from earnestness online, and problematic perspectives can be amplified just as easily as

pro-social ones. These new contours coexist alongside all that
has come before, a point of ambivalence that will underscore
each of the subsequent chapters.

The essentials of folklore

Some of Milner's earliest exposure to ambivalent folkloric
expression occurred during adolescence. When he came of
age around 12, he was permitted to join the men on his mom's
side of the family for their annual male bonding fishing trip.
Although not much one for fishing (or rigid gender segrega-
tion), Milner nonetheless enjoyed his nights around the fire
year after year in rural Missouri, trading jokes and stories as
the Jack Daniels flowed and the conversations grew more
ribald. Milner and his cousins were interrogated by various
uncles and fathers about their moral purity; those same uncles
and fathers then happily told story after story undercutting
their *own* moral purity. Barbs were traded about love, politics,
and "just what kind of bullshit" Milner's brother Eric had
added to the night's playlist of background music. On these
nights, Milner often found himself laughing along with the
family, despite some of the troubling commentary being
shared. And by the time Pappaw – mostly drunk and mostly
toothless – began to recite from Uncle Dave's hallowed dirty
limerick book, Milner was reciting right along: "There once
was a fellow named Skinner, who took a young lady to
dinner..."

   Phillips' introduction to folkloric ambivalence corresponded
with her burgeoning and now decades-long friendship with
fellow weirdo Katie – or as 12-year-old Phillips called her for
reasons neither can remember, "Bob" (Phillips, for similarly
nebulous reasons, was "Artie"). The two would spend their
all-day Saturday track meets giggling at stories from the *Weekly
World News*, a campy tabloid featuring accounts of Bat Children,
toilets haunted by plumbers' ghosts, and socialites impreg-
nated by Bigfoot, among countless other gems of anti-

journalism. They would also play pranks like tying a dollar bill to fishing wire, setting the bait, then tugging it away when someone would bend down for a pick-up (Phillips thinks this was something they learned from *The Simpsons*). And then there were their ongoing adventures with various adult enemies at meets and during practice, which they would chronicle in their self-published (that is to say, hand-drawn and shown to their mothers) newspaper, *The Larry Times* (don't ask); targets included a heartless fiend they dubbed "Achum," somebody's cranky mother who passed out jelly beans after practice and would squirrel away all the delicious reds for herself (Achum's name was derived from the sound the two assumed she made when she ate them).

To those who presume, as many people do, that folklore is comprised of "old stuff" like fairy tales, traditional dances, and spoken word performances, Milner's example might seem more obviously folkloric. It takes place around a campfire, involves alcohol and the spontaneous recitation of poetry, features an older generation bestowing dubious wisdom onto the younger generation, is vaguely ritualistic, and is gender-segregated (*rude*, Phillips snorts). Phillips' example, conversely, might not seem folkloric at all. It's restricted to inside jokes between two friends (and their bemused mothers), engages with mass media, and trades "traditional" locations like a campfire for youth track meets and practices. But both Phillips' and Milner's examples are folkloric, and understanding why is the first step in understanding the folkloric dimensions of ambivalent expression online.

The first point to mention is that there's no inherent rule that folk expression must consist of "old stuff." Rather than solely investigating the past, the discipline of folklore is concerned more broadly with the relationship between the *folk* – which prominent folklorist Alan Dundes famously described as "any group of people whatsoever who share at least one common factor" (1980, 6) – and their *lore*. Lore (also known as "folklore," like the discipline itself) is a fraught concept, but broadly defined consists of expressive creations (Radner 1993), expressive phenomena (Toelken 1996), and, perhaps most simply, the "stuff that people share" (Howard, quoted in Owens 2013) within a particular cultural circumstance. As Trevor J. Blank (2013) notes, this circumstance needn't necessarily span vast stretches of time, although of course it can. What matters most is that these expressions communicate "consistencies that allow a person or group to perceive expressions as traditional, locally derived, or community generated" (xiv). Both Milner's and Phillips' examples meet these criteria; each story revolves around a stable (if small) group with many factors in common, and each is steeped in consistent, locally derived traditions that in both cases have persisted for decades.

But tradition isn't folklore's only focus. Augmenting (and complicating) this focus, the discipline also foregrounds what Jan Harold Brunvand (2001) calls "multiple variation": the transformation of familiar expressions as they spread through new moments and audiences. Barre Toelken (1996) describes this process using the twin laws of *conservatism* and *dynamism*. As Toelken explains, conservative folkloric elements are stable; they are the aspects of a particular tradition that are passed down from generation to generation. Dynamic elements are those that evolve over time, and allow participants to personalize an event or behavior while still maintaining ties to tradition. Both Milner's and Phillips' experiences are underscored by these twin laws. In the case of Milner's family, fixed elements like excessive consumption of Jack Daniels, limerick readings, and the exchange of stories and life lessons were balanced by variations of the precise limericks, stories, and life lessons (read: unsolicited sex advice) that were shared and subsequently built upon during the next year's trip. For Phillips and Katie, their shared love of campy media and oddity generally, along with an eye for a particular kind of mischief, served as a consistent backdrop for the emergent jokes that evolved and became tangled into new expressions as the decades wore on.

The interplay between conservative precedent and dynamic transformation places folklore squarely within the realm of the *vernacular*. Folklorist Robert Glenn Howard (2008) foregrounds two common forms of vernacular expression, each consisting of dynamic innovations on conservative communicative standards: common vernacular and subaltern vernacular. As Howard explains, common vernacular is "held separate from the formal discursive products" (494) of existing institutions. It is, to use a very basic example, the difference between slang and words listed in a dictionary (or between "Achum" and whatever that poor woman's real name was). Subaltern vernacular, expression forwarded by individuals on the cultural margins, hinges as much on who is doing the communicating as it does on what, specifically, these individuals are expressing. Subaltern vernacular is doubly noninstitutional, in other words; the messages themselves run counter to formal or otherwise codified discourse, and so do the people transmitting the message. Reclamations of racist, sexist, or homophobic epithets by the groups these terms have been deployed against is an example of subaltern vernacular.

Both dimensions of vernacular expression are essential to the churning wheel of tradition and transformation that is folklore. And as they trace this churn, folklorists are ultimately tracing how different kinds of people make sense of the world and each other. Regardless of era or degree of mediation, regardless of whether the stuff folklorists study is hundreds of years old or something that happened yesterday, folklore is, to borrow Toelken's very broad framing, the study of "the living performance of tradition" (1996, xi) – for better and for worse and for everything in between, as we'll see below.

80 percent obscene and 100 percent ambivalent

The everyday expression of everyday people is not, by and large, house of worship talk. It's not ivory-tower talk. It's back-alley talk, around-the-campfire talk. Furtive talk when the boss isn't listening. Hybrid, unpolished, and unfinished, folklore is where formality goes to rest. Because it falls outside of, complicates, or is in direct conflict with more formal cultural elements, folkloric expression is often, quite literally, not safe for work (or church, or school, or any other seat of institutional power). Toelken (1996) estimates that the vast majority of orally transmitted folkloric material – up to 80 percent, he suggests – would in fact be considered obscene if encountered out of context. Of course, just as one person's weird is another person's Tuesday, one community's obscenity is another community's everyday expression; even the most seemingly dirty, inappropriate, or just plain weird traditions serve a specific social purpose within the communities that embrace them. That these expressions are both soil *and* dirt, indigenous *and* matter out of place, is the most foundational layer of folkloric ambivalence.

Another foundational layer of this ambivalence, highlighted by Howard (2008), is the fact that vernacular expressions are fundamentally hybrid, handily blurring the lines between structure and play, formal and folk, commercial and populist. In the context of Milner's annual fishing trip, for example, conservative middle American ideals of male bonding, family time, and intergenerational outdoorsiness are suffused with the integration of far less conservative elements, notably the mass consumption of alcohol, accounts of illegal exploits, and the disclosure of sexual experiences. Family members' adoption, adaptation, and performance of limericks published in a popular press book also blurs the line between folk creativity and mass produced content.[2] In the process, written tradition – borrowed from earlier oral sources – is reintegrated into new oral sources (and with the publication of this book, subsequently repurposed into a written academic tradition).

These same binaries are dismantled by Phillips and Katie's track and field troublemaking. The common experience (for youth athletes, anyway) of sitting through an all-day track meet or, more universally, navigating childhood under the looming threat of other people's mothers, was augmented by idiosyncratic pranks, silly stories, and subversive play. Inside jokes and references were intertwined with corporate content, including the insertion of personal adversaries like the truly frightening Achum into *Weekly World News*-worthy toilet ghost scenarios. And just as it was for Milner and his family, the line between the stories Phillips and Katie would tell each other and the stories they read in books or magazines was often nonexistent; corporate expression *was* personal expression.

The basic, inescapable hybridity of vernacular expression is also present in the case studies we highlighted in the Introduction; satirical Amazon reviews, antagonistic hashtags, and macabre fan art (along with myriad other examples yet unboxed) each infuse elements from corporate and populist expression. These cases, along with our own personal experiences, illustrate that while vernacularity may indeed provide an alternative to dominant power, such expression foregrounds and in fact is precipitated by the interdependence of the folkloric and the institutional. Playful Amazon reviews, for example, may subvert the intended purpose of Amazon's reviewing platform. But they also draw from precisely that platform. Henry Jenkins' (2006) assessment of "convergence culture," in which "new" participatory and "old" broadcast platforms feed into each other, further exemplifies this ambivalence. Like the fuzzy line between formal and informal language, these ostensibly distinct categories are, instead, reciprocal; you can't talk about one without talking about the other, or at least taking the other for granted. The hybridity of vernacular expression thus underscores its ambivalence; few expressive forms remain uninfluenced by at least some aspect of formal culture, so few cannot be regarded, on a basic level, as being "both, on both sides."

This is not, however, the only, or even the most significant, site of folkloric ambivalence. Much more vexing is the fact that folklore is, to quote Dundes, "always a reflection of the age in which it flourishes" (1987, 12) – one that often reveals anxieties about major social issues, for example concerns about the economy (Dundes and Pagter 1975), resistance to perceived threats to the status quo manifesting as racism, xenophobia, or homophobia (Dundes 1987; Oring 2008), and paternalistic handwringing over women's sexual, economic, and emotional autonomy (Brunvand 2001). Broader cultural issues are in this way encoded into everyday folkloric expression; the lore of the folk can never, should never, be separated from its broader communal or cultural context.

As it is charged with collecting, analyzing, and preserving for posterity this ambivalent intertwine, the discipline of folklore must navigate its own set of ambivalent contours. On the one hand, championing the everyday speech of everyday people is democratic, unpretentious, and ultimately humane. Everybody matters; everyone deserves to be heard. On the other hand, the everyday speech of everyday people can often be quite ugly. "Folksy" does not, after all, necessarily mean good, moral, or just. All it means is that people are doing something. And that can absolutely go any way, from the highest peaks of human compassion to the darkest pits of human intolerance to all the muddy places in between.

The fact that folk expression can perpetuate bigotry and intolerance immediately complicates folklorists' archival impulse, best articulated by the omnipresent Dundes' insistence that the study of human culture "must include *all* aspects of human activity" (1965, 92, original emphasis). Dundes and Uli Linke (1987) address this tension in their analysis of jokes about Auschwitz, the German World War II concentration camp. The authors provide an impassioned defense of engaging with "repugnant and distasteful" (29) folkloric content, a category into which Auschwitz jokes clearly fall. They concede that by publishing collections of Auschwitz jokes, they risk amplifying precisely the anti-Semitic sentiment they profess to abhor. But, they counter, these sick jokes will remain in circulation regardless of whether or not they are reported by folklorists; by collecting and analyzing them in order to hold prejudice "up to the light of reason" (38), there's a chance that folkloric intervention will call attention to, and in the process help stymie, bigoted thinking.

Cultural studies scholar Meaghan Morris ([1988] 2007) challenges the underlying assumption that bigoted expression can, and in fact should, be amplified by scholars on the grounds that it's what people are already doing. As she argues, merely affirming popular behavior risks reducing all expression – the good, the bad, and the ugly – to equally forgettable images in a flipbook. Nothing worth a second look; everything warranting clinical detachment. Beyond that, blithely chronicling and ventriloquizing the popular risks further normalizing the structural inequality, bias, and identity-based antagonisms that are embedded within so many mainstream discourses. This is a risk one takes regardless of motivation. "Even when done in the service of critical assessment," Milner argues, "reproducing these discourses continues their circulation, and therefore may continue to normalize their antagonisms and marginalizations" (2016, 123). From this perspective, Dundes and Linke's (1987) claim that they were, in fact, helping *combat* racism by archiving racism falls flat; by archiving, they are amplifying. And by amplifying, they're contributing to the overall problem.

We maintain, appropriately enough, an ambivalent perspective on this issue. It should go without saying that researchers in any discipline should carefully situate their own political standpoint alongside any and all research projects, and take every precaution not to amplify, replicate, or further normalize identity-based antagonisms. We also agree that sidestepping offensive content risks signaling complicity, and that airing uncomfortable cultural truths is often the first step toward combatting them. It might be better if there were more straightforward ethical solutions to issues of amplification. It certainly would be easier. But the ambivalence of these issues – the fact that an equally compelling argument could be made either way – highlights the futility of forwarding universalizing claims about human behavior, and, further, of forwarding universalizing claims about the best way to engage with this behavior. What is right, what is wrong, and what can or should be done, simply *depends* – requiring not rote proclamations, but context-sensitive, case-specific analyses. These are the analyses we hope to undertake, as we delve into the continuities between digital and embodied folkloric expression.

Digital continuities, bawdy and rough hewn

The previous section argued that the fundamental ambivalence of folkloric expression dismantles easy binaries between formal and folk, commercial and populist. This section will illustrate yet another binary complicated by folkloric ambivalence: the seemingly straightforward, but in fact quite convoluted, line between then and now. To do so, it will draw from a pair of contexts we know all too well: internet memes and subcultural trolling, each the subject of our respective 2012 doctoral dissertations, each the starting point for subsequent solo and collaborative research, and each the continuation of a long line of ambivalent precedent.

The meme connection

The faux Amazon reviews, satirical hashtags, and spree shooter fan art described in the Introduction are examples of *internet memes*, evolving tapestries of self-referential texts collectively created, circulated, and transformed by participants online. Famed biologist Richard Dawkins first introduced the term *meme* (a play on "gene") four decades ago to explain how "units of cultural transmission" (1976, 206) – like trends, fashions, and slang – spread from person to person, evolving as they travel. Dawkins' metaphor was one of virality; in his conceptualization, memes leap "from brain to brain" (206) as new participants imitate what they see and hear. In the years following Dawkins' initial argument, the meme metaphor resonated with participants on the fledgling internet, and by the early aughts the term became a favored descriptor for shared in-jokes, catchphrases, idiosyncratic habits, and of course participants' tendency to caption countless pictures of cats.

But memes are bigger than funny pictures on the internet, and are more complex than a leap from brain to brain. As Milner (2016) argues, memetic media instead comprise a thriving constellation of vernacular expression, spanning genres of communication and even degrees of mediation. Regardless of how divergent these media can be, they are unified by a few fundamental logics. They depend on *multimodality* (expression through diverse modes of communication, including written words and static images, as well as audio and video), *reappropriation* (the remix and recombination of existing cultural materials), *resonance* (the manifestation of strong personal affinity), *collectivism* (social creation and transformation), and *spread* (circulation through mass networks). Through these logics, participants create, circulate, and transform shared texts, adding unique and ever-evolving contributions to vast cultural tapestries.

Because this process is so situated, playful, and vernacular, the folkloric lens is a natural fit for internet memes – so much so that digital media scholar Limor Shifman describes memes as "(post)modern folklore" (2014, 15). Analyses of memetic participation have, after all, been folklorists' bread and butter for decades, whether or not they were using the term *meme*. Indeed, a year before Dawkins even coined the word, Alan Dundes and Carl Pagter were already talking about the "multiple existence," "variation," and "genetic interrelationships" (1975, xxi) of *Xeroxlore*, the folkloric art and commentary that spread across and between offices via photocopiers (for you kids out there, that's the *Xerox* in *Xeroxlore*, named after a popular photocopier brand). Common forms of Xeroxlore included mock letters, parodies of songs, comical definitions and taxonomies, and farcical office memos, all of which traveled from copier to copier, office to office, as participants – like they always have – created, circulated, and transformed their own everyday expressions.

These expressions would, for the record, have been right at home on Twitter, Tumblr, 4chan, Facebook, or at least an email forward. Not just because of the often not-safe-for-work (or life) nature of Xeroxlore. But also because Xeroxlore texts were subsumed by memetic logics, even if they existed decades before the mass adoption of digital media. Xeroxlore was multimodal, frequently combining written word and static image; one commonly circulated piece of Xeroxlore, for instance, is a drawing of a doughy cartoon man with a screw driven through his torso, captioned with some variation of the expression "work hard and you shall be rewarded." Xeroxlore was also reappropriational, featuring vernacular reinterpretations of pop cultural fixtures like *Peanuts* and *Looney Tunes* characters. It was resonant, connecting with participants' disdain for the bureaucracies underpinning college campuses, military branches, and commercial offices. It was collective, often being shared without signature or citation, and often lauding one social group at the expense of another. And it certainly spread, as variations of the most resonant jokes and stories popped up in different forms across different regions.

The overlaps between folklore and memetic media run even deeper than these fundamental logics. Before he ever even heard of Toelken's (1996) twin laws of conservatism and dynamism, for example, Milner (2016) pulled from discourse analyst Deborah Tannen ([1989] 2007) to argue that memetic media depend on the interplay between *fixity* and *novelty*, concepts essentially interchangeable with conservatism and dynamism. Tannen applied fixity and novelty to everyday conversations and the scripts we all live by. Fixed communicative motifs provide templates for, say, greeting acquaintances, sharing small talk in an elevator, or invoking common idioms. But, as standard as they might be to members within a given culture or community, these scripts are adapted in novel ways to make every interaction unique. Depending on the circumstance, we decide whether to greet with a handshake or a hug, whether we want to fill that elevator with talk about the rain or about the local baseball team, and whether "slow and steady wins the race" is a better piece of advice than "the early bird catches the worm."

Milner (2016) argues that memetic media balance the fixed and the novel in similar ways. Satirical Amazon reviews, for instance, are novel in their creative individual expression; they're fixed, however, in the constellation of odd products they target and the humorous hyperbole they employ. Each critical #AskThicke response was novel in its specific commentary, but the themes that resonated across these responses remained largely consistent, resulting in the repeated lampooning of Thicke's presumed misogyny, sexual desperation, lack of talent, and fashion *faux pas*. Holmies and Columbine shooter groupies, for their part, were novel in their professed affinity for mass murderers James Holmes, Eric Harris, and Dylan Klebold, but their expressions of devotion – love letters and floaty hearts – shared fixed dimensions premised on romantic motifs commonly applied to teenage heartthrobs. The balance of fixity and novelty in these and other cases allows participants to infuse collective online spaces with more idiosyncratic expression.

As it was fundamentally memetic and therefore fundamentally folkloric (and vice versa), Xeroxlore also hewed to a basic fixity of form, and also spun out novel iterations within a shared social context. Pop cultural references (to *Looney Tunes* and *Peanuts* characters, alongside countless others) and various stock office archetypes (the asshole boss, the bullying co-worker, the know-nothing secretary) were creatively transformed in the name of critique, parody, and play. Participants often edited broader Xeroxlore scripts so that they more specifically applied to their region, their company, or even their own uniquely incompetent middle management. The

fixity and novelty of these forms – or if you prefer, their conservatism and dynamism – served to create a *lingua franca*, a
bridge language between and within folk collectives: the same
then as now, immediately raising questions about that basic
demarcation.

Not only are internet memes and Xeroxlore premised on
similar fundamental logics, and a similar blend of fixity and
novelty, they're also similarly vernacular. And as such, are
often quite "bawdy and rough hewn" (to borrow a wonderful
phrase from Greenhill and Matrix 2010, 22). There's no rule
that they have to be, of course. But as expressions standing
in conflict with or in contrast to more formal cultural elements, their tone frequently veers – and veers spectacularly
– into Toelken's (1996) "80% obscene" territory. One preemi-
nent contemporary example is the collectively created (and
childhood-ruining) "Dolan Duck" family of comics (Figure
2). Dolan comics were popularized in 2010 on 4chan's "/b/"
("Random") board, a simple message board founded in 2003,
which quickly established itself as the go-to place for so-called
"trollish fuckery." These crudely drawn comics, some of which
are animated and voiced by glitchy voice-to-text translation
software, memetically chronicle the misadventures of homi-
cidal sex monster "Dolan Duck" (a play on Disney cartoon
staple Donald Duck) and his friends "Gooby" (Goofy), "Pruto"
(Pluto), and "Fogor" (Foghorn Leghorn, a *Looney Tunes* addition to the Walt Disney party) – all of whom are luminous
poster children for rule 34 (as Fogor and Gooby exist, there
is *indeed* porn of them).

Dolan comics often feature explicitly assaultive and sexually
violent imagery, which we will spare you (issues of amplification, after all). Figure 2, as tame as it might be compared to
other Dolan comics, nonetheless demonstrates the character's
memetic intertextuality and archetypical cruelty. The story
told in the 12 words and 4 scant panels of Figure 2 not only
pulls from Disney's Donald Duck, but also DC Comics' Batman.
Its narrative hinges on Batman's orphan backstory, knowledge

Figure 2. A Dolan comic, in which Dolan (or "doughlan" here) reminds the orphan superhero Batman (or "bertmun") that his parents are dead. Collected in 2012.

required to understand the mean-spirited poignancy of Dolan's characteristic taunting. It also replicates the nonstandard spelling and grammar so prevalent in Dolan comics and esoteric online vernacular more generally.

As uniquely absurd and grotesque as it might seem, Dolan's memetic vernacularity hews closely to the Xeroxlore American office workers created, circulated, and transformed a half-century ago; Dundes and Pagter (1975) note that much of the content they encountered was too sexually explicit, profanity laden, and gratuitously violent to print. Which is really saying something, considering the slew of profane, misanthropic written commentary and crudely sexualized drawings they *did* print. Popular reappropriations of *Looney Tunes* characters (like Road Runner and Wile E. Coyote) and *Peanuts* characters (like Charlie Brown and Lucy) exemplify this prurience: each was repeatedly placed into obscene circumstances, illustrating that rule 34 was alive and well long before 4chan. Memetic play resulted, for example, in Road Runner alternatively anally penetrating and being anally penetrated by Wile E. Coyote, and Charlie Brown constantly fighting an erection, or repeatedly impregnating his female friends ("Goddamn you, Charlie Brown" was a recurring punchline).

These examples, like the Dolan comics that exist in their lineage, may seem like shocking misappropriations, but as Dundes and Pagter argue, all it takes for a mass-produced work to pass into the populist tradition is for it to catch "the imagination of the folk" (145). A half-century later, the potential for collective narrative play – from the innocent to the grotesque – persists. There may be more ways to catch the imagination of more people, with more creative tools at their disposal, but the behavioral impulse remains the same.

And these impulses, regardless of era, directly reflect the contexts in which they thrive(d) – not necessarily as part of a conscious argument about the broader cultural reality, but as a backlit framing of its contours. As explained by Dundes and Pagter, Xeroxlore reflected the profound racial, sexual, and class tensions that permeated mid-century American office spaces. Right-wing populist sentiments were pervasive, as workers shared endless ethnic jokes and slurs. Through satirical accounts of "equal-opportunity Christmas memos" and "government poverty applications," they also skewered what is now derided as "political correctness" (paging Donald J. Trump and his legion of racist Twitter attack dogs). Misogyny reared its head in popular jokes about (allegedly) dumb blondes and (allegedly) promiscuous secretaries. And recurring jabs at redundant paperwork, incompetent middle managers, and corporate inefficiencies all point to a broader sense of alienation in the face of expanding white-collar bureaucracy.

Contemporary internet memes are similarly reflective of broader cultural motifs, illustrated by how often memetic content is steeped in familiar identity antagonisms. Dolan comics, for instance, often portray Dolan and his pals assaulting, dismembering, or murdering "Dasae" (i.e. Daisy Duck, girlfriend of Donald) because she displeased someone, sometimes simply by existing. Such misogynist expression is common on 4chan, which Phillips calls "unquestionably androcentric" (2015, 54). This isn't to assert that Dolan participants or 4chan users more broadly are necessarily violent or misogynist in their embodied lives, but rather that sexually violent motifs are especially resonant, and therefore especially common, on 4chan's forums. Similar discourses – about male dominance, violence, and sexual conquest – also persist on sites like Reddit and BodyBuilding.com, where the sizeism and ableism of Amazon Customer's initial Three Wolf Moon review first spread. These sorts of antagonistic memes weaponize existing cultural logics, and thus reflect the antagonisms pervasive in embodied spaces as well; the memes wouldn't remain so popular with so many participants if they didn't.

But within our contemporary media landscape, this picture isn't wholly discouraging. On the other end of the identity antagonism spectrum, hijacks of #AskThicke and Bill Cosby's ill-conceived request for participants to "meme him," as well as satirical reviews of BIC "Cristal for Her" pens, point to clashes around the same identity essentialisms that are predominant in many online spaces. Clash that is indicative of a cultural moment in which more people from historically underrepresented perspectives are asserting their right to be heard. Over the last half-century, many cultural realities have changed, and many (sadly) have not; but, for better or worse, folkloric (and therefore memetic) expression has consistently reflected those realities.

Expanding on this continuity, we will now turn to memetic play with death, another image reflected in the folkloric mirror. Although this image may strike many as especially outrageous, especially unpleasant, or even outright immoral, it too persists across eras and degrees of mediation – challenging, once more, any clear breakdown between what happened then and what's happening now.

LOL your dead

In 2010, a new and particularly virulent form of subcultural trolling began to overrun Facebook, the omnipresent social networking platform. Unlike contemporaneous subcultural trolling on 4chan's /b/ – whose anonymous, ephemeral interactions didn't extend beyond a particular coordinated attack against a chosen target – trolling on Facebook allowed for the creation of a relatively stable anti-social network in which trolls were easily able to form close-knit cabals targeting a whole host of on-site causes, public personalities, and affinity groups (Phillips 2015).

The most outrageous of these behaviors occurred on what Facebook called "memorial pages." These pages – sometimes known as "RIP pages" – allowed friends and family of the recently deceased to convene, collectively mourn, and share memories. In the wake of high-profile deaths, members of the wider public would often join these mourners, and would express their condolences alongside those who knew the victims personally. Facebook memorial trolls took umbrage at these public outpourings of sentimentality, and began taking aim. Most often, their targets consisted of so-called "grief tourists," those who didn't personally know the deceased. But some trolls focused on bereaved friends and family. Regardless of whom participating trolls chose to target, their behaviors encompassed a wide spectrum. They pretended to know the deceased to confuse posters who also didn't know the deceased; created fake memorial pages as a kind of grief tourist honeypot; posted silly, bizarre, or obscene photoshopped images onto official (created by friends or family) or unofficial (created by strangers or trolls) memorial pages; and, most upsettingly, flooded a page with cruelly photoshopped images of the crime or victim in question, or with crime scene photos taken of similar tragedies.

Unsurprisingly, RIP trolling generated a great deal of journalistic coverage and public debate focused on the singular, pointed question: exactly what was *wrong* with the people who would engage in these sorts of behaviors? Why would anyone do something like that? In her ethnographic research on the subject, Phillips found that, often, these kinds of questions would be followed by a lamentation that the internet was making everything terrible: people were getting meaner, and nobody had any respect. Reasonable conclusions to draw, given the behaviors in question, but ones that are not borne out by the folkloric record. RIP trolling is, in truth, highly precedented, a fact that doesn't mitigate its harm, but which does complicate any simplistic comparison between our presumably benighted present and presumably gentler past.

For instance, similarly profane behaviors were exhibited – and similarly fretted over – at late nineteenth- and early twentieth-century Newfoundland funeral wakes. As folklorist Peter Narváez (2003) explains, wake participants played games "with penalty of biting the corpse's toes," rigged corpses to scare unsuspecting guests, made the corpse "drink" alcoholic beverages, dressed the corpse in silly outfits, and played cruel practical jokes on selected attendees. Echoing memorial page trolling, these outrageous behaviors trounced taboos related to death and to the mourning process generally. Questions about motivations and what might be wrong with participants were just as pressing to horrified nineteenth- and twentieth-century onlookers as they were in response to contemporary Facebook memorial page trolling. In reviewing the existing literature, Narváez encountered two prevailing explanations: that mourners felt compelled to play within these sacred spaces, first, to placate the dead, or second, to challenge the ruling order.

While Narváez concedes that each explanation is plausible, especially when applied to their respective contexts (both arguments were forwarded by Irish scholars in response to Irish funeral behaviors), he asserts that neither adequately explains why Newfoundland wakes would inspire such bawdy and rough hewn fun, and why the tradition would persist – with some dynamic variation, of course – for so many generations. Perhaps there is a better theoretical explanation, Narváez contends; perhaps it would be possible to construct a socio-cultural analysis that elegantly explains why otherwise "normal" people would engage in such abnormal, or perhaps even sociopathic, behaviors. The problem, Narváez suggests, is that almost none of the informants' testimonies would support such a staid, academic reading. In accordance with their own explanations, people flocked to these sorts of wakes because they were *fun*. Some informants even expressed glee when a member of the community died, because a death meant a party, and a party meant drinking, and drinking meant there'd be pranks to play.

This does not mean that the behaviors couldn't also be reflective of larger cultural forces. As folkloric practices, they most certainly were. But in addition to the crisscross of cultural forces that influence behavior, play was also, well, at play. People like to feel good, Narváez notes, and like to do things that make them feel good. Sometimes "feeling good" is as simple as having a full stomach and nice buzz (what Narváez describes as "evasive" pleasures, like getting drunk on Jack Daniels and reciting vulgar limericks with the family). Sometimes "feeling good" means doing something you know you shouldn't be doing (described as "subversive" pleasures, like watching with glee as the coach who punishes you with never-ending warm-up drills bends over to collect their side-walk dollar prize and then is thwarted mid-snatch). Frequently, "feeling good" means both.

So, while a well-drawn theory will consider whether and how and why these pleasures reflect larger social forces, a fully embodied folkloric account must also acknowledge that pleasure is often a reason in and of itself. Questions as to why Newfoundlanders would engage in mischievous, rowdy behavior in the face of death could therefore be answered with (deceptive) simplicity: because they wanted to, which – as Phillips (2015) argues – was also a common attitude of the trolls who terrorized Facebook memorial pages. It was fun. It made them laugh. This laughter was often met by confoundment, rage, and disgust, with very good reason: the behaviors were often quite confounding, enraging, and disgusting. But for participating trolls, enjoyment was one very simple and almost always overlooked explanation for why they did what they did.

Narváez' account isn't the only study that provides precedent for memorial page trolling. Folklorist Elliott Oring's (1987) analysis of the "tasteless and cruel" humor surrounding the 1986 *Challenger* space disaster, in which seven shuttle crew members were killed instantly during an explosion at take-off, uncannily echoes the behavioral impetus and basic tone of RIP humor ("LOL your dead" – with "you're" deliberately misspelled – being a representative example). Many of the resulting jokes focused on middle school teacher Christa McAuliffe, winner of NASA's immediately abandoned "Teacher in Space" program. One of the jokes that Oring recounts asks, "What color were Christa McAuliffe's eyes?"; the answer: "Blue. One blew this way and the other blew that way" (280).

Rather than echoing the common perspective that such jokes were *either* evidence of sociopathy *or* provided a therapeutic release, Oring argues that these jokes allowed participants to play with and push back against a media apparatus that packages tragedy as a commodity and attempts to set an emotional agenda predicated on corporate interests. Whether or not the joke tellers self-consciously framed their actions as a pointed critique of sensationalist journalism is another question. Oring's argument is that these jokes weren't *necessarily* attacking McAuliffe and the other astronauts personally, as an act of targeted or otherwise sociopathic antagonism. Neither were they *necessarily* serving an explicitly therapeutic function. The truth was almost assuredly more nuanced than *either* versus *or*, *this* versus *that*.

The trolls Phillips (2015) interviewed for her study of memorial page trolling seemed to support Oring's hypothesis. Augmenting the trolls' insistence that they targeted memorial pages "for the lulz" – trolling parlance for antagonistic laughter derived from the infliction of emotional distress – they also cited news coverage as a behavioral catalyst. One troll, Paulie Socash, framed mainstream media outlets as "tragedy merchants" (161), and frequently discussed his disdain not just for journalistic sensationalism, but for the average Facebook users ("grief tourists") who bought into a given media narrative and inundated dead strangers' pages with what trolls derided as empty condolences. To the trolls Phillips interviewed, the oft-repeated expression "I didn't know you, but I am very sorry you're dead" bespoke excessive sentimentality and a lack of critical thinking, and therefore justified their trollish tauntings.

However carefully they rationalized their actions, of course, participating trolls were engaging in behaviors that had direct and often devastating real-world consequences for those affected by a tragedy. Trolls' behaviors also directly impacted those who weren't personally affected, but who nevertheless felt strong attachment to a story – despite trolls' myopic assertion that it is impossible to feel genuine compassion for a stranger. And it is at this point that the analogy between Oring's (1987) account of "sick" *Challenger* humor and RIP trolling breaks down; there is a big difference between recounting an off-color joke in a private setting and posting antagonistic commentary potentially or pointedly accessible to friends and family of the deceased. That said, like Narváez' (2003) account of Newfoundland wakes, Oring's (1987) account illustrates the fact that there is ample precedent for mischievous, antagonistic, and seemingly callous responses to death and tragedy. Memorial page trolls are certainly outrageous and upsetting, but they are far from the first group to make light of terrible things.

Timothy Tangherlini's 1998 study of Bay Area medics provides another embodied example of this impulse. As in the previous examples, the medics Tangherlini profiles laugh at (or, perhaps more accurately, around) dead people. Unlike the previous examples, these medics' dark and often grisly humor is shared by medics with other medics, often friends and co-workers, making it more of a tale-telling exercise than one of directed antagonism. So while not perfectly analogous to RIP trolling *per se*, the tradition of tale-telling Tangherlini explores can still be likened to the informal "grossest of the gross" contests (i.e. attempts to tell the worst story / show the nastiest image) that permeate the trollspace and other corners of the internet where shocking or scarring one's readers is the desired outcome. The following anecdote from Tangherlini's study illustrates this continuity:

> [describing a picture taken with a suicide victim]
> Darryl: We have this one picture where this chick had hung herself in a closet and she's like, err. And she'd been there for probably a day, and she was stiff – she was dead, dead, dead! And we took a picture of her hanging there with like me with my arm around my prom date. (161)

And this isn't even the most visceral story. One medic likens the brain of a woman run over by a train to a pile of chewed-up bubble gum; another compares the collapsed skull of a shotgun suicide to a salad bowl; and countless others recount one blood-splattered call after another, often sending their audience, always other medics, into giggling fits.

Based on the medics' shared experiences and emotional reactions, Tangherlini concludes that the stories medics tell provide an outlet for narrative one-upsmanship; create and maintain social hierarchies (within and outside the medic community); challenge, comment on, or subvert authority; and allow medics – whose jobs are otherwise never finished – to posit discrete endings (and therefore closure) for particularly difficult or otherwise jarring experiences. Perhaps most importantly, these stories, and the humor they contain, establish performative distance between the observer and that which has been observed, thus allowing the medic to do their job with a minimal amount of psychic trauma. Tangherlini's analysis also highlights the importance of taking audience into account when considering ambivalent behaviors. As he found, humor related to severed optic nerves, splattered brains, and otherwise disarticulated corpses – a few common narrative themes – depended entirely on context, namely the person telling the story and the people listening, how many times the story had been told, the current mood of the audience, what happened the previous shift, and so on – variables that are just as important when talking about memorial page trolling, or indeed any other ambivalent online behavior.

Although the subjects, objectives, and methods of their studies are widely divergent, Narváez (2003), Oring (1987), and Tangherlini (1998) reveal a great deal of behavioral and even tonal overlap between the pre-internet *then* and the contemporary post-internet *now*, and in the process provide a richer context through which to engage the seemingly unprecedented category of memorial page trolling. Precedent is not, however, the same as permissibility; the mere fact that certain behaviors span eras or degrees of mediation doesn't make the behaviors socially or politically acceptable. What this continuity does do is call attention to the fact that now and then are not so different after all, and must instead be considered on an uneven, ever-evolving continuum.

Digital divergences and folkloric expression

The conservative element of folkloric expression is that the tone, nature, and pleasures of ambivalent vernacularity have persisted over time, and span both historical eras and degrees of mediation. Echoing folklore itself, this conservatism exists in balance with dynamism; the brave new world of digital media adds its own topography to the landscape of folk practices, amplifying the ambivalence of already highly ambivalent expression. In the process, the already blurry lines between then and now, formal and folk, and commercial and populist, are rendered even more unstable. We'll explore these new blurs below, emphasizing the new technological affordances, new behavioral complications, and new ethical questions engendered by the ambivalent internet.

The affordances of digital mediation
Like all technologies, digital technologies are replete with specific *affordances*, a term meaning – most simply – what an object allows a person to do with it (Gaver 1991). Although these affordances don't dictate behavior, they certainly limit one's options; you can't, for example, very easily use a child's car seat to mail in your taxes or burn down your house. In the context of folkloric expression online, one of the most significant affordances is what new-media scholar Lev Manovich describes as *modularity*: the ability to manipulate, rearrange, and/or substitute digitized parts of a larger whole without disrupting or destroying the "overall structure of an object" (2001, 31). In his exploration of the open source software movement, Chris Kelty (2008) foregrounds the related concept of *modifiability*, the ability of open source software producers – really anyone engaging in any form of free and open collaboration – to repurpose and reappropriate aspects of an existing project toward some new end.

In addition to facilitating the modularity and modifiability of content, digitization also simplifies the *archivability* of content, or as communication scholar Nancy K. Baym (2015) puts it, how content online may be replicated and stored. Augmenting the ability to archive content is the *accessibility* of that content through categorization and searching. Online photo tagging, in which the people, places, or things in uploaded photographs are indexed within a searchable database, exemplifies this process (Shirky 2008). Taken together, these technological affordances – which have become more available to more people as the infrastructure of the web has shifted to favor social, and especially mobile, applications – allow online participants to create, circulate, and transform vernacular media much more easily than in previous eras. There were, of course, some early tools affording media manipulation (photocopier machines, for example). But these tools were restricted to a select few (in this case white-collar office workers), and furthermore afforded a fairly limited range of participation (copied images could be further copied, but if someone wanted to modify a drawing, they had to start from scratch or trace over the original).

So, while the three memetic images in Figure 3 certainly connect to an existing lineage of ambivalent folkloric expression, they also demonstrate how the affordances of digital media push folkloric ambivalence into hyperdrive, adding new dynamics to long-established practices.

Figure 3. Memetic images corrupting children's icons. Left: a *Berenstain Bears* book is gifted a crude title and crass cover art. Top right: an image of SpongeBob from the Nickelodeon cartoon *SpongeBob SquarePants* is captioned to explain SpongeBob's wrath toward his neighbor Squidward. Bottom right: an image of Bert and Cookie Monster from PBS' *Sesame Street* is captioned so that Cookie Monster now bellows about sugar in his rectum. Collected in 2015.

The convincing cover forgery corrupting the *Berenstain Bears* source text on the left side of Figure 3 illustrates modularity. Adapted from a 1998 book titled *The Berenstain Bears Get Their Kicks*, which features Sister kicking a ball past a stunned Brother as a delighted Mama and concerned Papa look on, the faux cover replicates fixed components of the original while adding dynamic, satirical elements. Even as "Get Their Kicks" is transformed into "Get Kicked in the Dick," the font, size, and placement of the title is precisely replicated. Brother is scooted to the left so that he's the one being kicked; to accommodate that change, the net and landscape have been reconstructed (the ball is altogether deleted). The facial expressions of three of the four characters have been altered to fit the new message. Only Papa's concerned grimace hasn't been touched. Mama's eyes are closed and her mouth widened to signal sadistic glee. Sister's eyes are narrowed and her teeth are exposed in a display of carnal ferocity. And instead of worriedly watching a soccer ball zoom through his legs, Brother is given the closed eyes and gritted teeth of a male who has just been, well, kicked in the dick. And to really drive that point home, the outline of a penis has been added under Brother's shorts. All thanks to a few minor photo manipulations.

The related affordance of modifiability allows for the collective repurposing of existing materials, helping facilitate the creation of the top right image in Figure 3. First, the image's original creator was able to screen capture a still from a 2002 *SpongeBob SquarePants* episode titled "Can You Spare a Dime?" It also allowed someone (perhaps the person who first captured the image, perhaps not) to add layers of text over the screen capture. Here the eponymous SpongeBob is looming over his neighbor/co-worker/rival Squidward, fists cocked, on the verge of breaking, screaming "Who Up?? You, muthafucka! So why the fucc didnt u clik *the muthafuckin* LIKE" (apparently SpongeBob is upset that Squidward is currently active on some social media platform but isn't "liking" SpongeBob's posts).

Finally, modifiability allowed the humor site ifunny.co to watermark the image when it was uploaded there (again, perhaps by the individual who screen captured it, perhaps by the individual who annotated it, and perhaps by some third or fourth or fifth or who-knows-how-many-th party). By the time Milner found the image on Tumblr in 2015, the affordance of modifiability had transformed the source text and its original meaning into a new form of vernacular creativity.

The bottom right image in Figure 3 augments Bert and Cookie Monster from *Sesame Street* with an anal-retentive proclamation. It was born from a circa-2007 meme about an unconventional form of intoxication: supposedly, one could get high by siphoning granulated sugar into one's rectum. Dating back to at least 2008, Cookie Monster was a chosen memetic vessel for this message; you can thank the affordance of archivability for gracing your life with its presence. Users' ability to encounter the image, connect with the image, download the image, and then repost the image, where it might remain for years undisturbed, in turn enabling others to find it, download it, possibly modify it, and subsequently recirculate it, has allowed the image to persist well beyond its esoteric origins. It's now made its way into an academic monograph, where it shall live on as an analog curio for decades to come. You're welcome.

"There's Sugar in My Ass," like all three images in Figure 3, is also indebted to the accessibility resulting from practices like tagging, cataloging, and indexing. These practices, coupled with archivability, mean that each one of those images is only a search inquiry away – provided one knows what terms to input. Accessibility also allows one to chart and trace the context surrounding these sorts of folkloric expressions in unprecedented ways. For example, after just a few moments of searching, Milner was able to uncover the unannotated *Berenstain Bears* cover (search term: "Berenstain Bears soccer"), the source episode for SpongeBob accosting a bed-bound

Squidward (search term: "SpongeBob yell Squidward bed"), and the earliest uploads of "There's Sugar in My Ass" (via a reverse image search on TinEye.com). Like nothing that has come before, accessibility puts the everyday expressions of everyday folk collectives right at users' fingertips.

Chaos in order

As they facilitate ease of search, storage, and playful reappropriation, these affordances allow participants to manipulate and continually remix an ever-expanding reservoir of source material, often without attributing what was found where, or made where, by whom. And once this newly remixed content is itself archived and search indexed, it can be found and further remixed by others – also without attributing what was found where, or made where, by whom. As a result, even with the affordances of archivability and accessibility, it is often impossible to track with complete certainty where a piece of content originated, where it subsequently traveled, or what meanings it might have communicated to the audiences who engaged with it.

The fact that digital media lend themselves to chaos as much as organization complicates Blank's assertion that the internet provides a "greater paper trail" (2009, 9) for researchers. Sometimes it does. But often digitization has the opposite effect, particularly given how easily vernacular content jumps between platforms and can be downloaded, remixed, and reposted in multiple locations by multiple participants, perhaps even simultaneously. The images in Figure 3, for example, may each contain traces of countless iterations made by countless participants unknown to each other, all culminating in an image that *appears* singular, but in fact is the remix of a remix of a remix over the course of an untold number of months or years. It's simply not possible to know just by looking at the "final" product (which may, of course, have continued evolving to meet subsequent folk groups' unique needs).

These broader technological affordances are themselves impacted – sometimes augmented, sometimes stymied – by specific platform affordances, essentially the menu of on-site behaviors from which users are able to choose. The most significant of these platform affordances is users' relative level of *anonymity* or *pseudonymity*. The more free-wheeling micro-blogging platform Twitter, for example, has no policy against the creation of pseudonymous accounts, resulting in a great deal of satirical, and often highly ambivalent, play. But even more controlled social networking platforms like Facebook – which ostensibly disallows "fake" profiles[3] – can be creatively misused. Users may be discouraged from creating fake profiles or subjected to punitive measures (like bannings or suspension) if they do, but that doesn't mean that they can't, or that all information included in a person's profile should be taken at face value. Ambivalence can still reign, even when platforms take preventative steps.

These platform affordances don't just impact what individual users can and cannot do on-site. They also impact what onlookers can know about these behaviors. For example, although the original satirical reviewer of the Three Wolf Moon t-shirt ultimately outed himself to the *New York Times* (Applebome 2009), the vast majority of Three Wolf Moon Amazon reviewers appear to be posting under so-called "sock puppets," throwaway accounts created for a singular specific purpose, usually shenanigans. Some of the commentators may have been "real" people, as suggested by multiple reviews spanning a period of months or years, but because Amazon accounts don't have to include legal names or other public-facing contact information, it's difficult to know what is really what, and who is really whom. All observers has is the text of the review, and any self-disclosed identifying information – which given the context, should be taken with a boulder of salt. Poster 50 Shades of Bic (2012), for example, proclaimed that "Shirt is awesome! However, Kevin Costner keeps following me around wanting to slow dance." While such a claim might be highly unlikely, it is not logically impossible – and further is difficult, if not impossible, to verify empirically.

Also difficult, if not impossible, to verify empirically is the exact number of participants contributing to a given thread, hashtag, or page, further precluding precise behavioral assessment. As Milner notes, online participants in anonymous or pseudonymous environments can easily have "multiturn conversations with themselves" (2016, 210) – maybe to seed a particular controversy, maybe to set up a particular joke, or maybe for some other inscrutable reason. In the context of Three Wolf Moon reviews, it may well be that some or all of the reviews were posted by the same person. This isn't to say that the reviews were indeed posted by the same person. Rather – echoing Kevin Costner's alleged love for 50 Shades of Bic – one can't prove it's *not* true.

Even when an individual does post under their legal name, or what seems to be their (or somebody's) legal name, motivations online remain extremely difficult to trace. So much so that questions about motivations are almost always nonstarters. And not just because people online can so easily misrepresent themselves and engage in various forms of mischief with the greatest of ease, as we'll discuss time and again in the chapters to follow. Rather, motivations are usually moot because, for observers, the truth looks the same as a lie, and there is no reliable way to fact-check what even needs fact-checking.

Milner (2016) foregrounds this ambivalence in his analysis of Poe's Law, an online axiom stipulating the difficulty of distinguishing irony from earnestness in public conversation online.[4] By posting something obnoxious to an internet forum, for example, a person might be messing with their audience for a laugh. On the other hand, they might sincerely hold an absurd or outright contemptible opinion. Both options are equally plausible, and, in most cases involving unknown strangers, equally unverifiable. Not that Poe's Law is exclusive to digital spaces, of course; it can be difficult to discern the difference between mischief and sincerity in embodied spaces as well, particularly when wildly divergent power dynamics require subversive rhetorical tactics.[5] But it is particularly potent in public conversations online, where observers have far fewer opportunities to consider paralinguistic signals alongside a particular statement, and just as importantly, rarely have access to the full relational context of a given interaction.

The vitriolic debate surrounding a rainbow tie-dye number cake recipe published to the website of a Melbourne radio station in 2014 illustrates the difficulty of parsing genuine outrage from straight-up silliness online, and in the process underscores the ambivalence of digitally mediated folkloric expression.[6] As Albert Burneko (2014) chronicles in *Deadspin*, the radio station's article was straightforward enough; it explained to readers that, to achieve the desired tie-dye number cake effect, one need only freeze said tie-dye numbers before-hand, and drop them in the middle of the cake tin before baking. The resulting comment thread, however – which, remember, was in response to a cake recipe posted by a radio station – quickly devolved into a shouting match between commenters about the relative merits of conservatism versus liberalism, the meaning of freedom in democratic societies, and whether or not certain commenters were, in fact, fascists ("Farts," commenter stuffnfartsinyomouth added to the fracas). Reading through the comments, many of which are posted in all-caps and are so frothy as to be almost unreadable, it's unclear who is genuinely angry and who is fanning the flames for a laugh. Because, again, it's a cake recipe. Posted by a radio station.

Ethical considerations, to be continued
The broad technological and specific platform affordances constituting digital media allow participants to share vernacular expression freely, easily, and immediately. While these affor-

dances can and often do yield explicitly positive outcomes, the same technologies that facilitate cooperation, connection, and community can also facilitate discord, anxiety, and alienation amongst those not comfortably situated within the ingroup. Sometimes these behaviors are willfully destructive – say when online mobs engage in harassing, professionally damaging, and in some cases explicitly illegal behaviors against chosen targets. In these cases, the ethical stakes are clear.

But in many cases, the ethical stakes are difficult to assess; echoing the above section, many stories are convoluted because participants' demographics are convoluted, because their motivations are convoluted, and because it's not always clear what kinds of messages are being communicated. The Australian Rainbow Tie-Dye Cake Comment Apocalypse illustrates this point. There's just not enough context to determine exactly who is playing, exactly who is serious, and exactly what difference that might make. Even attempts to understand a behavior through careful emic analyses – which consider an event or behavior using concepts and frames indigenous to the group in question – can fall flat; not having access to basic information like "Who is doing this?" and "What are they trying to accomplish?" means there's not even a breadcrumb trail to begin following. Sometimes all you have to work with is the content rolling past you on the screen, and sometimes all you can do is ¯_(ツ)_/¯ as it goes. Because what even *is* that?

The Columbine shooter fan art described in the Introduction further exemplifies this folk ambivalence. As Ryan Rico (2015) explains, much of this content was created, circulated, and transformed by anonymous or pseudonymous participants. While some of the resulting creative expression *appeared* to be a genuine expression of solidarity with the killers, it could also have been posted in an effort to anger other users, as an inside joke within an unknown affinity group, or because one individual was messing around online and felt like doing something weird, with no deeper motivation than that. Adding to the mystery, while these posters may have been the original content creators, they also may have been reposting found images for a laugh ("look what fucked up thing I found!!") or out of outrage (*"look at what fucked up thing I found"*), which in turn may have been reappropriated by other audience members for who knows what reason. The problem is that, more often than not, observers can't know, because observers can't ask. Even when they can, it's difficult to assess the veracity of what some random stranger (particularly some random stranger who may or may not be in mischief mode) posts to the internet – a phenomenon Phillips (2015) experienced all too frequently in her study of memorial page trolls.

Further, the ease with which digitally mediated content can be unmoored from its original context and memetically spun straight off a cliff raises another, familiar specter: the ethics of amplification. Amplification in digitally mediated spaces carries the potential for harm – *immediate* harm, persistent and searchable harm – distinct from anything experienced in embodied spaces. That harm can land in the inboxes or social media feeds of those personally impacted by a tragedy within minutes, even if the post was "just a joke," even if the poster was speaking to a very specific audience and didn't mean any harm. Playful engagement with mass shootings, or really any mass-mediated tragedy, exemplifies the potential impact of amplification; content floated as harmless can be anything but.

But it's not as simple as wagging a finger at callous online joke telling, or any behavior that actively courts controversy. The basic – and, one would think, value-neutral – act of commenting on a story also risks amplifying the story's reach to other members of one's social network. After all, the more engagement a story generates, the more likely it is to live on through the circulation and transformation underscoring online interaction; content spreads memetically whether participants share something to signal support, disgust, or anything on the spectrum in between.

A striking example of problematic spread occurred in the summer of 2016, when American actress Leslie Jones – a woman of color – faced an onslaught of racist abuse stemming from her upcoming appearance in an all-female *Ghostbusters* remake. This abuse was nasty enough on its own, but it soon merged with, and was significantly worsened by, the concurrently popular "Harambe" meme. Harambe was an adult male gorilla housed at the Cincinnati Zoo. He made news after being killed that May, when a black child fell into the animal's enclosure. Almost immediately, Harambe's likeness was incorporated into a flurry of images, songs, and mashups. Folkloric engagement with the Harambe meme reached such critical mass that the Cincinnati Zoo was forced to delete its Twitter account in August due to the deluge of participatory, and often directly antagonistic, vernacular expression. Some of this content was silly and playful; some took an activist, animal rights stance; and some was simply disturbing – for example, the iterations that likened Harambe to Jones (Rogers 2016).

The story only got worse from there. Two days after the Cincinnati Zoo deleted its account, hackers compromised Jones' personal website and posted to its front page unlawfully acquired personal information, nude photos of the star, and Harambe images. In an interview with Jason Koebler (2016) at *Motherboard*, Phillips raised the issue of amplification in relation to this story, noting that when journalists, cultural critics, and individual citizens alike shared the story, even in order to condemn the abuse, they were helping to perpetuate that racist imagery, and in an indirect way, helping to perpetuate the harassment itself – an outcome, Phillips suspects, that was likely part of the hackers' plan. Even if it wasn't, that is precisely what happened. The Jones case thus speaks to the underlying ethical question of whether and how to engage with explicitly damaging content online. This is a question we asked ourselves when weighing the ethical costs against the potential political benefits of including this example here; ultimately we decided to discuss the case, because it so clearly illustrates the embodied implications of vernacular participation online, as well as the broader – and often devastating – implications of amplification. But not without consequence, as we readily, and uncomfortably, concede.

In this way, digital mediation adds new shades of ambivalence to longstanding questions about amplification. Shining a light on cultural problems, such as the violent misogyny and virulent racism animating the Jones harassment case, is often the only way to affect awareness; sometimes, not speaking up is worse, since silence risks signaling complicity. But by engaging with vernacular ambivalence online, one is always on the precipice of amplifying ugliness, even inadvertently. On the other hand, by not engaging with vernacular ambivalence online, particularly when the stakes are as high as in the Jones case, one risks extinguishing important critiques, which can only spread if their audiences give them life. This is a line we walk throughout this book – imperfectly, we are sure – as we've had to decide what to amplify and what to ignore in the service of our own critical analysis.

It is here where our world is most new and most brave; and it is also here where folkloric expression online is most ambivalent. What this ambivalence means, and the lesson it ultimately conveys, is that no broad, overarching theory could ever comfortably subsume all instances of vernacular participation and play – not around a campfire, not at a track meet, and certainly not online. The only approach, and it is an unquestionably imperfect approach, is to work with this ambivalence, not against it. Most importantly, to resist the urge to assert that something is a particular thing, and therefore means a certain thing, just because it looks like that thing. Online, what something "really" is, what it "really" means, are often the first certainties to go. What can be gleaned, however, is the impact of folkloric expression: what groups are helped, what groups are harmed, and, most importantly, whose voices are empowered to speak as a result. In exchange for easy certainty, in other words, ambivalence can help illuminate truths that are much more valuable. Truths that are both, on both sides.

Chapter overview and looking forward

This chapter forwarded a number of ideas, tensions, and themes that will permeate the remainder of this book. Most conspicuously, it illustrated how ambivalence in both embodied and digitally mediated spaces complicates a number of seemingly straightforward binaries, including formal and folk, commercial and populist, and conservative and dynamic. It focused specifically on the erroneous demarcation between now and then, which it complicated by affirming the very real and very impactive differences between embodied spaces and tools and digitally mediated spaces and tools. It's a brave new world, the chapter argued, and there is nothing new under the sun.

The following chapter will take this tension for granted, focusing more directly on the erroneous breakdown between "online" and "offline" spaces, and the ways this ambivalence challenges normalized assumptions about identity expression. It will also avoid making any sweeping generalizations about ambivalent identity expression, regardless of media. Instead it will argue that the best response to questions about such ambivalence is a quick eyebrow raise, coupled with the assertion "yes, and…".

2

Identity Play

Take a moment to think about who you are. What are the most fundamental aspects of your personality? What differentiates your unique self from all the other unique selves you pass on the street? There are many ways you could break down and examine your *I*, for example by race, gender, class, size, ability, geography, sexuality, the things you laugh at, the clothes you wear, the stuff you buy, and all the ways those identity markers complement and complicate each other. Similarly, there are many ways you could break down and analyze the concept of identity more broadly. In this chapter, we will focus on the performance of identity: the process – to borrow sociologist Erving Goffman's (1959) framing – of implicitly asserting who a person is or wants to be seen as being. Say by engaging in some mild misrepresentation on a first date. Or behaving like a total fuckwad in anonymous online spaces. Or finding new and interesting ways to sext with strangers. Because that's just who you *are*, dammit. At least, that's what you're hoping to communicate about that version of yourself in that particular moment to that particular audience. This is the *play* in *identity play*; tied as much to "performing a role" as "messing around" or "making fun of."

And we will get to performing for audiences and messing around and certainly making fun of things. We will begin, however, with an exploration of the basic form and function of identity play, drawing from 2014's #YesAllWomen hashtag and "Not All Men" meme. Following this introduction, we will argue that identity play, like all the types of play highlighted in this book, can help and harm in equal measure.

We will then turn to the main points of continuity between embodied and digitally mediated identity expression, a discussion that will foreground the various differences ushered in by digital mediation. Through our analysis of the fundamental ambivalence of identity play, we will call attention to the breakdown between online and offline, authenticity and performance, and, finally, between the individual and the collectives they navigate.

Performing the self, collectively

In 2014, a young man named Elliot Rodger killed six people and injured seven more in Santa Barbara, California. In a sprawling manifesto and pre-taped YouTube confession video, Rodger cited his romantic disappointments as the reason for his murder spree. He wanted to sleep with women, he explained, but they didn't want to sleep with him. Somebody needed to die. Following feminist (and general human) outrage over the attacks, many men, particularly those associated with the so-called "men's rights" activist movement, responded defensively. Not *all* men are violent misogynists, they insisted. And yes, gold star. They aren't. But as feminist writer Laurie Penny (2014) argues, while Rodger's actions were extreme, his sense of sexual entitlement and misogynist rage was far from aberrational. Rather, it occupied the far end of a broad spectrum of – in many cases culturally normalized – sexist attitudes toward women. Attitudes that impact all women to differing degrees at different points in their lives.

This basic idea precipitated the #YesAllWomen hashtag, which resonated on Twitter in the wake of the attack. By using the hashtag, women across the globe were able to share experiences of navigating the spectrum most grotesquely exemplified by Rodger. Sure, the hashtag implicitly granted, *not all men* are guilty of violent misogyny; but *yes all women* have been direct or indirect victims of a broader culture of misogyny. Examples ranged from the physically and sexually violent to the more mundane, including condescending male tones of voice (i.e. "mansplaining") and unwanted sexual advances. Sasha Weiss (2014) of the *New Yorker* collected a litany of responses exemplifying #YesAllWomen's collective argument:

- #YesAllWomen because "I have a boyfriend" is more effective than "I'm not interested" – men respect other men more than my right to say no.
- #YesAllWomen because apparently the clothes I wear is a more valid form of consent than the words I say.
- #YesAllWomen because every time I try to say that I want gender equality I have to explain that I don't hate men.

The phrase "Not All Men" was directly and pointedly reappropriated into this discourse; its ironic use called attention to, and simultaneously repudiated, the underlying message of "shut up, woman trying to talk to me, I'm not part of the problem." In our analysis of the #YesAllWomen hashtag and "Not All Men" meme (Phillips and Milner 2017), we discuss two popular images satirizing the "Not All Men" meme in particular: in one, the animatronic shark from the film *Jaws* hurls himself onto the back of a fishing boat. "Not all men," the caption reads. The same caption is affixed to a cartoon rendering of The Kool-Aid Man soft drink mascot – red, smirking, and jug-shaped – as he crashes through a wall, shocking a room full of people. Both images, we argue, lampoon the tone-deafness of shouting down women's concerns in order to deny personal complicity in perpetuating those concerns.

Vernacular engagement with the #YesAllWomen hashtag in the wake of Rodger's attacks thus provided an outlet for participants to assert who they were, what they had experienced, and what they valued – and just as importantly, what they rejected. It also gestured toward participants' identities more broadly, including where someone was raised, what linguistic, technological, and cultural literacies they had, and the media they had access to. All of which influence not just how someone feels about a particular media text, and not just what they choose to do with it, but whether or not they even notice its presence. Images of Jaws and The Kool-Aid Man, for example, resonate as a counterargument only if one recognizes both references and can appropriately decode their subversion. For those not weaned on that particular segment of American popular culture, the visual joke would be dulled, if it was even recognized as a joke to begin with.

In addition to communicating aspects of identity, vernacular engagement with #YesAllWomen is performative in that it implies a real or imagined audience. The presence, or at least the possibility, of an audience is not to suggest that such expression is "fake" or inauthentic. Instead, it is to underscore Goffman's point that identity expression is about asserting who a person is, or at least who a person wants to be seen as being; it is "all the activity of a given participant on a given occasion which serves to influence in any way any of the other participants" (1959, 15). With its explicitly focused argument that, yes, *all* women have to deal with a spectrum of sexist behavior, #YesAllWomen certainly meets the criteria for "serving to influence other participants."

To do so, #YesAllWomen participants use what Goffman describes as *front*, the "expressive equipment of a standard kind intentionally or unwittingly employed by the individual during his performance" (22; side eyes to Goffman's default use of the male pronoun[7]). In the case of #YesAllWomen, front can include effective use of hashtagging, eye-catching visuals, or the adoption of a pro-feminist profile photo. No matter the specific circumstance, front is therefore akin to a mask, one that represents the "self we would like to be" (19). Or, more subtly, the self we feel we should be – even just for one evening, interaction, or tweet. This mask can consist of specific artifacts (clothes, cars, profile photos), or it can consist of semiotic and affective expressions (word choice, tone, gestures). We employ a variety of masks, regardless of their specific make-up, to perform a variety of roles.

And during these performances, audiences exert what Goffman describes as "reciprocal influence" (15) on the performer and their masks. In fact, audiences often help *create* performers' masks, perhaps by handing over a pre-formed mask, implicitly demanding "play this role!"; perhaps by snatching an existing mask away and etching on new markings, contouring the features, or adjusting the expression; perhaps by watching as the performer constructs their own mask, then pointing out the details that still need tweaking. Although masks are worn by individuals, the performances they help facilitate are therefore fundamentally collective – as reflective of all the groups, relationships, and communities being performed for as of the individuals doing the performing. In the case of tweets supporting #YesAllWomen, individual tweets, and the individual masks they represent, are placed in the context of, and ultimately are strengthened by, shared feminist experiences and concerns. One voice channeling a chorus of others – equally collective and self-contained. All identity performances, including the performance of gender, class, racial or national identity, sexuality, and the various and complicated intersections therein, are subject to this interplay.

As we will see in the sections that follow, some of these masks are explicitly positive. Some are explicitly negative. Some are both, sometimes simultaneously, depending on who might be looking. What unifies our masks – and we all wear more than one – is that they represent the performance of becoming ourselves. A self that only exists in relation to others; a self that isn't so singular after all.

The masks of ambivalence

The reciprocal influence between the collective audience and the individual performer is the first and most basic level of identity ambivalence. We are all special snowflakes with special personalities and hopes and dreams and fears, *and* these characteristics are predicated on groups of people, perhaps spanning generations, about whom we may not even be aware. Of course, we are often painfully aware of our audience, at least the immediate one. This awareness conjures the second level of ambivalence: the fact that our performances could go either way – indeed *many* ways – depending on whom we might be talking to, and what we might be trying to accomplish in any given moment. To play these different (and sometimes conflicting) parts, we all make conscious, unconscious, and sometimes semi-conscious behavioral and linguistic choices to highlight certain masks. And sometimes this goes swimmingly. But sometimes there are no clear winners. What might be a damn fine mask for one audience might be explicitly negative for another; both perceptions can occur simultaneously, and impact different audiences in an inversely proportional relationship, i.e. the better something is over here, the worse it is over there.

And sometimes, god help us, more than one mask is required at once. Say at a wedding – maybe your wedding – attended by a variety of social groups, with a variety of expectations for your behavior: your very conservative parents; the friends you were deeply unconservative with in college; a handful of bigoted relatives prejudiced against *X* race, nationality, or sexual orientation; a handful of friends of *X* race, nationality, or sexual orientation with whom you have spent years mocking said relatives; the cousins who judge you; the cousins whom you judge; a former partner or two who knew what you were like before you had kids / found Jesus / lost Jesus / stopped drinking / started drinking; your present partner who doesn't know about any of that, or how many other former partners there have been; and so on. In these cases, arguably the trickiest identity performances to manage, we must straddle the lines of our own fractured selves, perform appropriately to mixed audiences with divergent expectations, and try not to lose track of what *I* we are when.

The often inelegant, uncomfortable, or otherwise fumbling attempt to construct the appropriate mask for the appropriate audience is the serious, sincere implication of identity play. The specific performative behaviors might not appear serious or sincere, and might not even feel serious or sincere to participants. Tweeting about Robin Thicke's stupid sunglasses at the VMAs, for example; photoshopping an image of Brother Bear from the Berenstain Bears getting kicked in the dick; deciding to drink Jack Daniels around a campfire or play dollar bill track meet pranks. But these choices can lead to serious and sincere revelations about who a person is, or, just as importantly, who they want to be, or desperately want not to be, in that specific moment or more broadly in life.

In addition to identity play that ultimately results in revelations about the self (a self always embedded within broader collectives), there also exists a wide spectrum of identity play that is undertaken for fun, sport, or disruption for disruption's sake, building ambivalence on top of ambivalence on top of ambivalence. We ourselves have indulged in such activity. Phillips – mischievous by nature – recalls the pleasures of passing notes in sixth grade by rolling a small piece of paper around the inkwell of a ballpoint pen, which she'd then return to its plastic sheath, pass to one of her friends, and tee-hee Mr. Mueller would never know. She also revels in finding new and interesting ways to use curse words in academic writing; as a graduate student she resolved to use the word "fuck" in everything she ever published. And why, you might ask? I dunno, because it's funny? she asks right back, shrugging and checking this book off her list. Similarly, Milner – populist by nature – recalls finding ways to channel his punk-rock rage while unloading trucks at Wal-Mart during college. Because they were 19 and angry and knew the security camera blind spots, he and his co-workers often passed the time during their shifts with a game they called "Light Bulb Baseball": fluorescent tubes were bats, incandescent bulbs were balls, and the back wall of the delivery truck was Fenway Park's Green Monster.

And this is just a tiny fraction of how we have – and, were we to venture a guess, just about everyone reading this book has – articulated identity by playing with, or against, a specific target. These behaviors, in turn, help create and sustain the *I*; they reveal what a person values, and the groups with which they identify (ludic tinkerers, academic misfits, exploited workers). Who and what a person rejects is just as important; these antipathies help construct identity *via negativa*. Who someone is, based on who they're not, who they hate, and who they mess with. Say by playfully reappropriating anti-feminist perspectives to further the feminist cause, or by elaborately hiding notes in your pen because, I dunno, it's funny, or by smashing lightbulbs because you're no corporate drone.

As evidenced by these examples, identity construction *via negativa* can occupy all points on the ethical spectrum. The playfulness of feminists eager to use men's rights activists' words against them, for example, is pointedly political, even as it is also a source of levity and humor. Other forms of targeted identity play are mostly harmless fun, like passing notes in class because you're not supposed to (no offense to Mr. Mueller, Phillips always liked him). Other forms, like Light Bulb Baseball, might be fun, but certainly aren't harmless, at least if you're the one who has to take the loss on the broken product or has to sweep up the debris next shift. And still other forms are neither fun nor harmless, as "play," here, ultimately just means mask adjustment, and furthermore adjustment *toward* a particular audience, *against* a particular object. By shouting at women in order to argue that not all men shout at women, men's rights activists are playing with aspects of their identity. By writing his violently misogynist manifesto and taking six lives because he couldn't get a date, Elliot Rodger was playing with his. This spectrum highlights the point that identity play can absolutely go either way, in fact can go any way, and in the process can leave a trail of destruction in its wake.

Old standbys and online identity

At the most basic, performative level, there is little difference between identity play in digitally mediated spaces and identity play in embodied spaces. Online and off, identity is a series of masks. It is as much about collective others as it is about individual selves. It is just as consistent in its fracture. And it is every bit as ambivalent. This section will foreground three points of continuity between "online" and "offline" identity, in the process challenging the presumed binary between the internet and what is framed, conversely, as "real life." It will also continue exploring the breakdown between the mask of identity and the audience that shapes it, as well as the breakdown between "authentic" identity and its presumably inauthentic performative counterpart.

The first and most basic point of continuity between "online" and "offline" identity is that, even online, the physical body still matters. The physical body is still *paramount*. Digital media scholars like Lori Kendall (2002), T. L. Taylor (2006), danah boyd (2014), and many others have long argued precisely this point, and have pushed back against any stark divide between "online" and "offline," particularly in the context of identity expression. Even today, "online" and "offline" are frequently demarcated in public discourse as separate spaces with separate sets of rules. The common online exhortation that it's "just the internet" evidences this split, as does the impulse to describe embodied experiences as "irl," (i.e. "in real life") as opposed to the apparently less real life of that somewhere-else place called "The Internet."

But as #YesAllWomen shows, lived experiences of gender bias and other markers of embodied identity are directly encoded into every tweet, every comment, every image. Online and offline experiences are in fact so fundamentally intertwined that it's impossible to parse where the embodied ends and the digital begins; the one sustains and contextualizes the other. Beth E. Kolko, Lisa Nakamura, and Gilbert E. Rodman (2000) emphasize this point, arguing that a person's choices online inevitably draw from what that person already knows – or what they think they know – about the world. This is true even when a person adopts identity markers that don't line up with embodied experiences – say, if a cisgendered man creates a female videogame avatar, or if a white person claims to be a person of color in an online forum. Where a person goes (including the basic ability to go online at all), what language they speak once they get there, how they treat the people they encounter: everything comes back to the politically situated body.

The second point of continuity between digitally mediated and embodied identity play is how thoroughly this play is marked by performative fracture. Identity is no more complete and consistent online than it is offline. Which is to say: it isn't complete, and it isn't consistent, regardless of where the behaviors take place. Just as they do in embodied spaces, and using many of the same basic strategies, people online are constantly playing with – that is to say, highlighting, subverting, or downplaying – facets of the self. Not using the same tools, of course, but certainly with the same frequency. In the process, these identity performances call attention to the fact that "real" and "fake" are relative concepts in relation to identity, both offline and on; regardless of the degree of mediation, it's not a question of which mask is the most authentic mask, but rather which mask is the most appropriate mask within a particular context.

Even deliberate deception – presumed to be a significant risk in digital spaces – plays out similarly offline and on. As Nancy K. Baym argues, "it would be as naive to imagine that people do not deceive online as it is to think everyone is always honest offline. With the rare and well-publicized exception, however, most lies told are minor strategic manipulations rather than malevolent falsehoods" (2015, 128). In short, we all deceive, on the internet and in our own living rooms. We don't tell our oversensitive friend what we really think about their haircut. We don't tell our colleague we skipped their party because we felt like watching ghost shows. We don't admit to skimming that book someone we're dating told us we just *had* to read – and a thousand other mostly inconsequential stretchings of the truth.

Of course, some of our deceptions – wherever they occur, for whatever reason they are proffered – can be quite harmful, either intentionally, because we're mean, or inadvertently, because we don't know what else to do. But at bottom, even when we're up to no good, we are all twirling and bowing in the complex dance of performative identity. We might be working hard to impress someone at a bar or working hard to impress someone on Tinder. We might be managing our personal brands on Twitter or at the local farmer's market. We might be smoothing out a disagreement with a childhood friend over iMessage. Regardless of circumstance or cultural context, regardless of degree of mediation, regardless of how incongruous a person's *I* might appear to outsiders, we are all performing our roles in the best way we know how.

The third point of continuity between embodied and digitally mediated spaces surrounds age-old concerns about *deindividuation*. This might be a surprising claim to some, since deindividuation is often floated as a blanket explanation for why everything is so terrible now. But as it turns out, blanket explanations for why everything is so terrible now long predate the internet. And deindividuation has long been a principal concern. Well-established in social psychology (see Postmes and Spears 1998), deindividuation attributes "antinormative collective behaviors" (i.e. shitty group behavior) to the effects of being subsumed by a crowd. Offline, worry about deindividuation tends to center on violent, or potentially violent, groups. This can include mobs, protesters, pissed-off sports fans, Wal-Mart truck unloaders playing baseball with light bulbs, and so on, all of which pose – at least could potentially pose – a direct, physical threat to life and property. Online, these concerns are directed squarely at the deindividuating effects of anonymity, and further, the havoc one is able to wreak – the havoc one is afraid someone else will wreak – when sitting behind a computer screen. From this view, people behave badly online because they aren't physically there and can sidestep the emotional impact of their actions.

The presumed relationship between deindividuation and destructive behavior is so resonant, in both embodied and digitally mediated spaces, that the concept is often discussed in tandem with the "banality of evil" thesis. First proposed by political philosopher Hannah Arendt (1963) in response to the trial of Adolf Eichmann, one of the Holocaust's primary architects, the banality of evil thesis states that a person needn't *be* evil – psychotic or malicious – to commit horrendous acts. Rather, a person need only think in terms of social roles ("I was only following orders") instead of personal responsibility. Psychologist Stanley Milgram's (1963) infamous obedience experiment, in which research subjects seemed more than happy to administer what they thought to be fatal shocks to fellow test subjects at the direction of researchers, appeared to support Arendt's thesis. So too did psychologist Philip Zimbardo's (Haney, Banks, and Zimbardo 1973) equally infamous Stanford Prison Experiment, in which a group of students were arbitrarily divided into groups of guards and inmates. Taking their roles to heart, the guards became so vicious so quickly that the experiment was suspended after six days; this appeared to confirm the highly disturbing hypothesis that average, well-adjusted people can turn into monsters overnight, simply by losing track of who they are as individuals.

On the surface, the negative impacts of deindividuation and the banality of evil provide an intuitive explanation for violent, antagonistic, and destructive behavior, particularly when participants are anonymous and cannot be held accountable for their actions. Psychologist John Suler (2004) affirms this perspective, suggesting that the process of severing the embodied, named self from the dissociated and anonymous self fosters behaviors one would be much more likely to avoid in embodied spaces. The webcomic *Penny Arcade*'s "Greater Internet Fuckwad Theory" (Krahulik and Holkins 2004) parallels Suler's hypothesis. According to *Penny Arcade*, "Normal Person + Anonymity + Audience = Total Fuckwad." A joke, certainly, but one premised on the presumed dark side of deindividuation online.

The problem, however, is that despite their widespread acceptance, the evidence supporting these theories – whether applied online or off – is mixed at best. In a meta-analysis of 60 independent deindividuation studies, including those conducted by Zimbardo, psychologists Tom Postmes and Russell Spears (1998) found little to no direct correlation between deindividuation and destructive behavior in embodied spaces. Being subsumed by a group, they argue, doesn't in itself universally account for misbehavior. Rather, behavior – both beneficial and destructive – appears most strongly influenced by existing group norms, and furthermore by the degree to which individuals within the group already identify with those norms. Participants actively choose to wear that particular mask, in that particular moment, because it's a mask they *want* to wear.

Alex Haslam and Stephen Reicher (2012) echo these findings in their contestation of the banality of evil thesis, which they argue fails to account for the *relational* nature of tyranny: the fact that people follow orders not blindly, but as an active reflection of personal affinity. Mask alignment, in other words. In an interview discussing their study, Haslam applies his and Reicher's conclusions to 2006's Abu Ghraib torture photo controversy, in which American soldiers jocularly mugged alongside tortured detainees. While the soldiers clearly knew they were being filmed, Haslam states, "they had a sense that the people they were waving at and smiling at was an in-group who would approve of what they were doing. They were therefore in some sense doing it for them" (quoted in Gordon 2012). Similarly, he argues, while Milgram's and Zimbardo's studies *appear* to show their subjects' passive obedience to authority, they belie how extensively research participants identified with the researchers, and actively chose to play the role of dutiful test subject (and, in Zimbardo's case, dutiful *student* – adding an additional layer to the power dynamic). From this view, destructive behavior isn't a function of mob rule or sudden ethical lapses caused by deindividuation or the banality of "simply following orders." It's about who's holding the camera, and what you want that person to think about your pose.

Similarly, while anonymity in digitally mediated spaces *can* facilitate toxic expression, the disinhibiting effects of anonymity can also facilitate compassion and emotional openness as easily as aggression – a point Suler (2004) readily concedes. Anonymity can even facilitate explicitly supportive behaviors, as digital media researcher Mary Gray (2009) finds in her analysis of LGBTQ youth in rural America. For some of the teenagers Gray interviews, online spaces are more welcoming than embodied environments, since embodied environments are often replete with unsupportive, or even outright bigoted, individuals and institutions. If these teens are wearing a mask online, it's one that fits them a little better than the mask they're forced to wear in their closeted, embodied lives.

In short, deindividuated, anonymous participation online can facilitate the bad, the good, and the in-between, resulting in every permutation of communicative expression imaginable, from racist invectives to random acts of kindness – just as offline faces subsumed by the crowd can be criminals, first responders, or Good Samaritans. Regardless of the degree of mediation, identity performances depend on the complex intertwine of individual needs and audience expectations.

New complications to online identity

While the seemingly separate fiefdoms of "online" and "offline" identity play are subject to significant, demonstrable overlap, digital media simultaneously engender complications that simply don't exist in embodied contexts. Not only do modularity, modifiability, archivability, and accessibility usher in a brave new world of online identity expression, anonymity, pseudonymity, and all their resulting behavioral and motivational ambiguity further complicate the masks we wear and the masks others compel us to wear.

The most fundamental difference between identity expression online and off is the fact that there are more opportunities to play with identity online. Not because identity on the internet magically becomes more complicated, but because digital media afford what internet scholar Joseph Walther (1994) describes as a "communication imperative." Online, we only exist in so far as we actively communicate that existence. No matter what platform a person might be using, from email to Facebook to Twitter, no matter how many selfies or videos that person might post to Snapchat or any other smartphone application, digitally mediated interactions require participants to construct identity markers using available tools. Even on anonymous or pseudonymous platforms, participants are constantly performing something. They have to; that is, quite literally, the only way to render oneself visible online. These choices – which can include the adoption of specific email handles, usernames, profile pictures, etc. – are necessary regardless of how close a given identity might hew to the offline body doing the typing.

In the case of #YesAllWomen, for example, information about the embodied identities, perspectives, and experiences of those using the hashtag was largely restricted to the tweets themselves, as well as any information communicated through a particular user's Twitter bio and profile picture. Unless observers had embodied context to fall back on – i.e. a tweet

was coming from someone known in an embodied sense –
the only available context cues were those conveyed through
communication. Compare this to embodied spaces, where
individuals are able to extrapolate information about the people
they're interacting with based on someone's height, weight,
gender, ability, race, dress, and overall comportment – not
always fairly or accurately (often unfairly and inaccurately).
But regardless of what might be said or done, messages about
identity are communicated. In person, that just *happens*.

Online, this communication imperative affords an ambivalent paradox. On the one hand, digital media allow individuals
to control, in unprecedented ways, how they play with their
own identities. These media provide a set of tools that can be
used to earnestly express, deliberately deceive, or amorphously
blend biographical fact and biographical fiction. On the other
hand, these same media and tools can *strip* individuals of
control, also in unprecedented ways: they allow users to play
with the identities of others – essentially weaponizing someone
else's mask – by collapsing context, spreading secrets, and
hijacking selves. Regardless of whether they are used to build
up or tear down, these affordances further muddy, and at
times completely wash away, the line between the mask of
individual identity and the reciprocal influence of the
audience.

Masks you make yourself

Due to the disembodied nature of online expression, and
spurred on by the communication imperative, online participants are able to present their identities in a variety of ways,
using a variety of tools. They also have the option of sidestepping or outright disregarding existing social restrictions,
particularly those that might inhibit freedom of expression
in embodied spaces.

Internet scholar Pavel Curtis (1997) describes this affordance
as "reduced social risk." Just as online disinhibition can be
harnessed for positive or negative ends, the reduced social

risk of online communication carries similarly ambivalent potential. One can cloak oneself in the relative safety of the internet to do great harm, produce great good, or even just express an aspect of oneself with reduced worry about retribution or finger-pointing. In the case of #YesAllWomen, the mediated dimensions of the conversation allowed female participants to share sentiments and experiences they might avoid discussing in embodied spaces, perhaps due to lack of sympathetic allies, perhaps due to fears of backlash, perhaps due to preemptive irritation at the prospect of being intellectually dressed down, again, by some mansplaining dude in an ill-fitting suit. At the same time, these same platform affordances allowed antagonistic, anti-feminist participants to use #YesAllWomen to amplify overtly misogynist messages, with a similarly reduced potential for negative reprisal.

The ability to choose, at a granular level, how to render oneself publicly also has a direct and directly ambivalent impact on interpersonal relationships. Depending on the platform, users can decide what to engage with and what to disregard – and how public one wants to make those slights. On Skype, for example, users can set their online status to "available" yet ignore certain messages from certain people. On Twitter, they can "subtweet," posting passive-aggressive jabs without specifically mentioning their target. On Facebook, they can "hide" the posts of contacts without going as far as "unfriending" them. On all these platforms and others, users can simply "ghost," i.e. go silent without explanation, when they're angry or bored or done with a person – and in some cases, when they want the rest of the world to know it.[8] Each of these behaviors is a direct result of reduced social risk, itself a direct result of communication's centrality to online identity.

The affordances that allow individuals to easily choose and shape their masks online amplify existing identity fracture. One persistent concern hinges on identity subterfuge. Even if, as Baym (2015) reminds us, most lies online are small (if strategic), the risk for more malevolent falsehood is high on the list of resonant online panics. Addressing this potential, Judith Donath (1999) argues that online identity deception is a – if not *the* – primary threat to online community formation. The threat is so potent, she argues, a community doesn't even need to be deceived for negative effects to be felt; the mere possibility that someone could be lying about their true identity – whatever motivation a person might have for doing so – risks seeding a group with distrust and paranoia, and therefore can be just as damaging as the behavior itself.

The most extreme examples of online deceptiveness are known as "catfishing," in which an individual poses as a fictitious person, or steals the identity of a real person, in order to "hook" a given target. The motives for doing so can vary, from extortion to lust to wishful thinking to boredom. The term *catfish* was popularized in 2010 by a documentary film called (go figure) *Catfish*. In the film, a trio of 20-something New Yorkers capture the burgeoning online relationship between Nev, one of the men, and a young woman purportedly named Megan, but who turns out to be part of an elaborate hoax concocted by a middle-aged woman named Angela. In the film, Angela is framed as a catfish, whose threatening underwater antagonisms help keep other fish alert. She certainly keeps Nev alert, serving as a reminder that on the internet, nothing, and no one, should be taken at face value – and further suggesting that, while Angela's actions were wrong, she also "helped" her victim see how things "really were" online.

Problematic as that victim-blaming moral may be, *Catfish* put a name to a phenomenon that had plagued – or at least instilled paranoia in – internet users for decades. One of the first recorded cases of what would eventually be known as catfishing was chronicled in 1985 by reporter Lindsay Van Gelder. Van Gelder's "The Strange Case of the Electronic Lover" tells the story of a male psychologist in his fifties posing as Joan, a wheelchair-bound, severely brain-damaged neuropsychologist in her late twenties. For years, Joan deceived the online communities she belonged to – many of which were support groups for women with disabilities – and carried on a series of online affairs with the women she met through these chat rooms and listservs. Once revealed, news of Joan's deceit sent shockwaves through the communities that had come to love, trust, and appreciate Joan for the comfort she had provided to so many.

The similarly strange case of Manti Te'o, a star Notre Dame football player (see Burke and Dickey 2013), provides a more recent example. Over the course of a single terrible week in 2012, Te'o lost his grandmother and his girlfriend, Lennay Kekua, whom he'd been long-distance dating for over a year. In the days following her death, however, reports surfaced that Kekua – who had died of leukemia after barely surviving a terrible car crash – wasn't just not dead, but also wasn't an actual person. Instead, Kekua was the wholly made-up online creation of a male acquaintance, Ronaiah Tuiasosopo, who simply appropriated the profile pictures of an unaware, unconnected female bystander. Te'o claimed to be shellshocked by the news. Others questioned the timeline of events, and whether or not Te'o was in on the hoax. Even as reporters combed through the evidence, details remained confusing and unverifiable.

The media blitz surrounding the Te'o case fueled additional interest in the subject of catfishing, which proved so salacious, and so compelling to audiences, that it spawned a slew of catfish-related television shows beginning in 2012. Series include MTV's *Catfish*, which has aired five seasons since 2012 and is helmed by many of the same people who worked on the 2010 documentary; 2014's *Web of Lies* on Investigation Discovery, a Discovery Channel subsidiary focused on grisly true crime stories (a genre of television Phillips and her sister lovingly refer to as "Murderworld"); and 2016's *#killerpost* on the women-centric Oxygen Network. As rabid interest in the Te'o story and iterative crime-show viewership attests, people sure love catfishing, as long as it isn't happening to them (protip, courtesy of Phillips and Milner: just do a video call and have them put a shoe on their head or something).

Whether online deceptions are harmless or targeted or somewhere in between, determining why anonymous or pseudonymous actors do the things they do can be very difficult. Logistic questions, on the other hand, are much more straight-forward. Namely, people engage in various forms of identity construction and deception in digitally mediated spaces because they're able to: because the contours of the space allow it. Along with the more obvious platform affordances of anonymity and pseudonymity, the technological affordances of modularity, modifiability, archivability, and accessibility each play their part in this process. In the case of catfishing, modularity and modifiability underscore the freedom that deceivers have to craft new identities out of existing components. This could mean taking credit for other people's work – for example, in the film *Catfish* when Angela, posing as Megan, sends Nev a series of supposedly self-recorded songs that turn out to be pilfered from YouTube. In a similar fashion, one could use the "drop in" content structure of existing social media plat-forms – i.e. the ability to indicate with a single click whom one is related to or friends with – to weave a false relational network. In the case of *Catfish*, Angela invented an entire Facebook line-up of friends and family for Megan.

Archivability and accessibility, in turn, afford deceivers the ability to find, store, replicate, and recall the raw materials for their deception. In the Te'o case, catfisher Tuiasosopo decided to use – without seeking permission – images of one of his high school classmates to create his Kekua character. One might also use these affordances to seed a plausible history to assuage any lingering suspicions maintained by targets or post-hoc researchers. The communication impera-tive allows one to easily meet the criteria for verifiability – that is to say, the ability to be searched for on multiple platforms – as Angela did for Megan and Tuiasosopo did for Kekua.

Even if they unfold solely in digitally mediated spaces, these kinds of deceptions can have immediate embodied implications, once again illustrating the intertwine between "online" and "offline." They are also deeply unethical, in that they preclude participant consent, both for the direct targets and for those peripherally caught up in someone else's weird lie. These deceptions do, however, serve an instructive purpose (beyond the vaguely apologist assertion that "at least the catfish taught you an important lesson in the end!"): they illustrate the fact that creating oneself online – literally making oneself publicly visible – is as easy as clicking a few buttons. Tinkering with aspects of the self doesn't take much more effort than that, nor does creating an entirely new or alternative self; in many cases, all one needs to do is steal a few online pictures from wherever, fill in some data points, and boom. Suddenly you've got a profile – a "person" – who can be used to any mischievous or nefarious end. And thanks to reduced social risk, that new person can be deleted – thus covering whatever tracks, you monster – at any moment (well, provided law enforcement doesn't get involved; don't get too cocky). Of course, people are able to deceptively perform affinity, assert false biographical details, or alter their appearance in embodied spaces. But the fact remains that, on the internet, a person can be adjusted or constructed from scratch in just a few minutes – something we cannot do as easily offline, and which posits, at the very least, significant behavioral potential.

In addition to allowing users to tweak aspects of their identity online for a variety of generative, destructive, and neutral expressions, the control afforded by the communication imperative and reduced social risk allows people to create ironic or satirical identities alongside identities forwarded in earnest. This affordance is the engine behind that old internet stand-by, Poe's Law. As discussed last chapter, Poe's Law postulates that sincere extremism online (manifesting as bigotry, conspiracy theorizing, or simply being wrong about something) is often indistinguishable from satirical extremism. It's just not possible to know with any degree of certainty what an anonymous stranger on the internet means when, for example, they start screaming about immigrants in the comment thread of an article about rainbow tie-dye cake. Do they sincerely equate rainbow tie-dye cakes with fascism? Are they being difficult to entertain themselves? Is the answer – somewhere deep in their soul – "a little bit of both?" For a mix of old and new reasons, it's difficult to know exactly who is expressing exactly what about their "real" identity (or identities) online. This ambiguity kicks the ambivalence of online identity performance even further into hyperdrive.

The November 2015 controversy surrounding New York University's "Union of White Students" Facebook group illustrates just how difficult it can be to parse motives, meaning, and audiences when considering performances of identity online. The group, like similar groups purporting affiliation with other universities, was created in the wake of high-profile controversies at Yale University and the University of Missouri. On both campuses, students of color pushed back against racially insensitive university policies and administrators; many called for safe spaces in which issues of racial inequity could be addressed in a way that honored the students' experiences and foregrounded the pressing issue of campus diversity and inclusiveness. Protests weren't restricted to just these campuses, however; many participating students were also active in the broader Black Lives Matter movement, which was born in 2013 as a response to broad, systemic inequalities and relentless acts of police violence against people of color. But rather than addressing this fuller political context, or the students' stated – and, to editorialize, legitimate – grievances, much journalistic coverage of the Yale and University of Missouri demonstrations denigrated the protests and the protesters, arguing that participating students were hypersensitive, coddled, and as the *Atlantic*'s Conor Friedersdorf (2015) asserted, intolerant bullies.

It was out of this milieu that several "Union of White Students" Facebook groups emerged. The group claiming affiliation with NYU – and which NYU administrators explicitly condemned – received the most media attention. In its "About" section, this group promised to create a "safe space" for white students to celebrate the "pioneering will and greatness of our unique and virtuous people…We condemn the cowardly campaigns of moral subjugation and propaganda that seek to instill self-hatred and surrender within European-American youth and justify the continued invasion and degradation of the lands, institutions, and cultural heritage that is rightly ours" ("Union of White NYU Students" 2015).

Shortly after the NYU group was created, journalists began investigating the veracity of the groups' alleged university affiliations; very little evidence was found tying any of the groups to the universities in question (see O'Connor 2015). Rather, the groups were thought to be the work of unaffiliated troublemakers connected to 4chan, its more aggressive cousin 8chan, or white nationalists from the *Daily Stormer* (Weill 2015). But the "Union of White NYU Students" administrators were in it to win it; they continued pushing their claims to various news outlets, particularly the ultra-conservative *Breitbart* blog, which took the bait (see Bokhari 2015). The group even provided a highly redacted image of an alleged Facebook group administrator logged into the NYU student portal – really, in the end, only proving that someone was able to access or manufacture such an image.

As in many of the cases discussed thus far, figuring out the true identities behind the "Union of White NYU Students" group would be difficult enough; the Facebook groups' administrators easily could have lied about who they were, though one or more of the participants could have been enrolled at NYU, or any of the schools in question. Far more difficult is the question of motives. Was the NYU group the handiwork of sincere racists eager to publicize the white nationalist message following the Yale and University of Missouri demonstrations? Was it the handiwork of anti-racist activists eager to satirize the backwards absurdity of white nationalism? Was it the handiwork of a group of individuals eager to drum up more controversy because they thought it would be funny, regardless of politics?

Complicating matters more, the Facebook groups could also have been the handiwork of the then-burgeoning and already deeply confusing "alt-right"* movement, an amalgamation of (professed, though possibly sometimes satirical) Donald Trump-supporting white nationalists, neoreactionary monarchists (whatever that means), and run-of-the-mill deplorables (see Matthews 2016). Described by progressive activist Daryle Lamont Jenkins as "hipster Nazis" (quoted in Goldberg 2016), the alt-right rose to cultural prominence in 2016 by forwarding precisely the sentiments expressed on the "Union of White NYU Students" Facebook page. This potential connection is most strikingly expressed in the phrase "the continued invasion and degradation of the lands, institutions, and cultural heritage that is rightly ours." This statement is almost too perfectly, obliviously, stupidly racist *not* to be a joke (or a certain kind of person's idea of a joke, anyway; we're not laughing). Of course it could be both joke and argument, regardless of any explicit or latent connections to the alt-right: the result of sincere white nationalists trying to humorously co-opt discourses of marginalization, or other less explicitly white nationalist, but still ultimately misguided,

*Since the term was popularized online in early 2016, *alt-right* has become little more than a polite euphemism for white nationalism, if not outright Neo-Nazism. This increasingly threatening turn has expressed itself in a wave of embodied hate crimes in the wake of Donald Trump's Presidential victory. After the election, our misgivings about the term rose proportionally to the uptick in violence whitewashed by the "alt-right" framing; just as the term "trolling" minimizes the emotional impact of online antagonism, the term "alt-right" minimizes the visceral, toxic impact of bigotry. While this linguistic and behavioral shift occurred too late in the publication process to change the term throughout the text, we leave this note as an explicit disavowal, and encourage readers to replace *alt-right* with *white nationalist* whenever the term is encountered.

individuals confronting what they see as a "politically correct" double standard.

Assigning motive gets more complicated the farther down the rabbit hole you go, in this case and in fact all cases muddied by Poe's Law. What might start out as one thing for one individual or group can quickly evolve into another thing for another individual or group, splintering off into a million different directions, always allowing for the possibility that multiple participants can simultaneously bounce *between* groups, seeding conflicting motives as they go. When faced with such a relentless communicative flurry, satisfying conclusions are the last thing one can expect to find. Much more likely, instead, is the discovery of new questions. Questions, as we'll see below, made even more vexing when the person playing with identity becomes the person whose identity is being played *with*.

Masks made for you
Whether the end goal is outright deceit, mischievous fun, or something in between, digitally mediated communication offers new opportunities to experiment with any number of masks. While digital tools – spurred on by the communication imperative and reduced social risk – can be empowering, and often *are* empowering, the control they afford is not complete. #YesAllWomen, for example, allowed women to proudly wear the masks of feminism, solidarity, and survival. But these masks could just as easily be harnessed by others, and used as a weapon against their wearers. This final section will explore this potential, which is predicated on the paradox inherent to the communication imperative: the same tools that allow you to construct your mask *just so* also allow others to take your mask from you, and do with it whatever they please.

Underscoring this ambivalence is the fact that identity performances online can be much more difficult to manage than in embodied spaces, despite the level of control afforded by digital media. Often at the heart of this difficulty is *context collapse*, which digital media scholar Jessica Vitak describes as "the flattening out of mutual distinct audiences in one's social network, such that people from different contexts become part of a singular group of message recipients" (2012, 451). Vitak highlights the various identity complications stemming from context collapse. First, participants are not always able to know exactly who is engaging with content posted online, and therefore are not always able to cater their message to a given audience. Second, participants can't always know whether their audience is expecting their "public" and "professional" self or their "private" and "informal" self. As social media researchers Alice Marwick and danah boyd (2010) highlight in their analysis of identity performance on social media, the nature and consequences of this collapse can vary from platform to platform, person to person, and audience to audience; but regardless, the affordances of digital media complicate how individuals are able to express their identities.

This is not to minimize the complexity of embodied interactions; one is often required to switch between masks offline, or in situations populated by multiple audiences with conflicting expectations, to wear more than one mask at a time. The difference is that, in most embodied spaces under most normal circumstances, one knows who is present in the room, allowing one to anticipate performative roadblocks. At the very least, a person offline can count the number of eyes and ears present – a luxury and, in many cases, a basic sense of reassurance ("it's cool, we're all friends here") less certain in many digital spaces. Online, context is often the first thing to go, particularly when one is reacting to a single image, video clip, or tweet. D. E. Wittkower attributes this confusion to the "promiscuous intermixing of audiences" (2014, 4.6); a single piece of online content that makes perfect sense to one audience may end up being grossly misunderstood or misappropriated by any number of competing audiences (of which the text's originator may not even be aware).

This risk is ever-present in hypersocial, hypermediated, and frankly just hyper, digital spaces. As political scholar Zizi Papacharissi (2010) demonstrates, digital media texts don't always end up where they were intended to go; private information can easily become public, and vice versa. Even private behaviors conducted under a pseudonym can affix themselves to a person's public persona, which thanks to archivability and accessibility, can "stick" in ways that can be personally or professionally devastating. More devastating still – at least potentially – are cases where a person's likeness, words, or experiences are appropriated without that person's consent. In these moments, reduced risk is only traveling in one direction, and audiences that were never intended to be audiences are able, if they so choose, to use the affordances of digital media to decontextualize masks, hijack identities, and push context collapse to the extreme.

Sexting, the trading of sexually explicit messages, images, and videos, is one behavior particularly vulnerable to this outcome. A practice extremely popular with teens across the globe (and adults as well, let's be honest), sexting is intimately tied to performative identity. It is facilitated, and arguably amplified, by the prominence of various smartphone applications like Snapchat and Kik, which support the exchange of ephemeral content under chosen pseudonyms.[9] Unsurprisingly, the rising popularity of sexualized play, particularly exchanges involving teenage participants, and even more particularly, exchanges involving teenage girls, has spawned a great deal of handwringing. However, the nuanced reality provides an ambivalent bridge between potential control and potential victimization – between owning your own mask and having others wrest it from you.

Speaking to its potential for empowerment, researchers Justine Cassell and Meg Cramer (2008) complicate the moral panic surrounding teen girls' sexual experimentation online, and urge readers to rethink the impulse to shield young women from digitally mediated spaces where they might encounter aggressors, perverts, or run-of-the-mill weirdos. Yes there are dangers, Cassell and Cramer concede. But the benefits of sexual experimentation often outweigh the risks; the freedom to experiment and play encourages young women to "project more forceful agentive personalities" (16). This is something to encourage in girls, they contend, not to pathologize.

Regardless of the age and gender of participants, however, sexting requires bare emotion and connection (pun not intended, but certainly appropriate). And that vulnerability can open up identity play to significant, persistent abuse. Not just because the sting of an insult, pain of rejection, or flush of sexual excitement is just as visceral (and therefore just as *real*) when digitally mediated. But because, more and more, people's embodied lives are inextricable from their digitally mediated lives, a fact on conspicuous, and conspicuously painful, display when intimate details, including explicit images and videos shared in confidence, are unethically and unlawfully leaked.

In these cases, the affordances of digital mediation and the ever-present potential for context collapse feed into each other in the worst possible ways. Legal scholar Danielle Citron (2014) explores this collusion in her study of online hate speech and identity-based harassment. As Citron explains, for those subjected to coordinated online attacks – targets who are disproportionately female – embarrassing, compromising, or even straight-up libelous content lives on through sharing, indexing, and archiving. Compounding this initial violation, damaging online content can subsequently be appropriated, modified, and further amplified by any number of unseen, unknown harassers. 2014's iCloud hack, in which the nude photographs of a number of high-profile female celebrities were leaked online, is an extreme example of the identity violation described by Citron (see McCormick 2014). The 2016 Leslie Jones harassment case, described in the previous chapter, is another: not only was Jones subjected to racist and sexist attacks on social media, her private nude photos were unlawfully accessed and then posted to her website by a hacker (Rogers and Bromwich 2016).

The affordances of archivability and accessibility are integral to these violations. Online, participants have the ability to freely copy and paste, thereby removing things from their rightful place, without having to ask first. All that is logistically required is the desire to do so. In the process, unsuspecting, unconsenting individuals' identities can be flattened, fetishized, reduced to their constituent parts and ambivalently hijacked – resulting in the creation of an unwanted doppelganger: a mask not just shaped, but *conjured* by others. This mask needn't be directly sexualized in the moment to be harnessed, potentially, for future sexual violation. Milner's introductory media studies students, for example, and particularly his female students in their late teens and early twenties, express frustration at the invasive cameras that surround them at social gatherings. When you're at a party, they say, you have to pay attention to whether anyone might have their phone pointed at you and the kinds of pictures they might want to take. And if you do end up captured in someone else's phone, your image, your very sense of self, could – with a single click of a button – become *content*. In that case, suddenly, you're not a person; suddenly you're a collection of pixels that exists for someone else's pleasure. For someone else's who knows what.

This all-too-common scenario tramples notions of consent, since the process of harnessing and subsequently weaponizing someone else's identity strips away the victim's right to choose what happens to and with and on behalf of their own bodies – their bodies' photographic likenesses very much included. In an ideal world, consenting adults could take or pose for or share whatever kinds of photos they wanted, whenever they wanted, with whomever they wanted without fear of retribution from any audience, known or unknown. In an ambivalent world, the potential for abuse exists right alongside the potential for fun, for pleasure, for experimentation. For *play*.

Responding to this tension, one *could* take a seemingly prudent perspective, embodied by the furrowed rejoinders "Have you tried *not* sending naked pictures?" or "Well then don't have your photograph taken at parties," mediated equivalents to (and sometimes accompanied by) the oft-lobbed embodied suggestions that "Maybe just don't drink so much, that way you'll always have your wits about you" and "If you don't want that sort of attention, then don't wear such provocative clothing." But such behavioral injunctions, especially when the behaviors are sexual in nature, and *especially* especially when the injunctions are disproportionately directed at women, risk paternalism at best and misogynistic victim-blaming at worst. So we will not say any of those things.

What we will say, besides asserting unequivocally that no one should do anything – to someone else's likenesses, profiles, or body more broadly – without that person's consent, is that in cases where identities are hijacked and weaponized, the abuse is clear; it is willful, premeditated, and vicious. But those engaged in online identity play that takes another as its object needn't *intend* to harm anyone in order for someone to be harmed. Because regardless of participants' motivations, playing with someone else's identity risks conflating a *part* of that person – one facet of identity, one momentary performance – with the *whole* person. As a result, the totality of a person, including their parents, their friends, and their children, can be subjected to considerable embarrassment, distress, and misrepresentation, all in response to one articulation of one mask, or maybe even just a fragment of that mask.

The ambivalent potential of blithe identity hijacking is illustrated by "Bed Intruder," a popular 2010 meme. The "Bed Intruder" story began when a Huntsville, Alabama news station interviewed Antoine Dodson, a young gay man of color who lived in one of Huntsville's low-income housing projects with his family. An assailant had broken into Dodson's apartment and attempted to rape his sister. Antoine Dodson fought the intruder off, and when the local news crew arrived to report the story, he gave an impassioned interview. His statement, which opened with the line "Well, obviously, we have a rapist in Lincoln Park," was posted to Reddit shortly after the news segment aired. From there it spread, spawning a number of remix videos highlighting the most resonant soundbites, including the apparently hilarious statement "hide your kids, hide your wife, and hide your husbands 'cuz they're raping everybody out here."

This statement, and the Dodsons' experience more broadly, inspired a cascade of near-instantaneous memetic play. A musical remix of the newscast featuring short interspersed clips of the very white remix artists bobbing their heads along with the beat tore across the internet soon after Dodson's news interview was posted to Reddit; as of late 2016, this video, titled "BED INTRUDER SONG!!! (NOW ON ITUNES)" has amassed over 133 million views. And Dodson's most-quoted lines have become memes unto themselves – significant, given that the popularity of "Bed Intruder" hinged on finding comedic value in the attempted sexual assault of a young woman of color (see Carvin 2010). Placed in the full emotional, political, and intersectional context, there was nothing funny about the Dodsons' experience. But when people listened to the "Bed Intruder" remix and chose to laugh at, share, photoshop, and further amplify the story, they were not engaging with Antoine Dodson the person. Nor were they engaging with the very real and very embodied terror his sister experienced. They were engaging with a meme, and you can't hurt a meme's feelings, now can you?

This flattening, of course, overlooks the fact that the "Bed Intruder" meme isn't just a collection of pixels, it's the culmination of a series of embodied circumstances. A similar fact underscores cases where an individual is reduced not just to a flattened, memetic version of themselves, but to a flattened, memetic version of their very worst and most embarrassing moments. The "Ermahgerd" meme, for example, features an unflattering photo of a then-teenaged young woman enthusiastically fanning out several *Goosebumps* young adult horror books; "ermahgerd" became the go-to response for (perceived) excessive enthusiasm and general nerdiness (King 2015). In similar fashion, a then-teenager now known simply as "*Star Wars* Kid" recorded himself engaged in a one-sided lightsaber battle; that video, which was posted online without the teen's knowledge or consent, amassed hundreds of millions of views over the years. The unwanted exposure and attention ushered in by the video was a source of profound distress and humiliation for the teen, who ultimately required psychiatric hospitalization (Pasternack 2010). In these cases – as in many, many others – folkloric expression came at a very high cost, one ultimately borne by an unwitting, unknowing, unconsenting target.

But random slices of life aren't the only moments that can be flattened and harnessed online. As noted in Jon Ronson's 2015 book *So You've Been Publicly Shamed*, a growing chorus of people have been reduced to a single bad decision, bad joke, or general life miscalculation, often resulting in lost jobs, ruined reputations, and a shattered sense of privacy. All from the wrath of strangers – wrath that lives on through the affordances of digital media. Of course, as we'll argue in Chapter 5, certain behaviors are problematic; certain behaviors warrant a response. Sometimes a mass response. Sometimes a ferocious response. But in cases of identity hijacking, an individual's entire life is distilled down to one singular moment or decision, and treated as if this singular moment or decision represents the totality of that person's existence.

This is where digital mediation, identity, and ambivalence are most strongly intertwined. Online, it is often easier to separate people from their embodied experiences, or to mistake the part for the whole – or to never even see the whole, and therefore never understand the context from which a particular collection of pixels has been unmoored. And as a result, never understand or be forced to confront the inescapably embodied repercussions of one's own behavior. Phillips (2015) describes the behavioral implications of these affective gaps in her analysis of antagonistic humor in subcultural trolling circles. The greater the emotional distance between those who laugh and those who are laughed at, she argues, the louder and more antagonistic the laughter tends to be. And the louder and more antagonistic the laughter, the more likely it is that others will want to join in. And the more people that join in, the louder still the laughter, and greater still the affective gaps, as the snake takes a bite of its own tail: a self-sustaining dynamic we'll revisit in the following chapter.

The norms of a given group matter greatly, of course; who's laughing, and further who's holding that all-important camera, can have a significant impact on the implications of a particular interaction. But also significant are the technological affordances. These affordances facilitate context collapse, which easily creates further opportunities for further unmoored engagement. This process, in turn, transfigures *my* mask into *your* plaything, *ad infinitum*. In other words, ambivalent identity play – play with the self and with others – might not be exclusive to digitally mediated environments. But the affordances and limitations of digital mediation provide precisely the tools, and precisely the circumstances, in which ambivalence piles atop ambivalence, resulting in a truly brave, if often troubling, new world of identity performance.

Chapter overview and looking forward

No matter where it occurs, no matter what objects or groups it might take as its target, identity play is ambivalent business. As such, it challenges a host of assumptions that might make perfect sense on paper, but which are much more difficult to justify in practice: that sincere and performative expression are opposed (they aren't), that one's performative mask is both singular and self-contained (it isn't), and that online and offline spaces are fundamentally separable (oh boy). This final point is particularly pressing, and is the precondition for the first two, particularly as so many of our lives and associated masks become increasingly hybrid and increasingly intertwined with the hybrid lives and masks of others. So much so that the demarcation between "online" and "offline" is often little more than a spatial designation. I had this exchange with that person on Twitter; I had that exchange with this person at the grocery store. Regardless of the kinds of interactions these might have been, from neutral to delightful to traumatic, both are handily subsumed by all the significance and all the consequence and, of course, all the ambivalence as "real life," which pretty much covers everything.

The following chapter will continue exploring the intertwined, inextricable relationship between the individual and the collectives they navigate. It will focus specifically on the blend of personal resonance and collective understanding that draws groups together through laughter – and in the same moment, risks tearing them apart. In so doing, it will challenge any clear or comfortable demarcation between social and anti-social behavior, highlighting the fact that the same jokes that establish an *us* can just as quickly cast out a *them*.

3

Constitutive Humor

Although easily recognized and intuitively experienced – the ultimate in "you know it when you see it" – humor is notoriously difficult to pin down. From irony to children's pranks to filthy limericks that have no business being told to children, humor encompasses a broad range of subjects, behaviors, and moods. And worse, the second you try to explain *why* something is funny, the joke almost always shrivels up, lumbers into the audience, and starts heckling you to be less boring. This chapter tempts that fate, and explores the ambivalent social worlds built through constitutive humor.

Focusing specifically on the *fetishism, generativity*, and *magnetism* of jokes about your dad, the art film *The Room*, and the glory of Satan (of course), the chapter argues that in both embodied and digitally mediated spaces, constitutive humor complicates assumptions about the inherent pro-sociality of togetherness and sharing. Humor may, of course, be highly social for members of the ingroup. And that's terrific, people laughing together is fun! But this same laughter can be destructive and alienating for members of the outgroup, who are unable to laugh, and in some cases may be the object of ingroup laughter. The tension between generative and destructive laughter is especially conspicuous online, where digital divergences hopelessly blur the lines between *us* and *them*. The affordances of modularity, modifiability, archivability, accessibility, as well as the social realities of Poe's Law and problematic amplification, further erode any clear-cut demarcation between pro-social and anti-social humor, which reveals that our laughter is more loaded, and potentially more harmful, than we might like to admit.

A few notes about your dad

There we were, sitting at the kitchenette table of Phillips' Phoenix, Arizona hotel room, finalizing a PowerPoint for our upcoming presentation "Weird to whom, obscene to whom? Folkloristics and the study of online ambivalence." We were at the 2015 Association of Internet Researchers conference and were excited to present an overview of Chapter 1 of this book. Because the chapter – and book itself, if you haven't noticed – engages with strange and otherwise difficult-to-classify vernacular expression, we thought it would be appropriate, and also pretty funny, to present our findings using the weirdest, ugliest PowerPoint possible. We were talking about ambivalence, after all. And what better way to convey an argument about ambivalent folkloric expression than through ambivalent folkloric expression?

Possessing an anti-talent for absurdist creativity, Phillips had offered to assemble the presentation; this was the first time she'd walked Milner through her handiwork. And what a breathtaking effort it was. The slideshow theme of ugly gray eighties-looking checkerboard with weird science bubbles (atoms? planets?) was offset by tasteful bubble-gum pink shadowbox lettering – except, of course, for the few special slides that called for animated rainbow Comic Sans subject headers, the most aesthetically upsetting font combination that Phillips could think of. Slides were formatted asymmetrically, including words that spilled off the frame. There were glaring misspellings (Milner's first name became "Ryabn" on the introductory slide), and the whole thing featured precisely the kinds of ridiculous memetic images that pepper this book. It was perfect(ly bad). Confronted by Phillips' zest for life, Milner looked on half impressed and mostly horrified, occasionally pausing the slideshow to make blocking notes and editing suggestions.

Following two particularly absurd image-heavy slides – one featuring a trio of identical, graduated GIFs of martial arts star Jean-Claude van Damme dancing with a crowd on Venice Beach, and another boasting a collage of strange photoshops, including one of *The X-Files'* Fox Mulder staring blankly at a cat above the caption "hello are you a ufo" – the PowerPoint took a recursive turn. "Weird to whom, obscene to whom?" the subsequent slide asked, offset by a GIF of professional wrestler Hulk Hogan playing an electric guitar in front of an undulating American flag (Figure 4). "Your dad," the image caption read, a message Phillips included to indicate that your father, more than likely, thinks this content is weird and obscene – a stand-in for the broader idea that members of the outgroup, who don't share the same assumptions or aesthetic expectations as members of the ingroup, will likely react negatively to, or at least furrow their brows at, the ver-

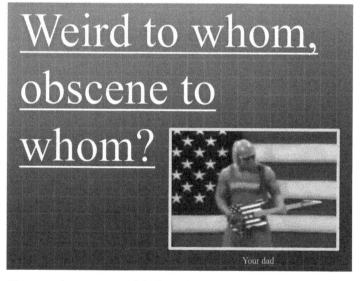

Figure 4. A PowerPoint slide from the presentation "Weird to whom, obscene to whom? Folkloristics and the study of online ambivalence," presented at the 2015 Association of Internet Researchers annual conference. Created October 2015.

nacular ambivalence of others. In this way, the image was meant to precipitate a discussion about the "both, on both sides" nature of ambivalence.

Milner, however, didn't pick up on anything close to any of that. On seeing the "your dad" caption beneath the Hulk Hogan GIF, he burst out laughing. "*Your dad*," he repeated. Phillips didn't know what to say. This was the thesis of the chapter, what was so damn funny about that? Milner's laughter persisted. "It's like we're like, 'that's your dad,'" he said, pointing at Hogan. He thought about the audience, and imagined how they'd react to this apparent *non sequitur* insult. The PowerPoint was already full of memes about murder ducks and Cookie Monsters screaming about sugar in their ass; now here was a random slander against somebody's father, universally personified by a balding, middle-aged former professional wrestler – one who had recently been publicly shamed for both a leaked sex tape and a racist tirade – shredding on a stars-and-stripes electric guitar. They wouldn't know what hit them. Phillips still had no idea why Milner was laughing, but his laughter made her laugh; usually *she* was the one doing the weird thing. After a good 20 seconds, Milner attempted to collect himself. "What if the next time we're walking around I'm like," he nodded at a hypothetical, repellent stranger, "'that's your dad.' Wouldn't that be *mean?*" This scenario flashed across his eyes as Phillips looked on, baffled. Milner started laughing again.

Like much of the ambivalent humor we'll assess in this chapter, "your dad" wasn't an obvious or straightforward joke. There was no narrative ("Your dad walks into a bar..."), no punchline, and neither of us was trying to make the other laugh. But laugh we did, for reasons neither of us could have explained at the time. Nor did we have any reason to try and explain these reasons; humor is experiential, not dryly argumentative. The relationship between humor and argument is so amorphous that, as Alan Dundes (1987) notes, participants often have no idea what their humor means, even when they think something is hilarious. Humor as a whole also remains a mystery, even to top humor scholars. Elliott Oring, for example, flatly states: "I do not accept the notion that the motivations, techniques, and functions of humor are fully known and understood" (1992, i), a point he echoes over a decade later, stating that "the question of how and what jokes communicate remains unresolved" (2003, 39). After another decade and a half of research, theory, and handwringing, that cat remains firmly planted in the bag. As humor theorist Giselinde Kuipers explains, "Ever since Plato and Aristotle, people have asked themselves these questions but it is very difficult, if not impossible, to answer them conclusively and definitively" (2015, 8).

There are, of course, a number of theories one could draw from. Many focus on psychological motivations, most notably the claims that humor is a function of aggression (clustered as "superiority theories"), or that humor provides an emotional outlet allowing participants to express socially taboo thoughts and feelings (clustered as "release theories"). We are not going to make either of those claims, or any claim that posits what humor "really" means objectively. Rather, we're interested in the *constitutive* characteristics of humor: how it functions as a communicative tool to help build and sustain social worlds, across degrees of mediation. To do so, we will draw from incongruity theories of humor, which postulate that humor is predicated on the recognition of a clash between elements (Raskin 1985; Morreall 1989). But not a random clash; Oring (1992, 2003) notes that, to successfully facilitate a "humor response," incongruity must be *appropriate*, that is, engage with and subvert the norms of a given sociocultural circumstance. The (ahem, false) assumption that Phillips was wedging a random slander against, I don't know, *anybody's father* into a professional PowerPoint presentation using a GIF of Hulk Hogan struck Milner as appropriately incongruous; it was exactly, perfectly, the wrong thing to be doing, given where we were and what we were trying to accomplish. At least it would have been, if that's what Phillips was actually trying to do.

By focusing squarely on the communicative elements of this moment, it is possible to see not just what social worlds were built through our laughter, but who was left out of the process. Speaking to the overall context of our hotel room exchange and subsequent presentation, we weren't saying random words or laughing indiscriminately. We were engaging with, and at times actively subverting, a whole host of cultural elements, from what constitutes a "good" academic PowerPoint to the various pop culture references contained in the slides themselves (a dancing Jean-Claude van Damme, *The X-Files*, Hulk Hogan, over-the-top patriotism, "your mom" jokes – of which "your dad" is a gendered inversion). These might have been in-jokes between Phillips and Milner, but like all comedic exchanges predicated on existing cultural logics and scripts, they were also inherently collective.

And not just collective, but ambivalent; not everyone was invited into our cozy laughing ingroup. Instead, we were speaking, pretty unapologetically, to our own specific interests and affinities as academics, mild iconoclasts, and friends. We were also hailing, as part of this *us*, audience members drawing from a similar cultural reservoir, and who furthermore were sympathetic to our broader argument about folkloric expression – as evidenced not just in the presentation topic, but the PowerPoint itself. This may have created a sense of community for the ingroup, but in so doing, it created at least the potential for an outgroup: those who weren't able to decode our flurry of memetic references, or who rejected our broader argument about vernacular creativity and folkloric expression, or who thought we were being too flippant (we were), and so on.

The following section will focus specifically on the ambivalent potential of constitutive humor, and how community formation, cultural exchange, and generally having a fun and funny time – presumably good things, pro-social things – can simultaneously serve to police community boundaries, encourage cultural myopia, and generally make outsiders miserable. A great party for some, in other words, also means a lonely night alone for others.

Fetishism, generativity, and magnetism (oh my)

The ambivalence of constitutive humor hinges most conspicuously on its *fetishism*: the process by which the full emotional, political, or cultural context of a given event or utterance is obscured, allowing participants to focus only on the amusing details. Just the incongruity; just the punchline. Phillips (2015) notes that this sense of the term is more akin to Karl Marx's (1867) "commodity fetish" than a religious or sexual fetish. For Marx, consumer goods are "made magic" by capitalism, rendering invisible all the labor conditions, systems of privilege and access, and environmental implications that underscore their production. Similarly, fetishized laughter is fundamentally myopic, allowing participants to focus just on the *us* who laugh, not on the *them* who do not, or how ingroup behaviors might personally impact the outgroup. For example, in her playful employment of the Hulk Hogan GIF, Phillips didn't think twice about how Hulk Hogan – legal name Terry Gene Bollea – might feel about being framed as anathema to intellectual pursuit, or, more broadly, about the people negatively impacted by his racist tirade or recently leaked sex tape – events that in Phillips' mind served mostly to ensure that more people in the audience would recognize the image. Had she stopped and considered these decidedly less amusing details, she likely would have chosen a different GIF.

Fetishism also, and simultaneously, cordons comedic expressions from expressions meant to be taken at face value. Or at least taken seriously. This fetishized play frame creates what folklorist Christie Davies (2008) describes as a "special world" subject to its own set of rules. Applying this frame to dogs' play, anthropologist Gregory Bateson notes that the "playful nip denotes the bite," i.e. replicates all the behaviors of aggression, "but it does not denote what would be denoted by the bite" (1972, 180), i.e. isn't interpreted as *actual* aggression. It is that which "would be denoted by the bite" – that is to say, the social, political, and interpersonal consequences and/or historical baggage of the utterance when removed from the play frame – that is fetishistically obscured. For example, the fact that Hulk Hogan is a person (if a fraught and complicated person, like most people), and not just a punchline saved to Phillips' hard drive.

Building on the fetishism of the play frame, and facilitating further ambivalence, is what Phillips (2015) describes as the *generative* and *magnetic* nature of constitutive humor. It is generative because it weaves an influx of new experiences, references, and often highly fetishized jokes into a collective *us*. One that, in turn, recontextualizes additional content, engenders subsequent laughter, and contributes to an even deeper sense of collective identity. And it is magnetic because these emerging worlds attract attention *from within* the group (cohering that *us* even more tightly), as well as *externally to* the group (drawing additional participants into the fold). Along with fetishism, generativity and magnetism are great for community formation. On the flip side, those who are not invited into the inner circle are cast as a *them* – further underscoring the fact that, while laughter builds social worlds, it also pushes out those unfamiliar or uncomfortable with the world being built.

To demonstrate the depth of this ambivalence, we'll devote the remainder of this section to constitutive laughter – both embodied and digitally mediated – directed at the beloved cult classic film *The Room*. As we'll see, giddy engagement with *The Room* exemplifies fetishism, generativity, and magnetism. It also exemplifies how constitutive humor both coheres and cuts, making it difficult to tell where social behavior ends and anti-social behavior begins.

Like getting stabbed in the head

As Phillips (2013) notes, there is a vast corpus of media texts that inspire "so bad it's good" audience play, both online and off. But there are few fandoms more ambivalent, or more rabid, than those surrounding 2003's *The Room*: a film so consistently boffo, so perfectly bizarre, that it is widely regarded as the "*Citizen Kane* of bad movies" (McCulloch 2011). This film didn't reach such great heights on its own, however. Rather, its legacy is underscored by a network of participation, from Hollywood word of mouth to global screenings to a salacious behind-the-scenes tell-all book to satirical Amazon reviews to mashups on YouTube to GIF sets on Tumblr. In this hybrid participation, the constitutive and destructive powers of ambivalent humor are on full display.

The Room was produced, directed, written, and financed by international man of mystery (emphasis on the "mystery"; no one seems to know what country he's from, how old he is, or where he gets his considerable funding) Tommy Wiseau. Wiseau also starred in the film, despite the fact that his acting, according to a book written by *The Room*'s co-star Greg Sestero (along with journalist Tom Bissell), is chaotically wrong, terrible, and reckless – and for that reason, "mesmerising" (2013, 41). Sestero – whose uneasy friendship with Wiseau predated *The Room* by several years – explains that Wiseau speaks with "an Eastern European accent that has been hit by a Parisian bus" (2), claims to be a vampire, and wears two belts simultaneously, one slung low below his waist (because it "keeps his ass up"). On the set of *The Room*, Wiseau was a paranoid, verbally abusive, incompetent petty tyrant whose acting was so consistently bad, and behavior so consistently bizarre, that his crew often struggled not to laugh, or cry, or shout curse words, or outright quit, depending on the moment in question.

In the film, Wiseau plays Johnny, a perfect gentleman and doting boyfriend to Lisa, a manipulative sex monster who initiates an affair with Johnny's best friend Mark. When Johnny learns of Lisa and Mark's betrayal, he goes berserk; after trashing his bedroom, (spoiler alert) he shoots himself in the head, and everybody learns their lesson. Supporting characters include Johnny and Lisa's underage, threesome-suggesting, sensual apple-eating apparently teenaged neighbor Denny, whom Johnny must save from a drug dealer named Chris-R; two of Lisa's friends who don't have any discernable backstory, other than the fact that they sometimes have sex on Lisa and Johnny's couch; and Lisa's mother, who midway through the film unceremoniously declares that she has breast cancer and never mentions it again.

Interspersed within the film's narrative are random games of pick-up football, nonsensical exterior shots, unexplained character replacements, recycled footage of the film's frequent and highly gratuitous sex scenes, and Johnny, in a fit of sui-cidal rage, grinding with tortured sensuality against one of Lisa's dresses. And if this fever-dream storytelling weren't enough, production details were similarly befuddling. For example, Wiseau chose, for no discernable reason, to simul-taneously shoot the film with a 35mm camera and an HD camera, requiring him to hire two separate crews, and result-ing in bizarre shifts in angles, lighting, and film quality. His set design was likewise nonsensical. For example, upon direct-ing the set designer to buy multiple framed photographs for Johnny's apartment, Wiseau refused to replace the stock photos contained therein. Consequently, the oft-used apart-ment set is overrun with a preponderance of shots containing framed pictures of spoons.

Sestero calls the final product of Wiseau's creative labors a "perfectly literal comedy of errors" (1), but Wiseau, for his part, was thrilled with the results. As Sestero notes, *The Room* was a deeply serious, deeply personal film for Wiseau, one born of personal heartbreak and what he believed to be the beauty of redemption; Sestero also notes that, upon screening the film's rough cut for the first time, Wiseau was "beaming … He was filled with such joy and pride" (257). But unsurprisingly to everyone, except maybe Wiseau, the film was a commercial flop. It netted $1,800 in its first two-week limited release in Los Angeles, even after Wiseau rented a giant billboard advertising the film on Highland Avenue in Hollywood.

The Room would have faded into immediate obscurity, Sestero muses, had two film students not walked past a movie theatre creatively advertising the film during its initial two-week run. Beside the film's screening times, the theatre posted a sign that read "NO REFUNDS." The sign also included a line from a recent review. "Watching this film is like getting stabbed in the head," it promised. The film students were intrigued and decided to check it out. And then were equally horrified, bewildered, and delighted. The students promptly began telling all their Hollywood friends, who told their friends, as magnetism attracted new viewers to the ambivalent laughter. Soon, countless screening parties, complete with an emerging repertoire of collective participatory traditions, were sprouting up; it wasn't long before the film became, according to Sestero, "an L.A. in-joke" revered by the "cream of the Hollywood comedy community" (xv).

Like audiences of 1973's similarly classic *The Rocky Horror Picture Show*, which has been inspiring elaborate fan engagement for decades, contemporary audiences of *The Room* crowd midnight theatre screenings and campily pantomime the film's action with interactive callouts, often augmenting their parallel performances with costumes and props. Unlike *Rocky Horror* audiences, however, whose engagement is overwhelmingly celebratory, audiences of *The Room* are engaged in a decidedly more ambivalent performance, one that centers on excitedly highlighting the film's various editing, pacing, acting, and logical shortcomings through a panoply of participatory traditions.

As anyone who has attended *The Room* screenings knows, these traditions are taken quite seriously. Not only are there multiple screening guides available online (House of Qwesi 2009; Newman 2010), many participating theatres in the US and UK pass out rule sheets – or at the very least explain the basics – to newcomers. Fixed rituals include throwing hundreds of plastic spoons into the air whenever a framed photograph of a spoon appears on screen; screaming "HE'S MY BEST FRIEND!" any time Johnny refers to Mark as "his best friend," which is constantly; and yelling "Focus! Unfocus!" whenever the shot jumps between 35mm and HD cameras. While most of the rituals can be performed from one's seat, a few require ambulatory action. During one scene late in the film, for example, Wiseau looks down, grins childishly, and waves at something on the ground near his left foot – apparently this something is the mark he kept missing as he tried to simultaneously learn his blocking and deliver his lines. Audience members exploit this moment by running down toward the front row, where they wait to wave back at Johnny.

Despite these conservative elements, each screening is a little different; the result, as Richard McCulloch (2011) notes, of an unpredictable interplay between the film itself, the venue, the broader geographic location, and the individuals who happen to be sitting in the audience that night. To test out McCulloch's last assertion, and also because she wanted to, Phillips attended two screenings in Atlanta, Georgia: one in October 2015 and another in April 2016. The latter was attended by Tommy Wiseau himself, live and in person. On both occasions, audience members engaged in all the expected tropes, but they also added their own dynamic twist to the proceedings – jokes and callouts Phillips later learned had evolved over the screening's several-year run at the Plaza Theatre. This included making exaggerated, rhythmic mouth sounds ("awmmmph" is the closest approximation text will allow) whenever any of the characters open-mouth kissed, collectively shrieking "CLOSE THE DOOR CLOSE THE

FUCKING DOOR" whenever characters would enter Johnny
and Lisa's apartment and then not close the fucking door,
and syncing running commentary to Johnny's breakdown
scene, wherein he violently disassembles the bedroom dresser
("One!" the audience shouted as Johnny yanks out one drawer;
"Two!" they shouted as he pulls out another; "FUCK IT!" they
shouted as he knocks the whole thing over).

Online play with *The Room* augments these and other
embodied rituals. Through digitally mediated word of mouth,
fans of *The Room* have cemented the film's ironic legacy. They
have also produced, unsurprisingly, countless GIFs capturing
and commenting on resonant moments from the film, as
well as mashups intertwining those moments with pop culture
texts like *Star Wars*, *Sesame Street*, and *My Little Pony*. Scene-by-
scene breakdowns on YouTube are also common, as are
romanticized fan creations on DeviantArt and photo captions
mocking Wiseau's delivery on *Know Your Meme* ("YOO
BETRAY ME EFFRIBODY BETRAY ME," one captioned photo
of a shouting Wiseau reads; "AHM FEDDAP WID DISS
WUROLD").

There are also scores of hyperbolically poetic Amazon
reviews for *The Room*'s DVD release, featuring narratives that
give the Three Wolf Moon canon a run for its money ("*The
Room* Reviews" 2009). "I now mark my life into two parts,"
reviewer Jonah Falcon says, "life before and after *The Room*.
After seeing *The Room*, things seem differently. Colors now
have taste. Taste no longer exists." A. Heil posits that "You
will call off work the next day. You will find yourself living a
life that cannot possibly be real. You will begin questioning
metaphysical reality as you find yourself trapped in a void of
hate and condemnation. Hate because you did not think of
creating *The Room* first. Condemnation as you relive your
past failures." And Chance McClain says of Wiseau, "The
forehead is a vast wasteland that serves no purpose other than
providing a platform to which the hair-mess is stapled."

Audiences of *The Room* across the globe – at midnight screenings and from the comfort of their own Amazon profiles – illustrate just how generative, magnetic, and fetishistic constitutive humor can be. The humor is generative because the years' worth of participatory play has created an evolving, and ever-expanding, performative repertoire. This, in turn, contributes to the overall sense of *us* sitting together in the theatre. It is magnetic because the resulting audience laughter has attracted additional jokes, sight gags, and callouts from existing audiences online and off and serves as a point of proselytization for potential future audiences. Most notably, however, this laughter is fetishistic; it stems from identifying with an *us* who laughs, and laughs uproariously, at a man's sincere cinematic efforts.

The fetishism of this laughter was particularly conspicuous during the April 2016 screening Phillips attended, the one featuring an appearance by Wiseau. As the audience filed into the theatre – Phillips estimates that there were around 200 attendees – everyone was ushered past a table piled high with *The Room* merchandise. Fans could choose between *The Room* DVDs, Tommy Wiseau underwear, Tommy Wiseau dogtags, signed headshots of Wiseau that had to have been taken 20 years earlier, and a Tommy Wiseau Eastern Orthodox blessing for the low low price of $40. Phillips couldn't afford *not* to buy a blessing from Tommy Wiseau, and now has a series of iPhone photos of him making the sign of the cross and draping dogtags around her neck.

After everyone had purchased their blessings and taken their seats – and after Wiseau shoutingly addressed a conspiracy theory that *The Room* didn't have a script, mumbled his way through a few audience questions, then forced everyone to watch the pilot for his yet-undistributed television sitcom *The Neighbors* – *The Room* finally began rolling. But something made this screening different from the one Phillips had attended a few months earlier in that same theatre. Maybe it was the fact that Wiseau's persona was every bit as disorienting in person. Maybe it was the added tension of knowing that the person you were laughing at in *The Room* was, literally, in the room. Whatever the reason, to a much greater, *palpable* extent than during her first screening, the audience was crackling with comedic energy the second the curtain raised. The callouts were so well rehearsed, the spoon-throwing so enthusiastic, the laughter so unbridled, that it had Phillips in stitches, at times even tears; it remains one of the most interesting, emotionally confusing, and funniest experiences of her life.

The constitutive dimensions of ambivalent humor helped make *The Room* a collective sensation. But as much as they build worlds around the film, as much as they create and sustain an *us* with whom Phillips, for one, felt surprisingly close by the time the film ended ("we've been through so much together!"), these dimensions are far from victimless. As convivial as the *us* might appear, it is predicated on a *them*. This is the flip side of generativity: identification through othering.

In the case of *The Room*, this othering centers on cinematic convention, proper English use and diction, and what it means, at a basic level, to behave like the humans do. By laughing at Wiseau and his film's perceived shortcomings, audiences are simultaneously gesturing toward existing cultural norms and logics – and implicitly framing as aberrant anything that fails to live up to those standards. The fact that *The Room* was initially embraced and amplified by people with a keen awareness of and investment in the markers of "good" cinema – film students and industry insiders – evidences this normative impulse. These are people whose entire livelihood is predicated on recognizing and upholding cinematic conventions. It is therefore unsurprising that the surrealism of *The Room* would prove so resonant for these audience members; given their own training and experience, Wiseau's aggressively unprofessional delivery could not be more appropriately incongruous with their own professional expectations.

Wiseau's artistic intent and life experiences and, more pressingly, how he might feel about this mockery are all left in the wake of fans' fetishistic participation. Whether through sloppily spelled photo captions or in-theatre chant-alongs, humorous play with Wiseau's persona yields a flattened caricature. Wiseau's identity has, in this way, been hijacked much like Antoine Dodson's in the wake of the "Bed Intruder" meme assessed last chapter. It certainly was during the April 2016 screening Phillips attended. Audience members were thrilled to be there, and thrilled to see Wiseau. But they expressed this enthusiasm through knowing winks and comic mugging, referring to him as "the great auteur" as they fought back laughter, and he just stood there, blinking. Wiseau was, throughout the night, and in fact every night, in every screening, the butt of a joke he may or may not even recognize – and may be crushed by if he does.

Wiseau isn't alone in this othering. In the context of *The Room*, even members of the laughing *us* are subject to policing. For instance, at the first screening Phillips attended, her gentleman companion – who before that weekend had never heard of *The Room* and in preparation had quickly scanned and apparently misread an online callout guide – started shouting the wrong things at the wrong times; more than a few heads turned to express reproach. Said gentleman companion got the message, and stopped talking (much to Phillips' relief; she was one of the people shooting side eyes). In the process, one more outsider was left in the wake of shared laughter.

The lesson of ambivalent engagement with *The Room* is that constitutive humor is not roundly, uniformly, or universally positive. It can also construct walls; assert restrictive, normative values; and fetishize those deemed to be *other* and, by extension, *less than*. The ethical stakes are relatively low when it comes to *The Room*, of course. Broader marginalizations, including the Auschwitz jokes described by Alan Dundes and Uli Linke (1987) and the memorial page trolling explored by Phillips (2015), amplify those stakes. In these cases, the constitutive nature of offensive or otherwise taboo jokes is easily deployed in the service of direct harassment, antagonization, and silencing. The bad side of the coin, without question. But even this point is subject to an ambivalent rejoinder. Because the same constitutive nature of these jokes can be harnessed to satirize the absurdity and intellectual feebleness of bigotry. Maybe constitutive humor does something else entirely; maybe it juggles more than one point of ambivalence at once.

Regardless, reproducing ambivalent humor – as an insider laughing, as a scholar analyzing, or as a mix of both – risks amplifying its ambivalence. We first addressed issues of amplification in Chapter 1, where we outlined Dundes and Linke's (1987) argument that all aspects of folkloric expression – even the most upsetting aspects – are worth collecting and analyzing. This position clashes with Meaghan Morris' ([1988] 2007) insistence that the amplification of popular content simply because it's something people are doing risks normalizing the most bigoted, ignorant, and overall harmful elements of populist expression. This same tension underscores constitutive humor, which, as we'll see below, becomes even more untenable in digitally mediated spaces.

The magical world of the mediated play frame

Regardless of era or degree of mediation, constitutive humor always carries ambivalence. Whether participants are populating a PowerPoint with opaque in-jokes or throwing spoons in the air at a cult movie screening, that which is social for one group can feel deeply anti-social for another – for example, those who don't get or don't like all those opaque in-jokes, or who go to the movies because they need a break from the kids, only to be thronged by hundreds of hipsters shouting at each other in broken English, then laughing. This section will consider this point of tension in digitally mediated spaces, exploring the continuities between ambivalent humor online and off, specifically its power to connect an *us* as it casts out a *them*.

Connecting the same old us

Although digitally mediated humor often precludes the full range of embodied paralinguistic cues – things like tone of voice, an encouraging smile, discouraging side eyes – participants fill in those blanks with tools like emojis, GIFs, and creative spelling, syntax, and grammar to communicate that "this is play" and furthermore that "I am one of you." Collectives predicated on mediation and distance are thus held together by generative group laughter, just as they are in embodied spaces.

As it is so fundamental to group formation, and as digital environments present no insurmountable roadblocks to its development, it's no surprise that humor has long been integral to digitally mediated communities. In the early eighties, William Fox (1983) explored how jokes exchanged on a high school computer network facilitated connections between participants. Nancy K. Baym (1995) describes a similar process in her study of humor on a Usenet board dedicated to discussing television soap operas. In their study of computer-mediated communication in a college setting, Mike Hubler and Diana Bell (2003) demonstrate how shared sets of behavioral norms emerge through threads of constitutive laughter. Likewise, E. Gabriella Coleman (2013) describes the importance of humor to communities of software programmers, dating back to the earliest days of the open source software movement.

Fitting comfortably within this lineage, contemporary online collectives are also constituted through the world-building power of humor. Further, the formal characteristics and communicative functions of this humor are in many ways indistinguishable not just from earlier mediated iterations, but also from embodied humor more broadly. Kumamon ("Kumamon" 2016), cartoon mascot of the Kumamoto

Prefecture in Japan, illustrates these connections. Well, not so much Kumamon himself, but rather the Satan worshiping, firestarting memetic derivative his likeness inspired in 2012, and which tore across a variety of social media platforms that same year (Figure 5). His big cute eyes appropriately incongruous with his apparent appetite for destruction, Kumamon resonated with the countless participants on 4chan, Reddit, and Tumblr who chose to create, circulate, and transform memetic iterations of the adorable villain.

The demonstrable fact that Kumamon *did* resonate doesn't explain *why* he resonated. Participants creating, circulating, or transforming Kumamon images could have been doing so for any number of reasons. Perhaps because the appropriate incongruity of sweetness and malevolence made them giggle. Perhaps because they thought Kumamon was already pretty

Figure 5. Three memetic images linking Kumamon, the mascot for Japan's Kumamoto Prefecture, with violence and destruction. Left: a vertical comic of Kumamon praising Satan at a bonfire. Top right: Kumamon basking in the flames engulfing his computer. Bottom right: Kumamon preparing to defend his territory. Collected in 2016.

malevolent (there's something dark, Milner insists, lurking behind those eyes). Perhaps because they appreciate Kumamon's flair for dramatic poses. Perhaps because they think that Satan is a pretty funny guy. Possible explanations for why participants might partake in Kumamon humor are, in short, endless – just as they are in embodied contexts. What is clear, however, is that through their shared participation with this Satanic muppet, individual participants were connected to broader collectives, reconfiguring Kumamon as yet another strand in a shared social tapestry.

Kumamon is most conspicuously collective in its relationship with existing memetic media. Arguably, its clearest analogue is "Disaster Girl," a meme popularized on the same platforms the year before Kumamon. "Disaster Girl" originated from a candid photograph of a little girl standing in front of a house fire. Head turned and eyes gazing directly into the camera, the girl's mouth is stretched into a dark, knowing smile. Like play with Kumamon, "Disaster Girl" iterations craft their humor from the incongruity between an innocent little girl and the destructive impulses applied to her. While it is impossible to confirm that Kumamon's firebug doppelganger was deliberately and explicitly based on "Disaster Girl," the two memes are used in similar ways, and feature a number of cross-pollinated memetic elements, thus establishing a bridge between members of the ingroup.

In addition to helping cohere this ingroup around a shared repertoire of texts, the spread of Kumamon highlights the role of the audience during humorous exchanges, and in particular, the importance of performing appropriately for that audience. This process unfolds identically in offline contexts. For example, speaking of embodied joking traditions amongst the Western Apache American Indian tribe, Keith Basso and Dell Hymes (1979) describe a number of similar performative markers, from word choice to specific cultural references to patterned communication modifications signaling that a joking exchange has begun. In the process, these markers do just that – mark the communicative exchange as taking place within a particular play frame, in turn establishing an ingroup able to appropriately, and collectively, decode a given incongruity. Posting a Kumamon image, or any so-called "subcultural batsignal" (Phillips 2015), asserts the same basic claim: that I am one of you, that we all comprise an *us*, and that, most importantly, this *us* exists within the magical world of the play frame.

Casting out the same old them
As we've seen, playing together can also push away outsiders. This ambivalence hinges, first and foremost, on the fact that decoding humor – regardless of where the humor unfolds, or through what tools it is communicated – requires a set of broader cultural literacies. Anthropologist Mahadev Apte emphasizes this point when he notes that "Familiarity with a cultural code is a prerequisite for the spontaneous mental restructuring of elements that results in amusement and laughter" (1985, 17). You have to know what you're looking at, in other words, to know when it makes sense to laugh.

The problem is that not all participants necessarily share the same cultural literacies. And when they don't, the play frame cannot be established, and neither can the *us* who collectively participates. In order to appropriately decode the left-side image in Figure 5, for example, one needs to know who Satan is – specifically the role he plays in the Christian tradition. And to fully decode subsequent iterations of the image, wherein the creepy little wide-eyed Kumamon is thrust into a hodgepodge of human suffering (the explosion of the Hindenburg airship, nuclear missile launches, and the terrorist attacks of September 11, 2001 all serve as backdrops), one must be familiar with the various historical and political references, and furthermore with the source image subsequent iterations are riffing on. On an even broader level, one must know how to read the visual grammar of these images, a process that might feel wholly automatic, but is in fact culturally contingent; different groups read different images in different ways. To appropriately decode Kumanon images, one's eye needs, essentially, to align with the eyes of the other participants. And if it doesn't, one's *eye* might need to find a new *we*.

Like all forms of humor, whether occurring online, offline, or some hybrid context in between, fully understanding the Kumamon meme demands familiarity with a number of broad cultural norms and references. These norms and references are requisite to the creation of the ingroup, which intertwines self and other through collective laughter. At the same time, this process highlights the fact that, while some people are pulled in by the laughing us, others are necessarily spit out.

The ambivalence foundational to online humor (indeed, to all humor) was especially prominent on niche shock sites like Stile Project, Something Awful, YTMND, and the quizzically cacophonous BodyBuilding.com, all popular in the late nineties and early aughts. On these sites, participants did their damnedest to create, circulate, and transform the weirdest, most disgusting, and overall funniest memetic content possible. Described as "proto-trolling" spaces by Phillips (2015), these forums and message boards were a harbinger of the antagonistic laughter later amplified on and around 4chan's /b/ board, which itself was further popularized on certain corners of Reddit, Tumblr, and YouTube. Laughter that, in each case, was used to push away at least as many participants as it pulled in.

In this litany of sites premised on ambivalent humor, 4chan is arguably the reigning (dark) prince. Since its creation by then 15-year-old Christopher "moot" Poole in 2003, 4chan's entire existence, particularly during the critical early years of subcultural formation in the mid- to late aughts, is predicated on humor. Humor was so important to subcultural formation on /b/ that Phillips (2015) was unable to undertake an ethnographic study of the space until after she began to understand the trolls' jokes. Digital media scholars Asaf Nissenbaum and Limor Shifman (2015) affirm this point in their argument that humorous play on /b/ serves as both cultural capital and a point of collective identity. And what fetishistic, generative, and magnetic play it has been. Emphasis on the fetishism, as the expressed purpose of trolling humor is the infliction of strong negative emotions (even amongst other trolls; "trolls trolling trolls trolling trolls" is its own genre of subcultural trolling). Consequently, participants must focus on nothing but their own amusement in order to remain appropriately trollish. Not context, not sympathy – just laughter in the face of their target's distress: the fetish in a nutshell.

/b/'s joyful taunting of GameStop employees provides an example. The premise of the longstanding game is as follows: participants post the phone number of a GameStop retail videogame store. Other participants make the calls, and one after another they ask employees about a (nonexistent) sequel to the 1990s franchise *Battletoads*. Clerks go from confused to frustrated to outright enraged as the requests continue and the prank becomes clear to them; participants either record audio of these calls or transcribe the (alleged) interactions and post their handiwork to the original thread. As the campaign unfolds, participants' fetishized laughter drowns out any concerns over the GameStop employees' state of mind. In fact, their anger becomes a punchline unto itself.

The "Be There in Thirty Minutes" meme provides another example of the laughing *us* creating a fetishized *them*. A recurring trend on 4chan in 2011, "Be There in Thirty Minutes" was born after a GIF of a Times Square cardstand being pushed over surfaced on the site. Many posters in many threads in the months that followed linked to street view webcams and promised similar vandalism; all viewers had to do was watch the webcam and wait 30 minutes for the vandal to show up. While most posters never delivered, a few did, and a meta-game emerged in trying to guess the reliability of a particular "Be There in Thirty Minutes" claim ("NYC Cardstand Earthcam Trolling" 2016).

Milner was present for one promise that was fulfilled. Early on in his dissertation research, he came across a thread containing a link to a live street view webcam. The link captured the exterior of a convenience store in New York and was accompanied only by the cryptic statement "be there in thirty minutes." After about, you guessed it, 30 minutes, Milner saw a person in a hoodie walk into view and push over the cardstand sitting outside the store, spilling postcards all over the street. His first thought – well, after the fetishized laughter – was that some poor, underpaid clerk would have to clean the mess up. A point that was, unsurprisingly, obscured by all the other fetishized laughter in the thread. Who cares what happens on the other side of the live-stream link? What matters is that watching people knock things over is *funny*. And watching some poor, underpaid clerk clean up your mess is even funnier. As long as that clerk isn't you.

This kind of world-building fetishization is hardly confined to explicitly antagonistic spaces like 4chan. Constitutive humor – and a particular sort of barbed humor at that – is so common on Twitter's microblogging platform that it prompted Phillips, in a piece co-authored with feminist media scholar Kate Miltner (2012), to describe the space as "Mystery Science Twitter 3000." This framing reflects the fact that, like the television program *Mystery Science Theatre 3000* – in which a human and his two robot friends watch terrible films and make fun of them – Twitter's participants often use the platform to assert an *us* who laughs at the expense of a *them* not in on the joke. Tim Highfield (2015) highlights comedic hashtagging, ironic @mentioning and retweeting, parody accounts, and other platform-specific instances of humor, affirming the connection between humor, the extended lifespan of tweets, and a general ingroup mentality. The funnier something is – humor that, Highfield notes, is often accompanied by snide tonality – the more likely it will be circulated and transformed by others, further evidencing the constitutive magnetism of massive social networks, and further evidencing that humor can both bring together and push apart.

From murder muppets to webcam cruelty to Mystery Science Twitter, the fact that so much traditional thought on humor can be seamlessly applied to digital media underscores the significant consistencies spanning era and degree of mediation. It's the same contextually determined incongruity, the same connected *us*, and the same cast-out *them*. However, as we've seen time and again, these points of continuity are dismantled, and at times outright destroyed, by the differences ushered in by digital mediation. Differences that conjure, and then subsequently amplify, the ethical concerns central to this book.

Digital divergences and ethical buzzkill

The same fetishism, generativity, and magnetism long prevalent in embodied humor are similarly prevalent in digitally mediated humor. But beyond creating more of the same, these characteristics are amplified online in ways simply impossible in embodied spaces. As they expand and refract in novel ways, these characteristics highlight how tenuous the seemingly clear-cut binaries between positive and negative, generative and destructive, and even social and anti-social really are. This section will address these new complications, emphasizing how digital tools kick ambivalent humor into hyperdrive, how context collapse and Poe's Law further complicate motive and meaning, and how harmful amplification becomes an even more pressing problem.

The ambivalence of tools, for example blunt objects
As we've seen, the modularity, modifiability, archivability, and accessibility of digital content facilitate a deluge of incongruous humor. With an endless repertoire of multimodal

source material to reappropriate, and an endless stream of prior participation to build on (and attempt to outdo), memetic media, from Kumamon captions to Dolan comics to gyrating Hogan GIFs, often push incongruity toward outright absurdity.

Figure 6 collects three such memetic absurdities, archetypical of the unique vernacular humor afforded by digital media. The left-hand image is a mashup crafted by *BuzzFeed*'s Jen Lewis, who manipulated a Getty Images photo so that performer Kanye West could kiss performer Kanye West (Lewis and Zarrell 2016). The joke plays with West's reputation for almost self-parodying levels of self-aggrandizement and narcissism. Its visually incongruous application of that theme is uniquely jarring, afforded just enough realism by digital tools

Figure 6. Three memetic images premised on absurdist humor. Left: *BuzzFeed* contributor Jen Lewis' 2015 Photoshop of a Getty Images photograph taken by Jason Merritt; it overlays Kanye West's head and hand on the body of his partner, Kim Kardashian West, allowing Kanye to kiss himself. Top right: Imgur user GuyGoald's Photoshop of garlic bread into a scene from the 2015 film *Star Wars: The Force Awakens*. Bottom right: an unknown creator's bedazzlement of Dana Scully, protagonist of the 1990s show *The X-Files*. Collected in 2016.

to enter the "uncanny valley," approximations of reality that get a little too close to the real thing. Because one Kanye West is, truly, enough.

The top right-hand image in Figure 6 also represents uniquely digital play. It was created by Imgur user GuyGoald (2016), who edited scenes from the 2015 film *Star Wars: The Force Awakens* into a GIF set featuring characters fighting with, oogling, and scrambling to recover pieces of garlic bread, yielding a remix called, fittingly, "The Garlic Awakens." Visually, the flimsily photoshopped two-dimensional bread cascading through the big-budget *Star Wars* universe makes little sense; thematically it's even more absurd. It may be a little more understandable in the context of all the *other* absurd memetic play surrounding garlic bread, a memetic subgenre resonant enough with enough participants for it to warrant its own entry on meme database *Know Your Meme* ("Garlic Bread" 2016). But, of course, the memetic resonance of *garlic bread* just raises its own set questions – most notably, "wait, what?" and "but why?" What *really* makes garlic bread (or anything) funny is as inscrutable now as it ever has been. What is different is GuyGoald's individual ability to amplify a resonant meme, and to do so by so thoroughly altering an apparently static media text.

The bottom right-hand image presents even more memetic vernacular creativity. It's one of scores of unflattering stills of Dana Scully from *The X-Files* shared on Tumblr, many of which use the GIF format to overlay her trademark red hair with shimmering sparkles. The thematic recurrence of unflattering Scully images is afforded by image capturing tools that allow participants to go through *X-Files* episodes frame by frame and immortally fix momentary facial contortions. The visual addition of shimmering sparkle hair amplifies the juxtaposition with another layer of unexpected – and uniquely digital – incongruity. The kind of absurdist collective humor illustrated by this image, by all the images featured in this section and in fact this whole book, certainly isn't new or confined to the internet; recall Chapter 1's *Peanuts* and *Looney Tunes* sex art. That said, the ease and ubiquity of multimodal reappropriation pushes that humor into hyperdrive online.

In the context of silly photoshops, incongruous image captions, and *non sequitur* GIFs, the fact that digital media tools facilitate absurdist humor seems like a rosy, or at least a neutral, declaration to make. So people are *weird*; isn't that funny? Or bemusing, or annoying, or who cares and what's for lunch?, depending on your perspective. But those are not the only contexts in which humor online occurs, and not the only contexts in which digital tools facilitate dizzying memetic absurdity. The fundamental ambivalence of these tools, and just as importantly, the chaos that can be loosed when appropriate incongruity spins out of control, is rendered much clearer when memetic humor is applied to moments of death, pain, and tragedy. In these cases, fetishism grows sharper teeth.

Playful remixes of the terrorist attacks of September 11, 2001, exemplify the flipside of the constitutive coin. Immediately following the attacks, these joking behaviors mirrored traditional "joke cycles," waves of humor often following high-profile events (see Ellis 2003 and Kuipers 2005 for an overview of initial joking reactions to 9/11). In the subsequent decade and a half, however, 9/11 humor online – particularly on 4chan and other forums that favor subversive or otherwise offensive content – has veered off any easily discernable course. Instead, participants have chosen to embrace, and in the process have highlighted the ambivalence of, the perpetual remix machine underscoring so much digital humor. Well-known pop culture figures, including Hulk Hogan, The Kool-Aid Man, and Kumamon have been photoshopped into images or animated GIFs of the collapsing towers, so that it looks like the figures are smashing the buildings to bits. Captions like "9/11 jokes are just 'plane' wrong," "9/11 Americans won't understand this joke," and "No you are a plane you can't work in an office, get out you don't even fit" have been overlaid on images of the moments of impact. The towers have been anthropomorphized in hand-drawn cartoons to express romantic sentiments, smoke marijuana, and fellate the incoming airplanes.

Not only do these images – which we have chosen not to reprint – illustrate the ambivalence of constitutive humor, they illustrate the ease with which modifiability and modularity can facilitate harmful fetishization. After all, the ability to extract a specific image or few-second video clip means that one is able to reduce any event to a quick visual punchline. This in turn allows one to sidestep the fuller political, historical, or emotional context – that which denotes an *actual* bite. Digital spaces do not require a fetishized gaze, of course. But as we saw with hijacked identities, the tools available for vernacular expression online easily lend themselves to the flattening of political, emotional, and interpersonal nuance into memetic granularity.

And the more myopic one's gaze, the easier it is to laugh at whatever might be in one's direct line of sight. Just a clever punchline. Just a funny still image. Just an amusing looped video. As evidenced by the "Bed Intruder" meme, the fetishized distancing between *text* (quote, image, tweet, short video) and *context* (the actual circumstance, including any mitigating factors and overall emotional impact) often inspires further laughter, further memetic reappropriation, and further affective distance – looping right back to the start of the cycle, one that is intimately connected to how easy it is to latch onto one component of a joke (an image, turn of phrase, clever hashtag) and spin it off into another, *ad infinitum*. The previous chapter referred to this process using the metaphor of a snake eating its own tail – known as the Ouroboros – to signal the cyclical, self-sustaining nature of constitutive online laughter. This chapter has added the additional point that, through the generativity and magnetism of this fetishized laughter, participants build communities *and* build walls. Ethically, the implications of this outcome depend entirely on what kind of community it is, and what kinds of walls this laughter might strengthen.

The technological affordances of digital media thus serve to further muddy the already brackish waters of constitutive humor. These affordances allow for the possibility that anything, from a civic mascot to a red-carpet photo to a national tragedy, can be harnessed for comedic ends. And not just harnessed, but immediately accessed and archived, allowing for a seemingly endless half-life of content that can disrupt or even destroy lives as quickly as it can engender harmless giggles – at least what feel harmless, just good silly internet fun – amongst globally dispersed audiences. Resulting, ultimately, in a fundamentally fetishistic and ever-churning trash-heap recycle bin, whose jokes have no bounds, and whose implications can never be predicted.

Context collapse + Poe's Law strikes again
It's not just digital media tools that amplify the ambivalence of humor online. The familiar combination of context collapse and Poe's Law is equally impactive. Because it's often impossible to know exactly who is present – and furthermore who is paying attention or cares – at any given moment on any given platform, it is very difficult to know how best to craft a particular message. It is similarly difficult to predict what might happen to that message once it is posted: things that were originally intended to be private, or at least semi-private, can easily be swept up into public discourse, where countless new observers may be pulled in. This magnetism can result in messages that are hopelessly unmoored from their original context, intended audience, and intended meaning. More problematic still, a person can't discern much from these messages online simply by looking at them – there is simply too much that *could* be happening.

On one hand, the unmoored nature of online vernacular facilitates a great deal of creative, constitutive play. Figure 6 above, for instance, highlights all the ways meaning and intention are up for grabs online. In these images, Kanye and Kim Kardashian West, Rey from *Star Wars*, and Scully from *The X-Files* are all brought into the service of incongruous humor. The process by which people connect with something online, put their spin on it, and then recirculate their personal variation on an existing collectivist theme is, in fact, the driving engine behind memetic resonance and vernacular creativity more broadly.

For these same reasons, though, memetic media can simultaneously precipitate as much confusion and strife as collective connection. When a national tragedy resulting in the deaths of thousands is juxtaposed with the cartoon mascot for a Japanese prefecture, or when found news footage chronicling the attempted rape of a young woman of color is set to a catchy beat, context collapse breeds fetishism. Further, as it's not always clear where something is coming from or what the original creator meant to communicate, it is often difficult to know how to interpret – and therefore respond appropriately to – a given text. Within different communities, groups, or dyads, the same memetic media could be deployed as a long-standing community in-joke, dadaist absurdity, or even as fighting words (or images, as the case may be). 9/11 jokes, for example, can serve each purpose, depending on the audience. And that's saying nothing of humor predicated on specific identity antagonisms, or other forms of communication that could be harnessed equally by bigots and satirists of bigots. These texts might still be constitutive, but as a result of rampant context collapse, it's not clear what worlds are being built by whom, what worlds are being challenged or dismantled, who's being invited into the conversation and who's being ridiculed, particularly when content begins zooming unattributed across and between online collectives.

The social and the anti-social are, in this way, always nipping at each other's heels online; what could be one thing one second, with one audience, could shift into the other with a simple retweet, unbeknownst to the original poster. As a result, the rejoinder that "I was just joking," or, just as frequently, "I was just trolling," becomes an even tougher sell. Even when both teller and listener are on the same basic page, the idea that one shouldn't be held accountable for one's own offensive speech and behavior and, furthermore, that if someone is offended it's that person's problem – for being oversensitive, for not knowing how to take a joke – is a highly self-involved, myopic framing.

And that's under the best circumstances. In the context of rapid-fire online exchange, particularly when participants have weak or nonexistent social ties to the people they're engaging with, the assertion that "I was just joking" is rendered nonsensical almost immediately. The joke may have been *intended* as an innocent jab ensconced by the play frame, but that point is moot if the audience does not and cannot decode that frame, or even recognize its basic existence. Due to the fact that humorous exchanges often focus on taboo, obscene, or otherwise offensive content, this Poe's Law fueled communication failure can get very serious very quickly. After all, once unmoored from the signal "this is play," content that was meant to be funny, not harmful, looks an awful lot like actual taboo, actual obscenity, actual offensiveness. An *actual* bite. And when confronted by what someone regards to be an actual bite, there is a strong tendency for aggrieved parties to actually bite right back. Not as a function of oversensitivity to humor, or the inability to take a joke. But rather the inability to know that a joke is even happening.

Issues of amplification, redux

And this is precisely why issues of amplification are so fraught in digitally mediated spaces. Regardless of why someone retweets, reposts, reblogs, remixes, or further reappropriates memetic media, any act of engagement – meant to condemn, to laugh at, to analyze, to complicate – ensures that what they're sharing spreads a little further. Depending on what the media might be, the implications of it becoming further inspiration for some future joke can range from neutral to positive to downright traumatic. In these more extreme cases – for example, the kinds of targeted, sexually violent identity hijackings described last chapter – these media are actively and maliciously harnessed to do ill. Much more frequently, however, negative outcomes are difficult to assess. Because like play with the "Bed Intruder" meme, these behaviors stem not from targeted malice, but from selective insensitivity – the result of not having to think about anything beyond the fetishized, myopic, modular punchline.

The difference between repeating a disaster joke in your living room and posting the same joke to one of your social media feeds provides an example. It also provides an example of how quickly an expression can veer from "social" to "antisocial," even if the poster's intentions are to tell (what they think is) a harmless joke intended for their friends' eyes only. In fully embodied, pre-internet circumstances, audience members might repeat the joke elsewhere, to people who may themselves repeat the joke. Meaning the joke can still spread, but not with the rapidity of similar content online, where one person can reach thousands of others at any given moment – sometimes without even knowing, or wanting to. Nor can an oral version of a joke be searched for by keyword – or worse, stumbled upon by the friends and family of those affected by a tragedy. For an example, consider the difference it would have made if the medic who took the suicide victim "prom picture" in Timothy Tangherlini's (1998) study was operating in the contemporary media landscape. Say, then, he posted that image to his Twitter or Instagram accounts. The basic behavior remains the same. But ethically something changes, ethically something *should* change, when something is loosed within a digital space designed to amplify content, and for which decontextualization isn't a bug, it's a feature.

In this mass and hyper and digitally mediated milieu, ambivalent content can be spread via average citizens and journalists alike. But the role of large media platforms in the amplification process cannot be overstated. The Holmies fandom described in the Introduction illustrates this point. Holmies – individuals who professed their love and admiration online for spree shooter James Holmes – initially constituted a small, self-contained group of Tumblr users. Based on her years of training and experience sniffing out the so-called "trollish fuckery," Phillips suspects that many of these users were less than earnest in their affections – though there's no way to verify this suspicion, bounded as we all are by Poe's Law. Regardless of motivations, however, the initial visibility and overall influence of participants' generative output was limited; it was a small, specific, inside reference, if not precisely an inside joke.

That is, it *was* an inside reference. Its scope widened when *BuzzFeed* published their July 31, 2012 article condemning (while still reprinting) the worst examples of Holmie fan art (Broderick 2012). After *BuzzFeed* posted their article, a number of other large outlets, including *Mashable* in the US (Pan 2012) and the *Daily Mail* in the UK (Warren 2012), followed suit with their own Holmie coverage. The limited magnetism of the fandom was now gravitational in its pull; suddenly, the Holmies *did* have an audience. And with this larger audience came those whose laughter was unquestionably taunting, notably denizens of 4chan's /b/. Denizens, it is worth noting, who didn't take too kindly to Phillips' attempts to debunk the manufactured outrage over the Holmies "phenomenon" – a phenomenon that only existed to the extent that news outlets ran with the story, and therefore turned it into one (Phillips 2012).

Regardless of how or by whom such ambivalent humor is amplified online, the takeaway is the same – one person's joke is another person's punch to the gut. So think before you click. Also don't stop clicking, because that's what sustains the most creative, and most interesting, humor online. An unsatisfying imperative, certainly. But one reflective of the fact that humor doesn't lend itself to tidy anything. Especially conclusions.

Chapter overview and looking forward

Many, if not most, if not all, of the ambivalent expressions described in this chapter are funny, or might be considered funny by someone. Maybe you. Maybe us. Maybe your dad. Simultaneously, many, if not most, if not all, of the examples in this chapter are offensive, or could be considered offensive by someone. The possibility that both could be true highlights the fact that the *us* and the *them* established by constitutive humor isn't much of a binary at all. Scratch that surface just slightly, and either *us* or *them* can facilitate constructive, pro-social engagement, just as either *us* or *them* can facilitate destructive, anti-social engagement. The ambivalence of constitutive laughter – the fact that it could go either way, or any way, with any group – also highlights the fact that designations of good/bad, social/anti-social, generative/destructive don't have much (or anything) to do with what a particular group or individual hopes to accomplish. Or even how a particular *us* sees themselves in relation to a particular *them*, if either group is even aware of this demarcation. Rather, what qualifies as what, both online and off, depends almost entirely on where a person is standing in relation to these actions, and what impact the actions ultimately end up having.

We will continue exploring these themes in the following chapter focused on collective storytelling. Just as constitutive humor challenges any easy demarcation between the aforementioned binaries, so too does the act of sharing and telling stories – a challenge amplified by the often massive populist participation that these stories can inspire. As we'll see – and also like constitutive humor – this populism can be equally thoughtful and confusing (or offensive, or regressive), can be just as empowering as it can be marginalizing, and is, despite its collective reach, also evidence of small strands of individual voice: one more storyteller in the circle.

4

Collective Storytelling

No matter who is holding the pen, aiming the camera, or striking the keys when telling a story, and no matter how audiences engage with these narratives – say by retelling a tale to a new group, or retelling a tale in a new way, or refusing to retell that tale at all – the stories we share are *collective*; audiences and tellers alike determine which narratives spread forth and which fade away.[10] We will begin the chapter by exploring the fundamentally hybrid and heteroglossic nature of this storytelling process, arguing that, rather than reflecting a niche folkloric framing, *all* instances of storytelling are in fact collective. Each draws from a variety of cultural references, textual callbacks, and narrative motifs, and each influences further references, callbacks, and motifs. As evidence, we will present examples featuring Bigfoot and Martha Stewart (naturally). We will subsequently show that this fundamental collectivism is, in turn, fundamentally ambivalent: stories are the work of individual voices and also of the chorus; are self-contained and densely referential; and draw from stable cultural meanings while simultaneously creating novel meanings for novel audiences. In these ways, stories deconstruct the seemingly straightforward binary between the singular and the multiple.

As we'll see, the ambivalence of storytelling spans eras and degrees of mediation. We will chronicle these continuities with an exploration of urban legends, creepypasta, and other deadly tales, paying particular attention to the overlaps between stories then and stories now. Simultaneously, we will highlight how digital mediation ushers in a number of divergences.

Not only do digital tools further exacerbate the already tenuous category of textual authorship, they hasten how collective stories are told and spread, and therefore facilitate what can only be described as runaway narratives – all shrouding digitally mediated storytelling in even more mystery, even more ambiguity, and even more ambivalence than in embodied contexts.

Stories, heteroglossia, and hybridity

As the bawdy campfire antics in Chapter 1 illustrate, Milner comes from a big, boisterous, storytelling family. When he was young, many of these stories centered on a Thanksgiving tradition known as Bigfoot Road. Each year, stomachs stuffed with turkey and pie, Milner and his gaggle of cousins would pile into Uncle Dave's van – seat-belt laws be damned – and sojourn down Bigfoot Road on the way to a sleepover. In reality, "Bigfoot Road" was one of many underdeveloped back roads in the northern suburbs of Kansas City, Missouri. But in the minds of Milner and his cousins, as the sun dipped below the treeline on a cold fall night, it was a ritual in terror and joy. As they made the trek, Uncle Dave would regale the cousins about the Bigfoot monster that roamed those lands. The car would slow to a crawl, stretching the ten-minute drive into an hour. *Here's where Bigfoot claimed his first victim. Here's the tree where he hanged an unfortunate hunter who got too close to his young.*

And then things would *really* get dark. When the van's tank ran out of gas – and it always ran out of gas – Uncle Dave would direct the cousins to get out and push, promising not to drive off like he did last year. And when he inevitably would, the cousins would break into a Darwinistic sprint toward the disappearing van, hoping to be one of the lucky few who survived the night. Even after they were nestled safely back in the van (Uncle Dave always, eventually, stopped to let them catch up), the mere prospect of seeing the monster would send the cousins into a frenzy; one year, Milner's younger brother Eric struggled to contain himself as Uncle Dave swerved the van violently and banged his fist against the door ("I threw up in my mouth!" Eric howled). Another year, one of Uncle Dave's hirsute friends hid shirtless in the bushes, ready to tear out in front of the van at just the right moment ("We had a confirmed sighting!" Milner proudly told his mom). But regardless of how elaborate the ruse became, it always had a happy ending. The troops would arrive safe and sound at Uncle Dave's house, and would spend the rest of the night drinking root beer floats and watching *Ren & Stimpy*.

Bigfoot Road stories resonate with Milner's family at multiple levels. The original Bigfoot Road tales themselves – told first by Uncle Dave and then by others as they came of age – were cobbled together from existing urban legends, loose folk archetypes, and winking personal touches. At a layer above that, stories about specific Bigfoot Road experiences have been passed along in family legend; at some point during almost every family gathering, someone proclaims to Eric "I threw up in my mouth!"

Like Milner's bawdy and rough-hewn campfire tales, Bigfoot Road aligns with "traditional" folkloric storytelling: it's transmitted orally, spans generations, and centers on a legendary monster. But similar kinds of collective storytelling can unfold in hybrid, digital, and ostensibly non-traditional vernacular contexts. Further, when contrasted with more traditional tales, these tangled narratives reveal the wide variety of stories subsumed by the collective storytelling category. For instance, Phillips' favorite constellation of shared stories is a multimedia narrative doozy, revolving around her somewhat sideways love for beige-toned lifestyle guru and convicted felon Martha Stewart. Stewart's maybe inadvertent, maybe deliberate humor and overall camp sensibility have been delighting Phillips since she was a teenager. This is also where Katie, Phillips' childhood friend mentioned in Chapter 1 – previously "Bob," now "Kato," though neither can remember what precipitated the nickname shift – re-enters the narrative. Because in addition to raising various stripes of hell on the track team, followed by various stripes of hell in high school, then college, then life after, the two have been exchanging giddy collective Martha Stewart stories for nearly two decades.

These bits of vernacular detritus include Martha Stewart-themed fanfiction and – when it was still airing – dramatic *Martha Stewart Living* show re-enactments (her old Halloween specials were always the most hilarious; the sadistic undertones of the holiday fit the series nicely). The two have also told a variety of deranged visual stories via Martha Stewart collages, the largest of which featured an image of Stewart clutching a bucket of eggs, and a cutout of her head taped to the body of a naked lady sipping tea in a lawn chair. Phillips and Katie's ever-expanding collection of multimodal texts also includes Martha Stewart framed art, including one fashion magazine spread wherein Stewart smirks directly into the camera as the grabby silhouette of some unseen sex-person wiggles his hand down the collar of her shirt. (Upon discovery of this gem, Phillips immediately picked up her phone. "Martha," she gasped into Katie's voicemail. "Trying to be sexy. Some guy – his hand. Kato his hand is down her shirt!" The next morning, Katie sent Phillips an email: "You should hang it above your bed," she suggested, prompting Phillips to go buy a gilded frame.) As analog has given way to digital media, Phillips and Katie continue to send each other Martha Stewart articles, GIFs, and tweets, particularly when Stewart is throwing icy shade at her enemies ("She's a national treasure," Katie recently mused via text).

Though Bigfoot legends and Martha Stewart fandom might seem to populate distinct narrative constellations, together they illustrate two foundational characteristics of the storytelling process. First, and most basically, they both demonstrate the collectiveness of storytelling; the existence of these stories depends on the audience as much as the teller. This claim might strike some readers as counterintuitive. Generally, the storyteller is regarded as the active narrative agent, while the audience is presumed to be more passive. The Bigfoot Road tradition, for example, wouldn't exist without Uncle Dave's initial Bigfoot stories, and Phillips and Katie's Martha Stewart play certainly wouldn't exist without Martha Stewart, whose decades of success have hinged on her ability to mold her domestic skills, business acumen, and upper crust white lady tastes into an aspirational lifestyle brand. But without active audiences – sideways or otherwise – to cast and recast those narrative seeds, neither constellation of stories could have resonated so powerfully. Uncle Dave's Bigfoot tales would have been shelved after they were told, and Martha Stewart wouldn't have had a fanbase for whom she could continue spinning her lifestyle yarns.

Second, both sets of stories fall squarely within the realm of contemporary vernacular expression, and are therefore a hybrid blend of media, meanings, and modes of participation. Even if Bigfoot Road tales seem "oral-traditional," Milner's Uncle Dave borrowed from literary and popular sources as he was crafting their original iterations, incorporating bits of campy horror flicks and the pulp serials he read growing up. The subsequent retellings of these stories by Milner and his cousins augmented certain details and omitted others, divergences that would be integrated into future years' stories, as Uncle Dave's now latent popular source material blended seamlessly with oral adaptation. Similarly, Phillips and Katie's Martha Stewart metanarratives draw from commercial sources spanning the television, book, and magazine publishing industries. As these sources were produced by dozens, maybe hundreds, of others, Phillips and Katie's stories are nothing less than a tangled amalgam of countless voices with countless narrative intentions, ones they subsequently reappropriated toward new meanings and new ends. And so it goes with all collective stories, which weave a variety of voices, jokes, and experiences into an ever-evolving constellation of narratives.

Collectivism and vernacularity are equally essential to stories
that don't seem obviously collective or vernacular. As literary
philosopher Mikhail Bakhtin argues, even the most apparently
tidy, self-contained texts are characterized by *heteroglossia*, a
"multiplicity of social voices" ([1935] 1981, 263) evident within
and between texts. Cultural critic and literary scholar Roland
Barthes (1977) forwards a similar perspective in his critique
of *Authorship* with a capital A. As Barthes insists, any attempt
to reduce a work of literature to the voice of a single author
overlooks the "multi-dimensional space in which a variety of
writings, none of them original, blend and clash" (146). Much
more accurate, he argues, is the comparison of *texts* to *textiles*,
"a tissue of quotations drawn from the innumerable centres
of culture" (146). For Barthes, as well as for Bakhtin, creative
expression is about weaving existing threads, not conjuring
a tapestry *ex nihilo*.

Literature is overrun with implicit and explicit heteroglossia. Author Jonathan Lethem (2008) chronicles several examples, beginning with Vladimir Nabokov's infamous 1962 novel
Lolita. As Lethem notes, Nabokov's work strongly echoes –
maybe deliberately, maybe unconsciously – a similar novel
written by a lesser known German author named Heinz von
Lichberg. Lethem also calls attention to William Burroughs'
1959 Beat Generation novel *Naked Lunch*, which was written
using what Burroughs called the "cut up method." This was
no figure of speech; a firm believer in collective storytelling,
Burroughs quite literally "cut up," with scissors, bits of other
people's writing and integrated it into his own without attri-
bution. In an essay published in 1963, Burroughs claims that
this method is reflective of creativity more broadly, gesturing
to Barthes' tissue of quotations. "All writing is in fact cut
ups," Burroughs explained, probably shrugging (347).

The same can be said of all mass media content; just as
every work of literature is a tissue of quotations, every film,
scripted television show, reality dating competition, streaming

webisode, podcast, and any other piece of emergent media content is a narrative bricolage, drawing from a vast range of cultural sources. The heteroglossia of these already densely referential source texts is further augmented through vernacular creativity. For instance, although remix is most often associated with digital media, something created with Adobe and housed on YouTube, participants have long been tinkering with mass media, crafting collective narratives along the way. Activist and artist Jonathan McIntosh (2012) provides an overview of early twentieth-century remixes, tracing the practice to 1920s Russia, where Soviet filmmakers would recut Hollywood films in order to critique class distinctions (again, "cut" as in literally cut the actual film into pieces, rearrange scenes, then splice the reel back together). Using these same techniques, McIntosh explains, Charles A. Ridley of the British Ministry of Information re-edited Nazi propaganda film in 1941 to make it seem as if Hitler and his soldiers were dancing to a popular Jewish song. In that same spirit, Cliff Roth produced a 1988 remix that recut footage of First Lady Nancy Reagan's hard-line anti-drug address to suggest that she is instead an avid marijuana user.

In short, while it might initially seem like a fairly narrow category of expression, collective storytelling is everywhere, from purely folk contexts to purely pop contexts to every hybrid context in between. Regardless of whose story it is or how original it might seem, the presumed autonomy of a given narrative disintegrates under the weight of so much tissue, and so many quotations. Of course, more quotations means more voices. And more voices produce more ambivalence. Digital media, which allow countless participants to ceaselessly reappropriate, remix, and transform existing texts, are especially cacophonous. But this collective flurry shapes analog storytelling as well, as authors across media blend with audiences, text blends with context, and individual meaning blends with collective narrative precedent. The following section will explore the breakdown of these seem-ingly clear-cut lines, illustrating how *this* is fundamentally tangled with *that*.

Hitchhikers, hooks, and one more kidney claimed

The collectivism and vernacularity of shared stories results in a fundamental multiplicity of authors and texts, as narra-tive seeds are flung every which way. While these seeds might mean certain things to those who throw them, all bets are off once they hit the wind. This is as true of the Martha Stewart brand as it is of Bigfoot Road, as true of Three Wolf Moon reviews as it is of Dolan comics, and as true of the "Bed Intruder" meme as it is of *The Room* fandom. Here we'll delve into the narrative dimensions of collective expression, focus-ing specifically on urban legends, a particularly collective strand of vernacular storytelling. As we'll see, each iteration of an urban legend defies singular authorship, exists almost exclusively as a tissue of quotations, and can only "really" mean what its multiple audiences decide it means.

As urban legend expert Jan Harold Brunvand (2001) explains, the glory days of oral-traditional urban legends lasted from the 1960s through the 1980s, though the narrative form has taken on new dimensions with the rise of digital media. Sometimes referred to as contemporary legends or modern legends (a nod to the fact that "urban" is a bit of a misnomer – these are not stories confined specifically to cities, but rather refer to the immediate or very recent past), urban legends are allegedly true events featuring scary, shocking, or supernatural elements. According to Brunvand, urban legends can be clas-sified into a number of general categories, including classic automobile legends, teenage horrors, dreadful contaminations, business rip-offs, bogus warnings, and others, and further classified into specific types or "cycles," multiple versions of the same basic story underscored by a "somewhat stable underlying form" (1981, 2). These stable narrative elements are augmented and incrementally transformed by participants' dynamic retellings. Each time a tale teller uses existing elements to fill in the blanks of their version of a particular legend, they are drawing from a reservoir of cultural tradition. Brunvand refers to this process as "communal re-creation" (12), underscoring its collective, vernacular, and therefore heteroglossic nature.

As such, urban legends always imply an *us* who speak and an *us* who listen, even when participants aren't fully aware of this plurality. A classic urban legend cycle called "The Vanishing Hitchhiker" provides an example. Its basic narrative centers on a hitchhiker – often a pretty young woman but in some versions an old man or religious figure (i.e. a Mormon disciple of Christ, or even Jesus himself) – who catches a ride from a stranger. Sometimes the hitchhiker warns the driver of a dangerous curve ahead, or makes other odd, prophetic statements. The hitchhiker then disappears from the car (or, in some retellings, is dropped off and then disappears). Often, the hitchhiker leaves "proof" in the car, like a book or purse or sweater. After the encounter, the driver learns that someone looking very much like the hitchhiker died years earlier in the spot where they were picked up or dropped off and/or, upon attempting to return the forgotten item to the address given by the hitchhiker, discovers that the hitchhiker has been dead for many years.

Despite its vast and varied retellings, Milner didn't know "The Vanishing Hitchhiker" was an urban legend until he came across it in Brunvand's book. As he read Brunvand's account of the tale, Milner froze. He recalled one of his overnight shifts at Wal-Mart and a conversation he had with John, an off-duty police officer who moonlit at the store as a security guard. Because there often wasn't much happening (overnight shift at Wal-Mart and all), John would entertain Milner with stories about some of the crazy things he'd seen while on duty. That night, John shared an allegedly true first-person account of "The Vanishing Hitchhiker." John swore he'd picked up a young female hitchhiker. John swore she had warned him of a curve. John swore the hitchhiker disappeared into the night after she was dropped off, and he swore that his subsequent investigation of incident reports revealed that a pretty young woman had died in a crash on that very curve years earlier.

At the time, Milner believed him, and over the next few days recounted John's story, wide-eyed, to various friends. In the process, he became part of a storytelling *us* he didn't even know existed: one more voice in the collective "Vanishing Hitchhiker" story. Milner's experiences illustrate that, while our stories – the ones we tell and the ones we hear and claim ownership over – are, unquestionably, *ours*, a reflection of our unique voices and life experiences, they also echo all the other voices that came before. This tension between *mine* and *ours* immediately complicates the question of what belongs to whom. After all, how could someone declare ownership over something that is, in the end, a patchwork of fragments? How do you claim strands in a tapestry, how do you lock down seeds in a breeze?

The communal re-creation and collective authorship evidenced by "The Vanishing Hitchhiker" are inextricably linked to the story's multiple, and often highly variable, iterations. A particularly hybrid and multimodal legend cycle, "The Kidney Heist," further illustrates this interconnection. Although the specific narrative details can vary, the basic story describes a person, usually a man, on a trip away from home, usually for business, and usually to a city or country regarded as "unsafe." At some point the individual gets drunk and, in most accounts, has sex with an anonymous stranger, usually a woman, in their hotel room. The next morning, the protagonist groggily awakens and realizes that one of their kidneys is missing, surprise! – the work, apparently, of black market organ farmers, who lure gullible people into compromising situations and then make with the quick extraction.

As Brunvand (2001) explains, this legend spans a wide variety of media. It served as the plot for a 1991 episode of *Law and Order* titled "Sonata for Solo Organ," regularly appeared in 1990s newspaper columns, and made its way through a fair share of chat rooms. "The Kidney Heist" is also one of many urban legends cataloged on the venerable Snopes.com, which has been debunking, and sometimes confirming, a variety of suspect claims since 1995 (Mikkelson 2008). In 1998, the legend was even the pivotal climax of a horror film titled, appropriately enough, *Urban Legend*. By 2001, when Brunvand's *Encyclopedia of Urban Legends* was published, more recent versions of the legend began including the names of specific medical personnel or law enforcement agents, and also introduced an additional narrative detail: that the organ farmers placed their victim in an ice-filled bathtub, and included a note telling the man to call 911 (how thoughtful). This is the version Phillips remembers hearing (and giggling nervously at) as a kid, and is one that has persisted in its own constellation of folk and popular retellings in the decade and a half since Brunvand noted the ice bath addition. Milner's first exposure to this version of the tale, for instance, was in a 2004 episode of the animated series *The Venture Bros.* called "Dia de los Dangerous!" that not only included the ice bath motif, but also amplified the racist assumption that Mexico is a seedy destination, where no kidney is safe.

Whether told around a campfire, in a newspaper, on prime-time TV, or over email, each iteration of "The Kidney Heist" is a present amalgam of past narrative participation, one that simultaneously primes its audience for their own future retellings. Further, the sheer number of iterations in such a wide variety of media complicates, even renders bizarre, the impulse to refer to "The Kidney Heist" in the singular (beyond ease of classification and analysis as a narrative cycle, of course). The specific version of the story an audience hears is the result of countless retellings, which themselves are the product of countless life experiences and cultural collisions, all fused into a seemingly singular, seemingly self-contained package that is, in the end, anything *but* singular.

And each time these multiple texts are reappropriated by new audiences, the basic idea of *meaning* is further muddled. A given iteration of a story might mean something specific to the teller, and might mean something specific to the listener, but it's not guaranteed that both teller and listener will be on the same page about that specific meaning, to say nothing of future tellers and future listeners, who reinterpret meaning as the story spreads. This is not a poststructuralist free-for-all, however. Resonant genres, iterations, and motifs – the conservative elements of collective storytelling, all drawn from a shared reservoir of cultural tradition – persist between stories and across eras. Simultaneously, dynamic personal meanings hinging on the dynamic contours of dynamic audiences flower in unique ways, as the needs of the individual intertwine with the traditions of the collective. In the context of collective storytelling, meaning exists at its destinations, not at its origins – echoing Barthes (1977) – *and* is embedded within persistent cultural resonance.

The dynamic variability of meaning within more conservative cultural strictures is illustrated by "The Hook," an urban legend in which a young couple drives to some secluded location to do what young couples do. "The night is warm with promise," winks one of Brunvand's collected examples (1981, 200). Suddenly, because these youths are apparently listening to the car radio, a newsflash blares from the speakers. A *very crazy murderer* just escaped from the local *insane asylum* – and he has a *hook* for a *hand*. Exclamation point! Realizing how far from the road they are, the girl asks to be taken home. The boy doesn't want to leave and throws some sort of penis tantrum (most iterations foreground the boy's sexual perseverations, then wounded protestations, which are sometimes followed by explicit anger; he expects the girl to have sex with him, and feels insulted when she doesn't). The girl hears a scratch at the door, and really lets the boy have it. He finally acquiesces, and they speed off. The boy drops the girl off at her house, and, although still an insensitive oaf, walks around to her side of the car so he can open her door. And *there*, dangling from the *handle*, is the *hook*, wrested from the arm of the murderer!!!

This basic story cycle has been in circulation in the US since the 1950s, and over the decades has grown increasingly multimodal. Iterations of "The Hook" have appeared across so many media – from comic books to television programs to email forwards – that, as Brunvand writes, "the very image of a hook dangling from a car-door handle is enough to suggest for most people the whole genre of urban legends" (200). Because there are so many recorded versions to analyze, Brunvand explains, the legend has also proven very popular with folklorists. But try as they might, no one can arrive at a consensus about what it all means. Alan Dundes (1971), for example, asserts that the murderer's hook is a phallic symbol, and – unsurprising to anyone who has ever read anything written by Dundes the Freudian – its amputation represents castration. Other scholars suggest that it is a warning about the dangers of youth sexuality; a reminder of stranger danger; or an expression of anxiety toward people with disabilities, among other explanations (Brunvand 1981).

As compelling as any of these arguments might be (or not), different audiences bring their own experiences and expectations to, and therefore extract their own personal meanings from, each iteration of each tale; analyses of specific tellers' motivations, the formal qualities of the text(s), and comparative overlap with similar legends might yield valuable localized insights, but no explanation will ever subsume every possible reaction in every possible moment. Depending on audience members' personal experiences, the unconsenting girlfriend could, for example, be decoded as a chaste Christian, an empowered feminist, a watchful citizen, or any combination thereof. Similarly, the couple's escape could be framed as an endorsement of sexual purity ("don't have sex before marriage, because if you do, you won't hear the warnings and the hook man will kill you"), lucky coincidence ("who the hook man kills is honestly just a coin toss"), or even an excuse to gather ye rosebuds while ye may ("we might as well have sex today, because who knows, maybe the hook man will get us tomorrow").

Simultaneous to this personal dynamism, however, meanings also draw from a more conservative reservoir of cultural tradition. "The Hook," for example, along with "The Vanishing Hitchhiker" and "The Kidney Heist," are all underscored by motifs addressing female and male sexuality, and the fact that the former is often pathologized and fretted over while the latter is often taken as a given (i.e. for women, sexuality is dangerous, while for men, sexuality is expected). These narrative motifs draw from widely accepted cultural frameworks, and for that reason resonate with tellers and listeners – regardless of how novel or personally idiosyncratic the specific narrative combinations might be, and regardless of what a storyteller or hearer might personally *feel* about the traditions their narratives evince.

Coupled with the ambivalence of texts and authorship, ambivalent meanings challenge any presumption of singularity within a storytelling context. Stories often seem singular, i.e. the audience only sees one author, hears one story, and posits one meaning. But even then, these stories are heteroglossic, densely referential, and open to an endless tangle of personal and traditional interpretations, regardless of era and degree of mediation. The following section will continue exploring the continuities between stories now and then, digital and analog, always taking for granted the ambivalence inherent to all authors, all texts, and all meanings.

On continuity and creepypasta

Collectivism and vernacularity – along with the multiplicities of authors, texts, and meanings these characteristics engender – are essential to online storytelling. The resulting heteroglossia inspires the same ambivalence it has for ages, as long-told tales are repackaged, rehashed, and recirculated in digital formats. This overlap speaks to the most obvious point of continuity between stories then and stories now, stories online and stories offline: the narrative elements that are integrated into those stories, and more broadly, the shared cultural reservoir from which they emerge. Mediation doesn't reinvent, and doesn't *need* to reinvent, those narrative wheels. The kinds of stories that speak to people around campfires, in books, or at movie theatres are equally resonant in digitally mediated spaces.

To emphasize these points of connection, this section will analyze a prevalent genre of digitally mediated storytelling strikingly similar to urban legends: *creepypasta*. As it will show, the ambivalence of creepypasta – like the ambivalence of the oral-traditional urban legends that precede it – hinges on multiplicity, tangle, and overlap: the fact that authors are more *we* than *me*, texts are never self-contained, and meaning is tethered to the audiences listening.

A tissue of authors, texts, and quotations

Creepypasta labels a loose constellation of suspenseful, scary, and, well, creepy stories created, circulated, and transformed by online participants. Originating on (you guessed it) esoteric forums like 4chan, Something Awful, and BodyBuilding.com in the early–mid 2000s, creepypasta is currently housed across a number of online repositories, notably 4chan's "/x/" ("Paranormal") board, but also on dedicated sites like Creepypasta.com, Creepypasta.org, and the Creepypasta Wikia. Reddit also features many subreddits – individual forums organized around a particular interest or theme, stylized with the prefix "/r/" – devoted to creepypasta narratives. In particular, /r/NoSleep and /r/LetsNotMeet archive dark tale after dark tale.

The name *creepypasta* is a derivation of *copypasta*, a playful shortening of "copy and paste." Copypasta content is so called because participants, presumably, use copy and paste shortcuts to move memorable (and mostly humorous) narratives within and between threads, or to bring old narratives to a new conversation. Copypasta is, therefore, definitionally memetic; to even earn the label, content has to resonate with multiple participants, who apply it again and again in novel contexts. While creepypasta and copypasta share similar memetic dimensions, creepypasta is more frequently presented as earnest narrative. "True stories," in other words, some quite fleshed-out, which seem more oriented toward eliciting a skin crawl than a belly laugh. As such, creepypasta stories are often framed as a single person's singularly terrifying experience, rather than playfully distributed copypasta. As *my* true story, not *our* inside joke – even if everyone participating is fully aware of the genre and fully aware of the "you spook, you lose" collective game being played.

This "everyone" is critical to creepypasta, which depends on countless tale tellers shaping countless existing narrative elements into new iterations, bridging the *me* telling the story to the *us* who came before. Sometimes this process is as easy as moving a chunk of text, unaltered, from one forum or thread to another, either by posting a hyperlink or by copying and pasting available content – not unlike borrowing a book of scary stories and then reading one aloud to an enraptured audience. Everyone knows full well that the story isn't "yours," but by telling it that night, in that way, to that group, the story is made new again. Sometimes this process entails making slight variations to an existing story depending on the night, the mood, and the group listening, just as tellers of oral-traditional urban legends have done for decades. Sometimes this process is fragmented and destabilized further, as authors take small motifs such as a hook or a hitchhiker and recombine them with all the creative license of Phillips' (scary in their own way) Martha Stewart mashups.

The Slender Man, a tall, thin, supernatural menace, exemplifies fragmented narrative multiplicity, and also illustrates how distributed authorship facilitates this multiplicity. The character, now a creepypasta mainstay, was first introduced in 2009 to a "Create Paranormal Images" thread on Something Awful, a web forum and content aggregator with close ties to 4chan (particularly at the height of both sites' popularity in the mid- to late aughts). He was initially photoshopped, looming and ghostly, into the corner of two pictures featuring groups of children. The first photo captures a handful of young teens scrambling to escape their blurry antagonist. "We didn't want to go, we didn't want to kill them, but its persistent silence and outstretched arms horrified and comforted us at the same time…" the caption reads, noting that the photographer was unknown but presumed dead. The second image captures children on a playground. Its short caption explains that all 14 of the children pictured vanished after a library fire in 1986, and suggests that the Slender Man was responsible for the attack. It also notes that the image was "confiscated as evidence," and that the photographer, Mary Thomas, has been missing since June 13, 1986 (Surge 2009).

The following day, another Something Awful user uploaded an image of a burning building to the thread, along with additional Slender Man backstory. Further narratives and images followed, and were layered onto the original narrative kernel; the thread quickly ballooned to 46 pages, as the Slender Man took on a life of its own. While the Slender Man narrative proved to be especially resonant, its collective conjuring isn't unique; creepypasta commenters frequently add layers to an emerging narrative alongside a given source text, with additions, subtractions, suggestions, and proddings becoming essential to the collective story. In these cases, authorship is multiple from the very beginning.

And as such, the stories' texts are multiple from the very beginning. This was certainly the case with the Slender Man canon (if you can call it that), which spiraled out in countless directions after emerging on Something Awful. Beyond more traditional text- and image-based narratives, the stories span

YouTube video series, podcasts, a range of fan art, and even alternate-reality games devoted to "Slendy," as he is sometimes called by his more affectionate fans. This framing itself illustrates the variety of new meanings that new storytellers have infused into the character. As media scholars Shira Chess and Eric Newsom (2014) explain in their analysis of Slender Man stories, sometimes these iterative retellings portray the Slender Man as a malevolent predator, sometimes as a misunderstood anti-hero, sometimes as an object of desire (trust us, rule 34 applies to the Slender Man), and sometimes as a little of everything. The Slender Man is thus quintessentially a narrative belonging to *me* (i.e. individual storytellers) and belonging to *us* (a broader, amorphous collective of participants). Speaking to the continuity of this vibrancy, Chess and Newsom muse that "This is the way that ghost stories have always been told" (5).

More broadly, this is the way that *all* stories have always been told: multiple authors borrowing and contributing multiple narrative threads. Even if individual authors and audiences don't think they're retelling an existing story, they are, in fact, reliant on narrative precedent. For instance, as Chess and Newsom outline, the Slender Man's original Something Awful photoshops were crafted by their creator as an homage to the 1979 horror film *Phantasm*. That narrative trace lives on in every subsequent Slender Man iteration; even when people producing those iterations have never seen the film, they are reproducing an aesthetic that precipitated the character's inception.

The dense referentiality that characterizes creepypasta specifically, and collective storytelling more generally, is illustrated by one of the most popular stories housed on /r/NoSleep, posted under the heading "My dead girlfriend keeps messaging me on Facebook. I've got the screenshots. I don't know what to do..." (we hope you'll forgive us if we shorten it to something more titular; say, "The Dead Girlfriend's

Facebook"). This story is an allegedly true first-person account of a bereaved boyfriend receiving Facebook communication from his dead girlfriend. The post was prompted, poster Natesw (2014) explains, by an especially frightening communication sent the previous day, which convinced him that it was finally time to share his story. He then provides an overview of all the events leading up to that point, beginning with his girlfriend's death in 2012 and spanning the subsequent two years of intermittent ghostly contact. For each major event, he includes a series of Facebook screenshots as evidence.

Even in its apparent singularity, "The Dead Girlfriend's Facebook" echoes a number of existing narrative motifs, many similar to those present in "The Vanishing Hitchhiker." First, like the hitchhiker in many iterations of the urban legend, the girlfriend in "The Dead Girlfriend's Facebook" is a woman who died in a car crash far too young. Also, like the hitchhiker's unsettling lamentations, amorphous warnings, and cryptic prophecies, the girlfriend's communication from beyond the grave is fragmented and unnerving; she tags herself in photos of her boyfriend as if she's standing right beside him, and resends old messages over and over, cobbling bits together to spell messages like "cold FRE EZIN G I don't know what's happening." Further, like the driver in many iterations of "The Vanishing Hitchhiker" who initially maintains skepticism until a preponderance of evidence renders skepticism impossible (e.g. a left-behind artifact, a found police report, a discussion with the hitchhiker's surviving parents), the narrator in "The Dead Girlfriend's Facebook" initially discounts the messages, thinking they're being sent by some cruel antagonist logged on to his girlfriend's account. But then, just as in "The Vanishing Hitchhiker," a preponderance of evidence begins to erode his skepticism (e.g. denials from others who might know the password, jarringly specific communication, the revelation of details unknown to anyone else). To be sure, "The Dead Girlfriend's Facebook" and "The

Vanishing Hitchhiker" contain vast differences. Even so, both draw from the same reservoir of cultural tradition, and as they do, are connected through common resonant motifs.

"The Dead Girlfriend's Facebook" thus provides another example of a storytelling *me* roped into a storytelling *we*. It further foregrounds the fact that the storyteller needn't be aware of this collective to be influenced by it, any more than Slender Man storytellers and audiences need to recognize the reference to *Phantasm* to collectively participate, or any more than Milner needed to know that "The Vanishing Hitchhiker" was an urban legend to connect with Officer John's apparently winking retelling. It is quite likely that few creating, circulating, and transforming collective content can accurately trace from whence particular narrative elements emerge. However, apparent to the audience or not, this overlap is present, and represents not just a tissue of quotations, but a tangle of one.

Indeed, beyond their connection to oral-traditional urban legends, the always macabre and sometimes disgusting dimensions of creepypasta stretch back centuries. The ATU (Aarne–Thompson–Uther; see Uther 2004) classification system catalogs these centuries of narrative overlap. Finnish folklorist Antti Aarne initially proposed this taxonomy of folk narratives in 1910, which he used to analyze and compare elements prominent in cross-cultural, inter-generational tales. American folklorist Stith Thompson expanded Aarne's index in 1928 and again in 1961. Pulling from an even deeper transglobal narrative reservoir, German folklorist Hans-Jörg Uther expanded the index once more in 2004. The current ATU index contains thousands of narrative elements persistent across cultures and eras.

As it is reflective of vernacular communication, the ATU is brimming with content that would be right at home on 4chan or Something Awful. Many of these stories feature the paranormal, including narratives about vampires, witches, ghosts, demonic sex criminals, and various other malevolent nightstalkers. Sexism and racism abound, and murder, incest, and bestiality are common. Your fairly jaded authors have spent years probing the depths of the ambivalent internet, and on our solo and collective travels have encountered some of the most unsettling, offensive, and straight-up bizarre tales that digital participation has to offer. We are happy to announce that our ancestors could give even these stories a run for their WTF money. Here are a few of our favorite examples from the wonderful world of the ATU:

- "The Corpse Eater" (ATU 363): A newlywed man eats corpses in three different churches while his bride watches. To make sure she won't tattle, he appears to her in the form of her mother and asks if she's seen her husband do anything strange. When she replies, "no yeah he eats corpses," he eats her too.
- "Making the Ogre Strong by Castration" (ATU 1133): A man tells an ogre his ox is strong because it's neutered. The ogre tells the man they should castrate each other and be strong too. The man agrees and says he'll come back tomorrow to complete the bargain. The man sends his wife, the ogre is castrated, and the wife already doesn't have a penis.
- "The Offended Skull" (ATU 470A): A drunken man finds a skull, kicks it, then invites it to dinner as an apology. The skull shows up to dinner, chastises the man for his bad behavior, then kills him.

As strange as many ATU tales might seem, they aren't a random litany of curios. The tale-types in the ATU represent, instead, the most successful narrative elements in the history of human storytelling (pretty much every Disney princess movie, for instance, has an ATU prototype). And as evidenced by this whole chapter, the paranormal elements on display in the ATU's pages have persisted, even thrived, across era, culture, and media.

Across lifespans as well; scary stories are and have remained just as popular with children as with adults. Alvin Schwartz' profoundly creepy 1981 children's classic *Scary Stories to Tell in the Dark* illustrates the intergenerational appeal of spooky-scary narrative elements. And not just their appeal, but the direct narrative continuity between the *we* of now and the *we* of then. As folkloric narratives (Schwartz notes in his introduction that he adapted his stories from American folktales), many even echo ATU entries. Schwartz' delightfully odd "May I Carry Your Basket?", for example, loosely follows the "The Offended Skull" narrative, although the skull is an old woman's severed head that the rest of her body is carrying in a basket (. . . ok), which, when dropped, gnaws the legs off the man who offered to help bear her burden ("Or invaded her personal space," Phillips mutters sympathetically).

Given its venerable lineage, it's no surprise that a number of creepypasta stories have integrated the sentient, assaultive severed head motif. One example housed on the Creepypasta Wikia is a 2012 post by the user RoboKy called "12 Minutes." In this tale, a religiously themed television program hosted by a charismatic Reverend premieres on a local network. As more episodes air, a disturbing trend emerges: beginning at the 12-minute mark of the show, pregnant viewers begin feeling nauseous and dizzy. Going through footage for clues, an intern finds that, 12 minutes in, frames showing a severed head are invisibly intercut into the rest of the program. The intern begins comparing the 12-minute mark of multiple episodes. Across each set of frames, the head mouths unintelligible words as it continues decomposing. Eventually the Reverend's endgame is revealed, as all those nauseous viewers miscarry their unborn children, bewitched by the severed head's "words of light."

Whether or not the author of "12 Minutes" ever encountered "May I Carry Your Basket?" – or any other iteration of "The Offended Skull" – is, to echo an earlier point about the connection between the Slender Man and *Phantasm*, irrelevant, just like Natesw's familiarity with "The Vanishing Hitchhiker" is irrelevant. Tellers and audiences of any given story may not know how and when – or even *that* – they have encountered existing narratives. They don't need to; the inclusion of these elements speaks, regardless, to all the stories that have come before, swept up again and again into countless tales based on countless tales. The differences between iterations might be slight, or might be significant, as a fundamental recombination of many narratives. In every case, storytelling is always as an act of borrowing from, and then feeding back into, a shared cultural tradition. In this way, the storytelling *we* functions as its own kind of phantom: an amorphous connection to an unseen past, which exerts its influence even on those who don't believe.

The multiple meanings of multiplicitous texts

The fact that prominent recurring motifs – for example, the "subliminal messaging on television" and "murderous zealots" motifs present in "12 Minutes" – have remained in circulation for so long hinges on the one characteristic that unifies even the most patchworked stories: storytellers include, and audiences share, content that resonates with them. This content must resonate, or else audience members wouldn't feel compelled to cast and recast those narrative seeds.

As straightforward as it might initially seem (*"obviously* people share the things they like"), the claim that resonance facilitates sharing explains how and why the ATU tale-type index contains the stories it contains. The ATU is not, as we've said, a random litany. Instead, it contains only the most memetically successful narrative elements: the stories people have shared the most, retold the most, and which were subsequently recorded by folklorists the most – all due to the fact that these were the references, conventions, and quotations that resonated most strongly, and which were, as a consequence, most frequently siphoned off from and returned to the collective cultural reservoir.

As evidenced by the preponderance of regressive narrative elements undergirding so many stories both within and outside the ATU, this collective reservoir is not always a source of purely nutritive water. That adds an additional layer of ambivalence to the already profoundly ambivalent collective storytelling process: the fact that these narrative building blocks contribute, implicitly or explicitly, to identity antagonisms and cultural boundary policing, even when the stories themselves don't *seem* politically prescriptive. In the context of urban legends, Brunvand (1981, 2001) notes that many stories are imbued with explicitly racist, classist, ableist, and sexist motifs. To this last point, and building on his analyses of gender stereotypes and "The Hook," Brunvand chronicles a number of legends in which women are punished (or at least pathologized) for exploring their sexuality and rewarded for maintaining their chastity. Indeed, the implicit injunction present in many urban legends is that women who step out of line – a line that may vary from story to story, but which almost always posits a "right" and a "wrong" way to behave not equally applied to male protagonists – are asking for trouble. Asking for *tragedy*.

Some, particularly those individuals who don't encounter them in their everyday lives, might be tempted to frame such sexist motifs (to say nothing of the other regressive motifs on display) as relics of a less enlightened era, or at least as an unfortunate but ultimately contained minority opinion ("not *all* men"). But these motifs have stood the test of time online and off, evidencing their persistent memetic resonance. Natesw's (2014) "The Dead Girlfriend's Facebook" provides an example. In this story, the speaker (presumably Natesw himself, as the story is presented as a sincere first-person account) goes to great lengths to cast its deceased heroine as unaffectionate, unsubmissive, and, most damningly, uninterested in sex. In fact, Natesw explains, she resisted any form of intimacy unless he was drinking (curiously, Natesw makes no mention of whether or not the girlfriend also needed to drink). "I got fake-drunk a lot," he explains, before recounting how he pretended to be drunk on Facebook chat to try and loosen up her ghost.

Even if these flourishes ostensibly add depth to the narrative, they also boil down to an implicit policing of the girlfriend's character and gendered communication style: while she rejected the gender norms that would have made her a "good" girlfriend (emotional warmth, sexual availability, general submissiveness), her unwanted photo tagging, constant cryptic messages, and simultaneous reticence to freely give her partner what he wanted marked her with a number of negative female stereotypes. Most conspicuously that, even after her death, she *still* wouldn't stop talking, specifically about things, and in ways, her boyfriend didn't like. Again, whether or not the author intended to rehash age-old sexist motifs, particularly the notions that "good girls" are quiet and sweet and carefully unobtrusive, their subtext and resonance persist. These motifs also persist in the vast corpus of urban legends that punish female protagonists for their talkativeness; as Brunvand (2001) catalogs, many a toddler has met a grotesque fate because the babysitter couldn't tear herself away from the telephone – a motif also implicit in the ATU's "The Corpse Eater"; when the bride was unable to keep her mouth shut, her husband literally ate her.

They may be strange; they may be creepy; they may even strike some readers as funny, if also pretty offensive. But these persistent regressive motifs cannot and should not be regarded as the fringe expression of fringe actors. If these kinds of narratives really were fringe, those seeds wouldn't have been continually cast and recast. They wouldn't have insinuated themselves into both vernacular and mass-market media. They wouldn't, as a result, have become ingrained in the broader culture. Not restricted to now, not restricted to then, but as an uncomfortable point of continuity spanning generation and degree of mediation. This is the crux of the ambivalence underscoring this whole book. Just as dirty or

otherwise taboo cultural elements point to and often complicate that which is regarded as clean, ambivalence – that which
is difficult to classify or is otherwise strange, creepy, or some
combination of funny and offensive – has more to say about
the center than it does about the periphery. In the case of
collective storytelling, it illustrates the persistent cultural
values on display when the same narrative seeds continue to
be cast and recast. For better and for worse and for everything
in between.

Digital divergences and runaway narratives

As we've seen throughout this book, digital media rarely, if
ever, create wholly new categories of vernacular expression.
Much more common is the process described by Henry
Jenkins (2009) in his discussion of the origins of YouTube:
new media, however emergent they might appear, are most
successful when they provide people faster and easier ways
of doing what they were already doing. In the case of collective storytelling online, people were, clearly, already telling
plenty of stories. Online spaces have harnessed this existing
narrative energy by allowing more participants to tell more
stories. And thanks to the affordances of digital media, have
punched the already blurred lines between individual creators
and the collective chorus, self-contained texts and their infinite
variations, and focused meanings and interpretive chaos, into
hyperdrive. These shifts foreground the speciousness of referring to any aspect of any online story as singular. Even more
so than in embodied spaces, stories online are never just one
thing.

A tissue of (even more) authors, texts, and quotations
If the notion of singular authorship was untenable offline,
online the very notion of specific, self-contained artifacts and
specific, self-contained creators is thrown straight out the
window. Millions and millions of Phillipses, remixing millions

and millions of absurdist Martha Stewart collages, nodding to each other approvingly all the while. We've seen this process before, with a panoply of (childhood-ruining) memetic variations of cultural figures like Donald Duck, *Peanuts* and *Looney Tunes* characters, SpongeBob SquarePants, the Berenstain Bears – the list goes on.

In similar cases of analog "cut up," texts are still marked by heteroglossia, and still densely referential. But no matter how many voices were implicitly contained in *Lolita* or *Naked Lunch*, or how many other texts they refer to or might influence, these novels can be attributed to what Barthes (1977) calls the scriptor, or "little *a* author." The person whose name is on the byline; the person with whom the narrative buck ultimately stops. What distinguishes digitally mediated content is that the narrative buck often doesn't stop – often *can't* be stopped – with one little *a* author, much to the chagrin of the person who originally produced a given narrative.

One example, reported by Zachary Crockett (2015), is the erotic fan fiction surrounding "Erin Esurance," the mid-2000s cartoon female spy mascot for the insurance company Esurance. The sexualized corpus devoted to Erin Esurance was so ubiquitous – and the character so fetishized, in so many different scenarios – that she had to be pulled from Esurance's marketing campaign. Erin Esurance's creator, Kristin Brewe, was mortified to learn that her character was being put to use for such explicit ends. A similar story, and similar mortification, unfolded in 2016 around the children's television program *Arthur*, which follows a cartoon aardvark as he navigates childhood. That summer, memetic images corrupting Arthur and his friends began to "take over the internet," at least according to *Paper*'s Sandra Song (2016). Many of these images followed the same trajectory as Dolan comics and Erin Esurance fan fiction, placing the otherwise innocent *Arthur* characters into a variety of compromising, and often explicitly sexual, scenarios. An untold number of participants had a field day remixing references to drug use, racist invectives, and incestuous couplings between Arthur and his younger sister into the source text (images redacted; we've put you through enough). So much so that the show's producers were forced to release a statement in July declaring that they were "disappointed" by the explicitness of the memetic play and urging participants to stop (which, of course, they did not).

What happened with Arthur, what happened with Erin Esurance, what happened with Dolan and the Berenstain Bears and SpongeBob SquarePants and Tommy Wiseau and Antoine Dodson and yes even Martha Stewart, God bless and keep her, all follow the pattern of identity hijacking described in Chapter 2. And they all follow the pattern of fetishistic, generative, and magnetic laughter described in Chapter 3. Each of these cases also highlights the ease with which producers big and small, both at the individual level and from the monochrome boardrooms of multinational corporations, can utterly, irreparably, lose control over their own narrative, thanks to collective vernacular expression online. This potential for amplified reappropriation lends even more salience to the age-old question: at what point does something of *theirs* become something of *mine*?

Beyond opening the chorus to every possible interested voice, digital media tools allow for an infinitely remixed and reappropriated textual cacophony. In the case of the Slender Man, countless narrative threads are woven into an ever-unfurling textual tapestry. Even when restricted to a single platform, it can be difficult, even dizzying, to keep track of the various narrative offshoots; on YouTube alone, there are millions of videos devoted to the collective Slender Man constellation. These videos represent a vast range of narrative content, from clips of broadcast news footage exploring the Slender Man phenomenon to purported "Slender Man in real life" found footage to shots of other people reacting in horror to the videos about the Slender Man that other YouTubers have posted. There are also short dramatic films, some of which boast sophisticated visual effects, as well as Slender

Man music videos, operating under a range of production budgets. These clips may have been edited, recut, remixed, and uploaded by a single individual (though they might also represent a tweak on someone else's existing work), but once online, Slender Man participants across the globe are free to make this content their own by integrating existing clips into new narratives, integrating existing ideas into new narratives, or simply reacting, on camera, to other people's narratives.

As we've already seen, this visual heteroglossia has its roots in practices as old as cinema itself. But just as Xeroxlore is dwarfed by the deluge of memetic imagery ushered in by digital media, so too were early analog remix videos outside the skillsets and, quite literally, the toolsets, of most people. Digital technologies have narrowed that gap. Some digital remix videos require a good deal of technological skill, of course, or at least ample patience and time. Take, for example, YouTube user Metkuratsu Mizuiro's 2013 mashup called "SLENDER MAN visits the Krusty Krab," which intercuts scenes from *SpongeBob SquarePants* with existing Slender Man imagery. Overlaid on a television backdrop "to avoid copyright," as the description explains, this video opens in the Krusty Krab (SpongeBob's place of employment) as his cranky neighbor and co-worker Squidward grows increasingly frightened while reading a book. After falsely accusing SpongeBob of flickering the lights, the phone rings. It's SpongeBob's best friend Patrick, a starfish, who screams for protection against the Slender Man. "He's just standing there," Patrick bellows. "*Menacingly!*" Sirens can be heard blaring in the background. Squidward looks up, terrified. And there, in the doorway, is the Slender Man himself. What will Squidward and SpongeBob do??

In order to tell its dark tale, "SLENDER MAN visits the Krusty Krab" required a careful search of available SpongeBob footage and then a laborious manipulation of that footage so that it coheres with a typical Slender Man narrative. But in other cases – say, for example, reaction shot Slender

Man videos, in which a webcam is trained to the face of someone watching someone else's video and captures their fearful reaction (reactions that also often include a great deal of nervous laughter in addition to shrieks, wide eyes, and full-body wincing) – vast technical know-how is not a necessary requirement. And vast technical know-how is certainly not required to copy a link and paste a link, immediately intertwining one individual story with the stories of others.

Not every multimodal remix of an existing story is an obviously recognizable or traditional narrative – one with a clear protagonist, plot, and some form of resolution. However, each remix is cobbled together from existing stories, and each has the potential to shape subsequent understandings of existing narratives (that's the "ruined" in "you ruined my childhood," Arthur). And as they spread, these novel (yet still cobbled together, still "old") narrative threads may in turn influence countless other threads of countless other stories. In the process, one digital text can transform into thousands of digital texts for thousands of people overnight – say it with us, for better and for worse. Online, that makes all the difference.

The (even more) multiple meanings of (even more)
multiplicitous texts
Each time these resonant seeds are gathered by a new audience and retrofitted to align with listeners' political or emotional needs, meaning becomes that much more ambivalent, even more markedly than in embodied environments.

One conspicuous source for this ambivalence hyperdrive is Poe's Law, which has haunted this book (it's always just standing there, *menacingly*). It's simply not possible to know – particularly when a poster is anonymous, but also when a poster is named but unfamiliar – why someone is posting, for example, a frightening narrative to /x/ or /r/NoSleep. Maybe that person really had an experience they can't explain.

Maybe they didn't, but want to entertain their readers. Maybe they want to revel in their readers' gullibility. Maybe something else entirely; maybe there is no reason – not one the poster could consciously identify, anyway. Regardless of what kind of story is being presented, regardless of the collectives in question, these motives are often impossible to ascertain just by observing. So much so that in many cases, a poster's intended meaning is moot, or at least is a nonstarter: there's often no way to satisfactorily verify or refute one's suspicions.

In his analysis of the "bogus warnings" circulated on photocopied flyers, as well as other urban legends featuring dubious stories of crimes, scams, and health concerns, Brunvand (2001) provides an analog outcropping of Poe's Law. Whether or not a story is true, or at least is *believed* to be true by the teller, certainly isn't always clear offline. That said, most of the false (or at least probably false) narratives Brunvand describes are shared within the context of embodied relationships and spaces. This in turn influences how listeners evaluate the information. For example, if your co-worker, who you think is an idiot, shares a warning about cordless phones causing children's brains to overheat, you are much less likely to take the message seriously. Conversely, if a person you know and trust seems genuinely concerned about a particular crime statistic (or a murderous Bigfoot or a vanishing hitchhiker – Milner has been burned many times), you are more likely to give the warning credence, even if it turns out to be false.

On anonymous online message boards, however, it's not clear who is sharing what, for what purpose. 4chan's /b/ exemplifies how fraught the "bogus warning" narrative genre can be online. After all, while much of the content posted to /b/ is false, and aggressively so, some is true, complete with documentation. However, through the magic of photo manipulation, sometimes that documentation isn't authentic either. Often it's impossible to know what's play and what's truth and what's both, and therefore impossible to know whether /b/'s boilerplate disclaimer – "The stories and information posted here are artistic works of fiction and falsehood. Only a fool would take anything posted here as fact" – is itself a convenient lie. Nothing on /b/ is ever true; that is, until it is. ¯_(ツ)_/¯. Good luck.

This ambivalence is reflected in the countless warnings, rumors, and life tips that are posted to the board. Some of them tried-and-true copypasta, these narratives often include images, annotated instructions, or other ostensibly helpful information. Sometimes they're very slick, and sometimes very amateur (depending on the context, either could communicate more authenticity). The most successful of these narratives – the most likely to be engaged with and reposted on the site and elsewhere – convey just enough context to make the ruse plausible. One classic copypasta example admonishes Windows users to delete their "System32" file, a move that would, if heeded, destroy one's operating system and completely brick their machine. This outcome is of course masked in the surrounding narrative, as this archetypical account – one collected by Milner on /b/ in 2011 – demonstrates:

> When Microsoft was first getting started, they knew they wouldn't make enough money just from the profits of their operating system. Everybody knows people pirate Windows. So they had to get creative. A guy named Chris Liddel came up with the idea to put a folder called "System32" in the Windows folder that literally slows down your machine – on purpose. "System32" holds 32 GIGABYTES of deleted files, internet history, uninstalled programs, and other worthless crap that intentionally clogs up your machine. Why did they do it? Because Microsoft owns several PC "cleaning" tools, like TuneUp Utilities, Norton Antivirus, etc. More money for them. /b/ isn't cool with that, however. Here's how to out-smart those assholes once and for all:
>
> Open Notepad
> Type the following text:

```
@echo off
del c:\\WINDOWS\system32
```
Save as "speedup.bat" (select "all files" instead of "text document")
Double-click the .bat file

Reboot, and your PC is twice as fast. (You didn't hear it from us)

The narrative elements of the disastrous advice lend plausibility to the prank. A justification for why this file needs to be deleted is provided (one that is both marginally believable and anti-elite). Specific names are dropped in to bolster credibility (from a supposed Microsoft employee to recognizable brands that Microsoft allegedly owns). Affiliation is created between the addressee and speaker (let's "out-smart those assholes once and for all"), who is doing the addressee a favor that they really don't have to or shouldn't be doing ("You didn't hear it from us"). Further, the first-person plural associated with /b/ signals that the advice comes from a member of the supportive ingroup. Even if audience members already know the game, or simply just know better, the narrative instills hope that others might follow the advice, and suffer the consequences.

Sometimes, responses to bad advice become legendary themselves (and are equally compelling in their "just might be true" claims to authenticity). For instance, the text below comes from a screen capture of a purported 2009 post to /b/, which Milner collected in 2015. Assuming the screen capture isn't itself photoshopped, the text furnishes an account of someone who followed – or claims to have followed – a posted (and *highly* dangerous) recipe for making "really cool crystals" at home:

WELL THANKS ALOT B.

I come every day on this site for like 2 months and I always participate in stuff this site says but this time is almost fucking killed me.

I am writing this shit from the hospital because I almost fucking died.

some shitface posted something to make crystals from some regular stuff everyone has. If I remember correctly it were: soda, salt, some pennies (the copper I needed), ammonia and a bit of laundry bleach.

I had to mix it and blow through a straw until I became dizzy because then there would be more CO_2 in there so there would be nice colours in the crystal.

The docter said they found mustardgas or something in my body (WAT THE FUCK) and I was passed out for a few days.

Have to stay here for like 1 week more and my parants cut of the internet.

Thnx alot motherfuckers…hope everyone of you die

Picture related…it's the crystal he said I was going to get but instead I got something which almost killed me.

Produced by and for an environment where Poe's Law casts a long shadow, the implied authenticity of the text echoes the infamous Jenkem scare of 2007 (see Phillips 2015 for more on /b/'s supposed designer drug, concocted from fermented urine and feces). This apparent authenticity hinges on several communicative markers. The poster was patient; the response was posted a few days after the original recipe made its rounds on the site. It is formatted in the fractured style of 4chan narratives, containing site-specific vernacular grammar and spelling, and is tonally consistent with the site's typical post. Readers are given just enough context, and just enough confirmatory detail, to encourage suspension of their disbelief. Like when the man in the ATU tale-type tricks the ogre into self-castration, these texts revel in the possibility of harming those not smart enough to avoid harming themselves. Maybe this time the prank had worked; dare to dream.

The collective re-creation of these bogus warnings – accompanied by re-creations of their supposed effects – might be a halcyon delight to the ingroup, but echoing discussions of constitutive humor in Chapter 3, can be intensely marginalizing to those cast as outsiders – say those poor souls who do try to delete System32, or any other of the "life hacks" designed to actually ruin, or even snuff out, one's life. These tensions are hardly restricted to digitally mediated spaces, of course. Collective storytelling online is in many ways an extension of collective storytelling in embodied spaces: that is to say, full of texts and practices that straddle the line between community and divisiveness, enjoyment and critique, veracity and, frankly, bullshit. But things are faster online, and they are more tangled, and while one should always do one's best to look before one leaps, this reminder is even more pressing on the internet. And whatever you do, friends and neighbors, never inhale anything recommended on a message board.

Chapter overview and looking forward

Because they draw from hybrid vernacular sources and creatively reconfigure existing narrative tropes, all stories are collective, at least implicitly. And because these collective stories occupy both sides of the singular and multiple, fixed and dynamic, and old and new divides, they are definitionally ambivalent. And because they are definitionally ambivalent, they reveal that apparently straightforward demarcations between author and audience, between this text and that text, between universal meaning and audience-specific meaning, don't need much jostling before they start to crumble. Stories are many things, to many people; and so they signal and accomplish and complicate many things. They signal and accomplish and complicate even more things online, where the line between *me* and *us*, this and that, one and many, is even more blurred.

Things get fuzzier still when we push beyond the stories people tell to the values they hold dear. The following chapter will explore this most cacophonous chorus of voices, the chorus of public debate. Building on all the vernacular practices we have described thus far, the chapter will unpack the fundamental ambivalence of voice: that which can help, harm, build up, cut down, empower, marginalize, and everything in between, often all at once. A final nod to all that is new, and all that is not, about the ambivalent internet.

5

Public Debate

This final chapter is focused on the public debates that occur when everyday citizens come together to discuss resonant social and political issues. While we will consider conversations unfolding in hybrid and embodied spaces, we are most interested in online debate, and the impact digital media have on public discourse. Drawing from the saga surrounding UK research vessel Boaty McBoatface, we will illustrate how the blending and clashing of groups within groups, publics within publics, can engender profound discord, confusion, and the unfair marginalization of some and unfair aggrandizement of others. Simultaneously (and there is always a simultaneously), we will show that there's vibrancy in this complication. Even if it represents fracture and contestation, a public multiplicity can empower marginalized identities, facilitate a greater range of public expression, and ultimately strengthen the democratic process.

The ambivalent claim that public multiplicity complicates democratic participation and also provides the raw materials for such participation is augmented by two further points of ambivalence: the evil twins of *conflict and unity* and *affect and rationality*, each collapsing under the weight of the other. To demonstrate the conceptual bedevilment of both, we'll focus on the highly contentious and often highly bizarre 2016 US Presidential election, with special attention paid to the ultimately successful campaign of gaudy gilded businessperson, actual reality television villain, and as of, well, yesterday (these words were typed just before the book's final submission deadline on November 9, 2016), President-Elect Donald J.

Trump.[11] We will then explore how the ambivalence of public debate persists across eras and degrees of mediation, keeping our side eyes on Trump all the while. True to form, we will follow this discussion with the rejoinder that, *not so fast*, digital mediation sends ambivalence into hyperdrive – one final look at our brave new world, with nothing new under the sun.

Publics and their problems

On March 17, 2016, the UK's National Environment Research Council (NERC) took a pretty big risk: it turned to the public to help name its state-of-the-art £200 million polar research vessel. To that end, NERC set up a site, NameOurShip.nerc.ac.uk, and invited interested parties across the globe to submit something "catchy" to call the boat. The campaign was an immediate hit. "We've had thousands of suggestions made on the website since we officially launched," NERC's director of corporate affairs Alison Robinson revealed in an interview with NPR's Laura Wagner (2016). "Many of them reflect the importance of the ship's scientific role by celebrating great British explorers and scientists. Others are more unusual but we're pleased that people are embracing the idea in a spirit of fun." One of these names, submitted by former BBC Radio host James Hand, was spirited and fun indeed: Boaty McBoatface. This particular name proved so popular with voters that, in the days following its submission, the NERC site nearly crashed – its servers could barely contain the public's enthusiasm (Walker 2016). Unsurprisingly, Boaty McBoatface ended up winning the competition in a landslide, garnering over 124,000 votes.

While voters and rubberneckers alike celebrated Boaty's triumph, NERC wasn't amused. Echoing broadcaster and naturalist Sir David Attenborough's insistence that the research vessel deserved a more prestigious name – particularly one that "lasts longer than a social media news cycle" – UK Science Minister Jo Johnson indicated that NERC would sidestep the poll's results and instead choose a more traditional name for the boat (Plunkett 2016). In protest, apparent Boaty supporters took to the internet. They posted to the #JeSuisBoaty Twitter hashtag, a riff on 2015's freedom-of-speech-focused #JeSuisCharlie, which spread in the wake of the tragic mass shooting that occurred in the offices of satirical French newspaper *Charlie Hebdo*. They changed their Facebook profile pictures to an image of a boat captioned with the statement, "I Sail with Boaty." They lashed out at NERC authorities, as geek-chic celebrity Wil Wheaton (2016) did when he addressed Boaty's demise on his popular tumblog. "fuck you, you stupid goddamn science minister," he wrote after NERC sank Boaty. "If you put it up for a vote on the Internet, and you don't get 'HMS 420 Moot Fucked Your Mom' as the winner, consider yourself lucky, and honor the fucking vote."[12]

Journalists entered the discursive fray as well, adding their own spin to participants' indignation. In a cheeky article on the controversy, *Guardian* contributor Stuart Heritage (2016) connects the defeat to broader tramplings of public will. "We all need to face up to the desperate fact that our voices are doomed to be forever unheard," he writes. "The anti-war demonstration in 2003 was ignored by the government. Protests and marches and movements are routinely ignored by the government. And now we can't even give a jaunty name to a sodding boat without the government blowing it up in our faces." Heritage concedes that the name Boaty McBoatface is an "infuriatingly twee…godawful name for a boat" in no way befitting its mission. But that's not the point. The point is that the people voted for Boaty, and those votes should be respected.

For Heritage, "the people" is a singular collective, existing in clear opposition to the fun-ruining, democracy-thwarting powers that be. However, the actual participant breakdown in the Boaty saga – as in all cases featuring discussions of "the people" or "the public" – is more complicated than that.

Instead of being some monolithic, undifferentiated mass, "the public" is in fact comprised of a number of different perspectives and collectives, a cacophony of voices and interests constituting multiple publics. Even within smaller, subset publics unified by some common factor (akin to a bounded folk group), each seemingly singular public can always be broken down into further publics unified by more specific common factors. Singular framings of "the people" and "the public" obscure how many publics there are, or could be, depending on what common factor one chooses to foreground; the public sphere is at once nesting doll, spider web, and ball pit of overlapping Venn diagrams. And these are not always – in fact, these are rarely – wholly harmonious points of difference.

In the case of the Boaty debates, some participants seemed to genuinely care about the outcome and perceived threat to populist expression. Others were more ambivalent in their creation, circulation, and transformation of Boaty content on Twitter and Facebook. Perhaps they participated for a laugh, perhaps to get a reaction from their followers, perhaps simply because that's what people were playing with on Twitter and Facebook that day. And still others took a more contrarian stance, or refused to take a stance either way. Because, like Heritage says, it's a sodding boat.

Communication scholars Robert Asen and Daniel C. Brouwer (2001) argue that, chaotic as these publics might be, the resulting clash of motives and perspectives creates important opportunities for dissent via *counterpublics*. Nineteenth-century political philosopher John Stuart Mill anticipates a similar point when he frames divisive "sectarian" debate as an opportunity to "share the truth" ([1859] 2009, 47) between groups. This sharing, according to Mill, can inspire more nuanced arguments, more critical thinking, and more self-reflection, in turn allowing "disinterested bystanders," i.e. everyday citizens not swept up in whatever discursive flurry, to arrive at a more perfect truth. In the case of Boaty, this more perfect truth could be achieved by weighing UK Science Minister Jo Johnson's insistence that the name of a £200 million polar research vessel shouldn't be an internet punchline *and* Wil Wheaton's reminder that, no fuck you, it really could have been worse *and* Sir David Attenborough's charge to grow up, science is serious *and* Stuart Heritage's conviction that the will of the people must be respected, even if the people are, as he says, "idiots." Democracy at its finest.

In the end, NERC asserted its will; on May 6, the Council announced that the boat would be christened the RSS *Sir David Attenborough* (the same man who protested against the Boaty submission on the grounds that the vessel's namesake should befit its station – a criterion met, apparently, by himself). They did, however, throw Boaty supporters a life raft, announcing that Boaty McBoatface would live on as the name of a "high-tech remotely operated undersea vehicle" affixed to the main vessel (Chappell 2016). The most vocal Boaty supporters remained unsatisfied; in response to NERC's tweet announcing Boaty's reboot as Subby McSubface, commenters on Twitter lamented the failure of democracy, accused NERC of "cowardly desperation," and suggested that they might as well be living in totalitarian regime North Korea. One group even formally petitioned that Sir David Attenborough change *his* name to Boaty McBoatface (Doctorow 2016).

Boaty's torpedoing illustrates the limits of utopian democratic framings. Within the public sphere, different publics and different voices within those publics *can* share their truths. But just because someone is speaking doesn't mean that others can or are willing to hear. Not all citizens – and not all publics – are treated with equal respect, or afforded equal volume.

There are two basic factors contributing to this discrepancy. The first is the fact that some people are simply louder and pushier than others. This is certainly true in contemporary online debates; the vast majority of public participation online is produced by what Todd Graham and Scott Wright (2014) call "super participants," a highly polarized minority. Small in numbers as they might be, these super participants are especially loud and especially visible, and can easily drown out dissenting perspectives, thus skewing – or seeming to skew – a particular debate. In the case of Boaty McBoatface, yes, there were a lot of people shouting rude and sarcastic and sometimes, admittedly, pretty funny things on Twitter. But there were many more people, millions more people, who responded to the story with a shruggie, if they bothered to respond at all – which was certainly not the impression communicated by many Twitter feeds.

But loudness isn't the only explanation worth considering. Also critical to this picture is access, and the agency tied to that access. Specifically, those who have an existing audience and platform – stemming from who that person is, what kinds of experiences they've had, and where they fit within the socioeconomic hierarchy – are more likely to command attention. Wil Wheaton, for example, enjoys a large audience across multiple social media platforms, and so his perspective, even if it was an extreme perspective, garnered much more attention than those of participants who were more moderate but less known. Relatedly, the positions of power or privilege one occupies directly influence who is willing to listen, and more importantly, who is able to take action as a result. Regarding Boaty, when it came time to make a decision, the more traditional seat of public power – literally the public face of the British Crown – was able to set the agenda. They had the power to say "yeah actually no" to Boaty supporters, despite the fact that those supporters considerably outnumbered NERC representatives. Regardless of how compelling Pro-Boaty publics might have been (or not, Wil Wheaton), those voices were stifled by the establishment, and forced to begrudgingly accept the high-tech remotely operated undersea vehicle consolation prize.

Beyond illustrating the multiplicity of publics, the Boaty McBoatface saga reveals that public debate is predicated on ambivalence; it's a process that empowers and marginalizes in equal measure. And beneath this already highly ambivalent umbrella is, unsurprisingly, more ambivalence. The following section will take a deeper dive into these points of ambivalence, highlighting how quickly the conflict/unity and affect/rationality binaries fall apart when considering the complex realities of public debate.

The evil twins of public debate

The fundamental multiplicity of public debate is the engine behind its ambivalence: the fact that many groups (within groups, within groups) with many different, often clashing, motives can support, reassure, and embolden insiders while simultaneously condemning, antagonizing, and even injuring outsiders. Complicating this picture, and echoing discussions of identity play in Chapter 2, these demarcations are not stable across time; insiders can become outsiders, and outsiders can become insiders, depending on even the slightest changes within groups and also within the individuals who comprise them. However *us* and *them* might be configured in a given moment, a further layer of ambivalence is engendered by the apparent binaries of *conflict and unity* and *affect and rationality*. Each component of each set represents the flip side of the other; each component equally inhabits both sides of the coin. And each has for generations played the role of the bad twin and the good twin within public debate, in the process carving a highly ambivalent public sphere that both facilitates and hinders democratic participation.

The following two sections will focus on these two sets of evil twins, drawing from cases related to the 2016 US Presidential election. Not only do these examples illustrate the ambivalence of public debate, they also illustrate the increasing hybridity of the public sphere. Breaking political news stories, for example, may begin in embodied spaces, but once they hit Twitter or Facebook or CNN.com, they are swept up into a frenzy of digitally mediated participation, thus becoming an "internet thing." Conversely, stories that begin online, like barbs publicly traded between elected officials on Twitter, can be picked up by traditional media outlets and reconfigured as office water-cooler chatter. And by that we mean iMessage chatter or email chatter between colleagues sitting across the room from each other. In short, whatever tenuous boundaries exist between "online" and "offline" are obliterated in the context of public debate, where digital participation is integrated into embodied experiences, and embodied experiences are integrated into digital mediation.

Conflict and unity

For many, the idea that "unity" within the public sphere is an evil twin of anything might seem like a stretch, particularly in the context of unitary democracy: people coming together to find consensus on important issues. Political theorist Jane Mansbridge (1983) expands on this ideal, noting that unitary democratic systems value common ground, equal respect, and the trust and sacrifice inherent to friendship. When disagreement does emerge, such systems rely on what classicist Danielle Allen describes as "the instruments of agreeability" (2004, 118) in the quest for peaceful consensus.

On the surface, that all sounds lovely. But even the most unitary democratic system can go either way. Because however inclusive it might appear, ingroup unity can come at the cost of ignoring, disregarding, or actively silencing dissenting – and particularly dissenting outsider – perspectives. To this point, political philosopher Chantal Mouffe (2005) asserts that consensus, regardless of its warm and fuzzy connotations, can be just another name for hegemony. Critical theorist Nancy Fraser likewise argues that "deliberation can serve as a mask for domination" (1993, 119). Conflict and unity, in other words, are far from diametrically opposed; even when the goals are unitary for some, behavior in the service of that unity can easily veer toward the antagonization of others.

This overlap played out during the 2016 US Presidential election, particularly through the campaign of Republican nominee Donald Trump. At various points in his campaign, Trump asserted that the US should ban all Muslim immigrants from crossing American borders; pledged to build an enormous wall on the US–Mexico border (that he insisted he'd make Mexico pay for); connected Mexican immigrants with criminality, murder, and rape ("And some, I assume, are good people," he stated in a 2015 speech announcing his candidacy, with the qualification "I assume" seeming to imply that, if there are any good Mexican immigrants out there, Trump has never personally encountered any); promised to strongly police African American communities, which he continuously – and erroneously – equated with his own cartoonish hellscape vision of crime-ridden "inner cities"; warned his followers about the "international bankers" (a longstanding dog whistle for anti-Semitic sentiment) allegedly controlling the US economy; and upon suggesting that the election was rigged, urged his supporters to descend on polling places to "keep an eye" on "other communities." Alongside these and other equally egregious assertions, Trump has repeatedly invoked the nationalist, and ultimately racist, proclamation that he, and he alone, can "make America great again." In so doing, Trump has unified his overwhelmingly white working-class supporters around a cause – a xenophobic, racist, and fear-based cause, but a resonant cause nonetheless. The same holds for Trump's overall political platform, which rejects "political correctness" and affirms the economic struggle of many of his supporters, who feel abandoned by their government and alienated by the increasingly diverse culture that surrounds them.

By establishing common ground between himself and his supporters, by vowing to sacrifice his own needs to help fight for others, and by making supporters feel understood and fundamentally worthy – all goals of unitary democracy – Trump has created a strong sense of *us*. He has also created an even stronger sense of *them*. For those outside Trump's *us*, the implication that all those who qualify as *them* deserve less protection, less respect, and fewer (or even no) basic human rights most certainly does not create a sense of unity. It creates a sense of disconnect, conflict, and, for many, outright fear.

Just as unity can be a mixed bag, conflict is similarly ambivalent. While the conflict Trump courts is premised on a silencing denigration, many progressive political theorists advocate, and even outright celebrate, conflict premised on equal clash. Mouffe (2005), for example, is a staunch proponent of agonistic debate, which she frames as healthy, productive conflict between adversaries (as opposed to explicitly antagonistic conflict between enemies). Similarly, communication scholar Karen Tracy (2010) advocates for what she calls *reasonable hostility* in public debate, a framing that also embraces the adversarial register in conflicts between oppositional counterpublics. As with Mouffe, Tracy's adversarialism is not *carte blanche* antagonism; she says that for such hostilities to be "reasonable," they have to respond to rather than initiate injustice or threat, push back against an action or event without devolving into unrelated personal insults, and remain sensitive to the socially rooted contextual standards of judgment surrounding the debate.

Khizr Khan's 2016 Democratic National Convention address provides an example. Khan, a Muslim immigrant from Pakistan, spoke of his son Humayun Khan, a US soldier who died in the line of duty in 2004. Noting his son's sacrifice and bravery while enlisted, Khan asserted: "If it was up to Donald Trump, he never would have been in America." Khan then pivoted to Trump's draconian foreign policy platform, stating "He vows to build walls, and ban us from this country." With that, Khan pulled out a pocket copy of the constitution. "Have you ever been to Arlington Cemetery? You will see all faiths, genders, and ethnicities. You have sacrificed nothing. And no one."[13] This statement was met by thunderous cheers from the audience, and resonated strongly with mediated viewers as well; almost immediately, the hashtag #KhizrKhan began trending, and the text and video of Khan's speech was shared tens of thousands of times across multiple social media platforms.

Embodying Tracy's reasonable hostility, Khan eviscerated Trump, yet he did so fairly, accurately, and without stripping Trump of his humanity. He simply reminded the audience of what Trump has actually said and done. His speech also illustrates the fact that agonistic debate and reasonable hostility can be especially powerful tools when employed by members of historically underrepresented populations. Not only do they empower individuals to speak truth to power, they affirm these individuals' perspectives and experiences, in the process holding dominant institutions and individuals accountable for unjust action. All suggesting that, for certain voices to be heard, conversations might sometimes need to get a little heated.

Just like unity, conflict is far from ethically straightforward. Both categories are, instead, fundamentally ambivalent. As a result, ethical assessment of circumstances resulting in conflict and unity (and this is often an *and*, rather than an *or*) depends on who is participating, what participants hope to achieve, and, most significantly, who stands to be empowered and who stands to be silenced as a result. There are simply too many variables to easily demarcate or universally characterize these equally, evilly, disorienting twins.

Affect and rationality

Like the evil twins of conflict and unity, affect and rationality are complementary, contradictory, and highly ambivalent, both separately and together. Each serves as the basis for productive public debate as well as the roadblock to that debate, and each collapses into and complicates the other, right from the outset. This, again, is not the traditional story, particularly in the West. Since the Enlightenment, sentimentality and emotion have often been cleaved from the thinking, reasoning mind, which is typically privileged over the feeling heart. It is only through cool, calm calculation that one arrives at the correct answer; excessive sentiment is a rhetorical liability. From this view, geek-chic celebrities shouldn't go around swearing on Tumblr, but instead should articulate their perspectives dispassionately, like a true person of science. Rationality, in short, is the means by which Mill's ([1859] 2009) "disinterested bystander" can parse the truth from all the rancor.

A fine theory, in theory, but less so when put into practice. Because instead of being a distraction from or encumbrance to productive public participation, affect is often a driving force behind that participation. Mouffe (2005) affirms this position, foregrounding the persistent centrality of passion in politics. Likewise, communication scholar Peter Dahlgren (2013) defends the value of the emotional register in public discussions. He argues that people need to be informed, and need to weigh their options deliberatively, but they also need to feel emotionally invested and "sufficiently empowered to make a difference" (76). Zizi Papacharissi (2015) further dismantles any clear demarcation between affect and political argumentation, noting that cognition is a significant aspect of emotional experience, and that emotional experience influences critical thinking.

Emotional experience is, in fact, precisely what compelled Khizr Khan to deliver such a powerful speech – and masterclass rhetorical check – at the 2016 Democratic National Convention. Not just to pay tribute to his son's sacrifice, although he did that beautifully, but to directly address his adversary by name. And *to his face*, on national television, dismantle Trump's assertion that the country would be less safe if there were more Muslims within its borders. Our country is *more* safe because of my son, Khan countered, what have you ever done? – a point he delivered not calmly, not dispassionately, but as a fully invested and, frankly, pissed-off bystander. In the process, Khan was able to give voice not just to his own disgust, but to all Muslim Americans – to all Americans more broadly – similarly disgusted by Trump's racist statements. A tepid speech reminding Americans that they could vote for Democratic nominee Hillary Clinton in November if they wanted to, presented without personal comment, presented in the tone of a robot, would not have galvanized the audience as it did. It would not have happened to begin with, if something hadn't first been galvanized in Khan.

Similar passion – and similar pain – underscores the organization Mothers of the Movement, and the related Black Lives Matter movement. This group, which was also given a prime-time slot at the Democratic National Convention, is comprised of the mothers of young men and women of color killed by police officers (and in one instance, a citizen vigilante). The purpose of the group is to work with law enforcement agencies and members of the black community to proactively combat the statistical reality that black people in the US are much more likely to be killed by police than are their white peers (see Lopez 2016).

On stage, these seven women spoke about coping with the loss of their children Trayvon Martin, Eric Garner, Jordan Davis, Mike Brown, Hadiya Pendleton, Dontré Hamilton, and Sandra Bland. They also spoke of a galvanization similar to Khan's – one that prompted the spontaneous eruption of the phrase "Black lives matter! Black lives matter!" throughout the convention hall (Kaleem 2016). It was their sadness and frustration, the mothers explained, translated into political action, that is helping them work to ensure that there will be fewer mothers like them in the future. Similarly, it is sadness and frustration, translated into political action, that spurs all participants across all media in the broader Black Lives Matter movement. Without deep, personal investment in a given issue, people are less likely to engage with underlying cultural issues and inequities. And they are much less likely to make arguments.

But, of course, not all arguments are created equal, and neither is all affect. Trump exemplifies the failings of both: bad arguments coupled with excessively affective behavior. Not only does he express nationalistic, racist, and xenophobic sentiments, he is also virulently sexist. In one well-publicized instance, he berated Fox News contributor Megyn Kelly after she asked him about his sexist discourse (including his well-publicized tendency to attack women he dislikes with gendered slurs); instead of answering her question, he called her a "bimbo" and later accused her of having "blood coming out of her wherever" (Easton 2015).

And then, in October 2016, came the kicker: a 2005 audio tape released that month captured Trump bragging to *Access Hollywood* reporter Billy Bush (cousin of former US President George W. Bush) about kissing women and "grabbing them by the pussy" without waiting for consent – because he was a star, and could do whatever he wanted to them ("Transcript …women" 2016). Following the surprise release of these tapes – which describe behaviors that meet the legal criteria of sexual assault – a number of women came forward accusing Trump of precisely what he and Billy Bush had chuckled so heartily over. Trump responded to the accusation that he was, in fact, a man of his word by threatening to sue his accusers, as well as the *New York Times* for running several of the women's stories. In an open letter, the *Times*' general counsel responded, in turn, by arguing that Trump's reputation has been so damaged for so many decades by Trump's own behavior that he could not possibly be libeled by anyone (Rappeport 2016b). Trump underscored this point when he mocked an accuser's appearance during a post-scandal campaign rally. "Believe me, she wouldn't be my first choice," he said, suggesting that she wasn't attractive enough to assault (DelReal 2016) – a statement that also implicitly suggested that he has standards for the kinds of women he *would* be willing to assault.

As illustrated by his hyper-affective, hyper-defensive response to the growing litany of sexual assault allegations, Trump flings insults in every possible direction whenever he is challenged. Following Khizr Khan's speech, for example, Trump directed his ire at Khizr's wife Ghazala, who stood by her husband on stage during his speech (*BBC News* 2016). "If you look at his wife, she was standing there," Trump said during an interview; "She had nothing to say…Maybe she wasn't allowed to have anything to say. You tell me." The remark – a not-so-subtle jab at the supposed sexism of the Khans' Muslim faith – was insult as usual for Trump, who deflected Khizr Khan's critiques by once again trotting out anti-Muslim prejudice, editorializing by proxy through a suggestive "You tell me." In response, Ghazala Khan told the press that "When I was standing there, all of America felt my pain, without a single word. I don't know how he missed that."

In another memorable instance during a March 3, 2016, Republican Presidential primary debate, Trump responded to fellow candidate and Florida Senator Marco Rubio's suggestion that his hands are small with an assurance to the American people that his penis size was more than adequate. "I guarantee you there's no problem," he barked. "I guarantee you" (Krieg 2016). These embodied behaviors are reflective of Trump's online persona as well; when mediated through his Twitter account (which as of this writing boasts 12.7 million followers), Trump is what *Politico* writer Joe Keohane (2016) describes as a "cry-bully," someone who is equally insensitive and sensitive, aggressive and easily wounded – expressed through incessant boasting, the assertion that his detractors are sad and disgusting, and a broken record of "crowing, cajoling, whining and threatening."

Sharpening this picture, Zachary Crockett (2016) of *Vox* analyzed seven months of Trump's tweets, and posited that 45 percent contained explicitly negative sentiment, mostly expressed through insults. By Crockett's count, Trump's two most frequently used negative words were "bad" and "sad," trailed closely behind by "weak," "little," "dumb," "horrible," "nasty," and "unfair." These insults, as *Rolling Stone*'s Tessa Stuart (2016) explains, follow a few basic trajectories: that the target doesn't have "it," that they're a dog, that they're a failure, that they have no credibility, that they are the worst, and that they've asked him for favors before. By the standards of reasonable hostility, over-the-top affect precludes Trump from engaging in meaningful public debate; he's too busy huffing and puffing and, in an ironic twist, accusing others of being sad and disgusting.

But judging affect based solely on Trump would be as incomplete as judging the US based solely on Trump (please don't). Passion – and the spectrum of emotions it subsumes, from profound pain to profound love to profound anger to the profound sense that things could be better, that things *should* be better – is critical to every social movement and every meaningful conversation. It's also a potential hindrance to every social movement and every meaningful conversation. Just like unity and its evil twin conflict, each can be used as a weapon, and each can be harnessed in the service of social justice. And in the process, each highlights the fact that these binaries aren't binaries at all. They are different sides of the same coin, as they always have been.

Make America pretty much the same again

As Trump's Presidential candidacy attests, the contemporary public sphere is a brave new world of digitally mediated vernacular participation. However, public debate also exhibits many continuities across eras and media, particularly around the evil twins of conflict and unity and affect and rationality. These evil twins were just as inextricable then as they are now – and just as confounding to each generation of cultural theorists who looked around, furrowed their brows, and wondered just what in the hell the world was coming to.

Conflict and unity, same as it ever was
The fact that unity within a collective or around a perspective can simultaneously breed deep conflict has persisted for

generations. This point is evidenced by the countless jousts, scuffles, slap fights, bar brawls, and various stripes of honorific duels that have long peppered public debate – and which have subsequently resulted in some people cheering and giving each other high fives, and other people slinking back home to nurse their wounds.

In the US, few of these partisan altercations are as symbolically significant as the 1856 caning of Charles Sumner. This event preceded the American Civil War by five years and presaged the level of rancor that would consume both Northern and Southern factions. Sumner, an abolitionist Massachusetts Senator, had just given an impassioned speech denouncing the recently passed pro-slavery Kansas–Nebraska Act. He criticized the political power of slave owners, including the authors of the Act, one of whom was Senator Andrew Butler of South Carolina. In addition to attacking his role in the creation of the Act, Sumner insinuated that Butler was having sex with his slaves, and according to Senate historian Richard A. Baker, denounced him as a "noise-some, squat, and nameless animal...not a proper model for an American senator" (2006, 61). Butler's distant cousin, South Carolina Representative Preston Brooks, was incensed. Believing that Sumner wasn't a gentleman and therefore didn't *deserve* to be challenged to a duel, he decided to mete out the kind of punishment he would reserve for a dog (his words, not ours; everything about that is awful). So two days after Sumner's speech, Brooks and several supporters stormed into the Senate chamber and beat Sumner to the brink of death with a cane; according to historian James M. McPherson (2003), this attack consisted of at least 30 lashes directly to the head. Bleeding profusely, Sumner had to be carried away. Brooks strutted right out of the Senate chamber, as onlookers were simply too stunned to try and detain him.

This story is significant not just because the attack was carried out by an elected official on the Senate floor, and not just because of the physical and mental pain Sumner suffered as a result. It is also significant because Brooks wasn't just *not* ostracized for his behavior, he was embraced as a Southern hero. Newspapers in South Carolina printed gushing editorials supporting Brooks' "noble" defense of his home state, and Virginia's *Richmond Enquirer* exclaimed that the caning was "good in conception, better in execution, and best of all in consequence. The vulgar Abolitionists in the Senate are getting above themselves...They have grown saucy, and dare to be impudent to gentlemen!" (quoted in McPherson, 151). According to Brooks, his genteel Southern compatriots even begged for fragments of his cane to use as "sacred relics." After winning reelection in South Carolina – he initially chose to resign facing censure, but his constituents would hear nothing of it – Brooks was sent hundreds of new canes, some inscribed with messages like "Hit Him Again" and "Use Knock-Down Arguments."

Like Brooks' bombastic, sectarian violence, Trump's various identity performances online and off – particularly those foregrounding his blustering racism, sexism, xenophobia, and "screw you I'll say what I want" attitude toward detractors – have inspired ingroup unity by way of outgroup hostility. Trump has proven to be a particularly unifying force for the Ku Klux Klan, splinter white nationalist groups, and the cacophony of reactionists, antagonists, and neo-supremacists that have come to be known as the alt-right, all of whom have declared, publicly and enthusiastically, their support for a candidate who "gets it."

To be fair, aligning his performative mask to such audiences hasn't always been comfortable for Trump; throughout the campaign, he tried, sometimes more and sometimes less successfully, to publicly distance himself from these groups and their support.[14] But he has also thrown these groups plenty of bones that have helped strengthen their particular and very limited sense of *us* – for example, by retweeting messages from Twitter users with white nationalist ties, even ones with explicitly white nationalist handles. And, in one especially infamous case, by tweeting an anti-Semitic image of Hillary Clinton superimposed with the Star of David, originally posted to a white nationalist website. The sense of unity engendered by Trump's racist expression runs deep, and is deeply ambivalent; when Clinton denounced these and other bigoted actions in an August 2016 speech connecting Trump with white nationalism generally and the alt-right specifically, alt-right boosters were, as the *New York Times'* Alan Rappeport (2016a) reported, "thrilled." By making that connection, they argued, she had given their movement greater visibility – and, in turn, greater legitimacy – than it had ever enjoyed.

Trump's actions in the above instances (really, throughout his whole campaign) speak to concerns often attributed to the contemporary historical moment, but which in fact persist across generations. Arguably, the most pressing of these concerns center on when, if, and how observers should intervene when debate gets a little too contentious, and at what point adversarial clash becomes a threat to the common good. These questions are particularly pressing when considering counterpublic pushback against dominant marginalization. However forceful their messages might be, however uncomfortable these messages might make some citizens, voices of historically marginalized groups should be heard; these voices are necessary to the overall health of a democracy. The systemic injustices raised by the Black Lives Matter movement (and the Civil Rights movement decades before that) clearly fall into this camp. Even if – even when – the discussions get not just a little, but a *lot* heated.

That said – and this is where problems creep in – just because a group is in conflict with the mainstream doesn't make that group *good*. The mainstream might have its problems, but not to such an extent that it warrants "the enemy of my enemy is my friend" transitive logic. Explicit white nationalism, for example, whether expressed through embodied action or digital participation, most certainly runs counter to mainstream sensibilities, and thankfully so. In that sense, white nationalists are marginalized; hence their delight at being regarded, suddenly, as sufficiently influential to be vocally condemned by one US Presidential nominee and implicitly embraced by another.

But regardless of the relative marginalization of white nationalists and the alt-right, questions about how best to respond, or *if* to respond, to antagonistic conflict remain as vexing now as they were back when Preston Brooks nearly murdered Charles Sumner. On many digitally mediated platforms, these questions are especially complex, as the oversight of public debate is often in the hands of private businesses, not government entities. Until and unless online behavior breaks existing laws, platforms must decide if and how to respond to users' antagonistic speech. Often, those decisions are tethered more to bad press than to legal (or even broadly ethical) concerns. Reddit, for example, has faced considerable backlash over the years for hosting content that might not be explicitly unlawful, but certainly skirts the line between protected speech and speech that is, to be very generous, problematic (Massanari 2015). Twitter has also uncomfortably walked this line, and in response to high-profile cases, including the harassment of Leslie Jones, has been forced to revise existing on-site moderation policies (Warzel 2016). Because they are reacting to particular controversies, these changes are often undertaken swiftly, without much time for users to respond, or even to realize that the changes have been implemented.

Amplifying this confusion is the fact that moderation policies can vary widely between platforms, as each platform is guided by a different and ever-evolving outlook on speech protections and general sense of responsibility for enforcing these protections. With so few consistently reliable reporting options, it's unclear how individual Twitter users should respond to instances of personal abuse, let alone abuse lobbed against others – for example, the alt-right's harassment of

Leslie Jones, or its systematic, even gleeful, opposition to Black Lives Matter. Should antagonistic posters be named and shamed? Counter-antagonized? Should their impact be minimized, so the broader public can't see offending posts? Should their impact be maximized in order to call the greatest amount of attention to bad behavior? Should the most offensive contributors be reported and reported and reported until they're finally, maybe, banned?

The prospect of silencing conflict, regardless of circumstance, regardless of severity, might cause some to bristle. Indeed, for many scholars, censorship is itself an offensive proposition. Mill ([1859] 2009) famously falls into this camp. In his foundational "On Liberty," he argues that the silencing of equal clash "is an assumption of infallibility" (21), and asserts that censorship creates a "mental slavery" that chokes out an "intellectually active people" (36). According to Mill, it's not the violent conflict between parts of the truth that is the formidable evil. It is, rather, suppression of half the truth. Mill thus comes down on the side of more clash, not less; louder speech, not selective muting. This is not to say that Mill, or other free speech advocates, are necessarily apologists for antagonism. A nuanced version of the "more clash, not less" position – which acknowledges that nasty speech is, indeed, quite nasty – is best summarized by the early twentieth-century British writer Evelyn Beatrice Hall (1906), who asserted that "I disapprove of what you say, but I will defend to the death your right to say it" (1906, 199).[15]

On paper, such positions seem to represent a noble compromise, one underscoring vibrant democracy. It's the loss of precisely this idealized vibrancy – one predicated on ever more and ever louder clash – that many alt-right advocates mourn when their Twitter accounts or subreddits are banned, or simply when their comments are deleted from a particular thread. Regardless of who is making the argument (or how earnest they might be, as members of the alt-right often trot out democratic ideals to justify their presumably unalienable right to attack others, and others' presumably unalienable obligation to tolerate their abuse), blanket assertions that *more* speech is the best response to *bad* speech often overlook differential power relations, and falsely presume that being heard is merely a function of speaking up and adding your voice to the clash. Of course this is possible for some, particularly those already in positions of privilege and power. But others could spend their lives screaming and never be heard. Not through lack of trying, as proponents of the "more clash, not less" position implicitly suggest, but through lack of access to a prominent platform, and, most importantly, an audience willing to listen.

That said, and even when they overlook issues of power and access, the most vocal supporters of the "more clash, not less" position are often willing to place some limits on unfettered speech. This is particularly true when speech is premised on the foundational belief that some people shouldn't be part of the debate, and perhaps shouldn't be allowed to *live*. For Mouffe (2005), violently extremist, regressive perspectives merit silencing because they undermine *conflictual consensus*. She argues that democracies need agreed-upon values – "all people are created equal," for instance, or "all people are entitled life, liberty, and the pursuit of happiness" – before productive, agonistic conflict is even possible. Therefore it's appropriate, and in fact is necessary, to draw a line between those who reject the basic ground rules and those who work within them. If you fail to play by the rules, in other words, you forfeit your right to step on the field.

Mill, open clash advocate that he is, takes a similar position, arguing that public debate premised on "want of candour, or malignity, bigotry, or intolerance of feeling" ([1859] 2009, 55) isn't within the rules of the game. This is speech that silences, and therefore may justifiably be silenced. The question is, at what point is something objectively silencing, as opposed to "merely" infuriating? There is no question that much of what the alt-right posts online, for example (to say nothing of what Trump regularly says on Twitter and during rallies), is premised on want of candor, as well as malignity, bigotry, and intolerance of feeling. But is it wanting of candor *enough*? Malignant, bigoted, and intolerant *enough*? Who gets to make that determination, and how might that person's lived experiences influence their ability to parse outright silencing practices – which render a person physically unable or psychologically unwilling to speak – from other affective or argumentative responses?

Further complicating this picture, what if the same behavior silences some audience members, but spurs someone like Khizr Khan to face his antagonist on a national stage and call him, essentially, a blustering, un-American coward? The same could be said about divergent reactions to Trump's gleeful, chest-thumping boastings about sexual assault. Even if these statements were, as Trump later insisted, "just locker room banter," some women – and not just his (many) accusers – may have felt silenced, violated by proxy. But some were empowered to push back against Trump and the toxic masculinity he embodies. This is where the seemingly intuitive rhetorical baseline between silencing / not silencing breaks down, a sudden clatter amplified by our second set of evil twins: affect and rationality.

Affect and rationality, same as it ever was
In each case described in this chapter – in fact, in all instances of contentious public debate – conflict and unity are tightly coiled with affect and rationality, and are both equally essential to clash and commiseration. This connection functions like clockwork, regardless of who is participating in what debate, under what circumstances, in what decade – or even century. In the process, the overlap between conflict, unity, affect, and rationality further dismantles not just the demarcation between each set of evil twins, but also any clear demarcation between each individual concept.

To illustrate this continuity, we turn again to Trump, specifically his notorious Twitter antagonisms. Trump's targets (restricting ourselves solely to elected officials from the state of Massachusetts; we only have so much space) include Senator Barney Frank (in a December 21, 2011, tweet: "Barney Frank looked disgusting – nipples protruding – in his blue shirt before Congress. Very very disrespectful"), former Governor and 2012 Presidential candidate Mitt Romney (in a February 25, 2016, tweet: "Mitt Romney, who was one of the dumbest and worst candidates in the history of Republican politics, is now pushing me on tax returns. Dope!"), and Senator and person of Native American heritage Elizabeth Warren (in a May 6, 2016, tweet: "Goofy Elizabeth Warren, Hillary Clinton's flunky, has a career that is totally based on a lie. She is not Native American").

Even if Trump's adversarialism seems to have taken affect to new heights (or new depths), the 2016 election is certainly not the first characterized by name-calling and mudslinging. For example – and this is just one example among many in US history – the 1800 Presidential election, which pitted sitting President John Adams against sitting Vice President Thomas Jefferson, would have done Trump proud. Or at least, prompted him to shout variations of the words "Sad!" and "Failure!" while vowing to make the new republic great again. As historian Kerwin Swint (2006, 2008) chronicles in his countdown of the 25 dirtiest US campaigns of all time, the 1800 election featured personal attacks mocking candidates' religious views, intelligence, sexual appetites, and even their gender identities. Candidates were also referred to in the press with a variety of increasingly creative slurs; for instance, a Federalist handbill wrote that Jefferson was, in addition to not being white enough, "raised wholly on hoe-cake made of coarse ground Southern corn, bacon and hominy, with an occasional change of fricasseed bullfrog" (2006, 183). Trump might take the name-calling to the 21st-century extreme, but he certainly didn't invent foaming-at-the-mouth affection.

Nor is he the first to inspire concerns about these sorts of behaviors. Beyond worries about the "dirtiness" of professional politics (an old adage indeed), the fear that people are too irrational, too mean, and conversely too sensitive to accomplish anything positive, has long haunted political theory. Mill ([1859] 2009) encountered enough nastiness in nineteenth-century public discourse to comment on it; Mansbridge (1983) uncovered drama, fighting, bullying, domination, outbursts, and people afraid to speak up for fear of reprisal or judgment in the midst of idyllic, tight-knit 1970s town hall meetings; and Tracy developed her theory of reasonable hostility by looking at the "emotionally marked, critical commentary" (2010, 203) prevalent during 1990s school board meetings.

Of course, some of this is confirmation bias; empirical research conducted by Papacharissi (2004), Carlos Ruiz et al. (2011), and Dimitra Milioni (2009), all exploring a variety of mediated environments, suggests that audiences tend to overstate the inflammatory dimensions of public debate. Not everyone debating public issues, online or off, is Wil Wheaton screaming at UK Science Minister Jo Johnson. That said, as evidenced by generations of theorists' handwringing, the vocal, contentious minority is especially visible, and therefore especially concerning – and is, presumably, why so many cultural problems remain unresolved.

Again, maybe this is true in theory. But in practice, things aren't so simple. Khizr Khan's disgusted takedown of Trump's racism, Black Lives Matter activists' passionate pushback against systemic injustice, and incensed reactions to a US Presidential candidate bragging about sexually assaulting women, all show that pointed – even impolite – responses to systemic antagonism can absolutely serve public ends. Of course, it would be better if all those systemic antagonisms were already resolved. And it would certainly be better if marginalized groups didn't bear a disproportionate burden in continuing to combat the antagonisms and violence that disproportionately affect them. But until justice is equally just for everyone, the discomfort resulting from heated exchanges reminds us all that there is still more work – much more work – that needs to be done.

Affect isn't just passion or anger, of course. Affect covers the full range of human emotional experience – play and playfulness very much included. And, just as anger and frustration can facilitate meaningful public debate, so too can engagement that appears to be "just" playful. Theorists across disciplines have long affirmed the political potential of play, immediately complicating the notion that play is, or should be, framed as "just" anything. Game theorist Miguel Sicart, for example, argues that play is "a critical liberating force that can be used to explore the ultimate possibility of human freedom" (2014, 72), making it the perfect conduit for political expression. Political scientist Marcus Schulzke (2012) likewise asserts that playful audience engagement with satirical political programs like *The Colbert Report* promotes civic awareness. And Papacharissi suggests that playfulness can be a "strategy for dealing with the fixity of norms" (2015, 95) that often constrict public debate, thus helping connect individual creativity to collective expression.

Digitally mediated play with the 2016 US Presidential election certainly demonstrated such a connection. Evidencing this affective participation, Figure 7 collects images inspired by a few memetic moments during the 2016 primary elections. First, when New Jersey Governor Chris Christie dropped out of the Presidential race after many deeply contentious clashes with Trump, then endorsed his former rival, then was insulted by Trump on a hot mic, and then still stood behind him – visibly stupefied – during a victory speech, citizens embraced the opportunity to play. As Trump spoke, Christie blinking vacantly beside him, participants across social media platforms wove satirical tales about Christie being held hostage by his future overlord. A #FreeChrisChristie hashtag emerged, allowing Twitter users to express mock concern. Commenters implored the governor to blink in Morse code if he was in distress, wondered if he was regretting every decision in his

Figure 7. Four memetic images shared during the 2016 US Presidential primary elections. Top left: a still from a televised Donald Trump speech; the recently defeated Chris Christie stands – perhaps not willingly – behind Trump. Top right: a Photoshop transposing Marco Rubio into an oversized child's swing; also added are a lollipop and propeller hat. Bottom left: a Ted Cruz quote overlaying a photo of a blobfish to create an unfavorable comparison. Bottom right: a Photoshop comparing the alleged stances of Bernie Sanders and Hillary Clinton on wolves. Collected in 2016.

life that had led him to that moment, speculated that he was maybe just dreaming about the pho he wanted for dinner, and photoshopped the pair as a master/slave couple in BDSM latex. *Digg* compiled looping Vine videos that zoomed in on Christie's face while emotive music – from a slasher horror soundtrack to the bumbling horn-driven theme of HBO's *Curb Your Enthusiasm* to the sullen, existential opening lines of Simon and Garfunkel's "The Sound of Silence" – played over the governor's blank expression (Cosco 2016).

Fellow Republican Presidential candidate Ted Cruz also found himself on the receiving end of ample memetic play. Not only was he – for no discernable reason other than the fact that people didn't like him – widely purported to be the Zodiac serial killer from the 1970s, he was also compared to a white, slimy blobfish. Images of such fish were captioned with quotes from Cruz' various stump speeches. Similarly, after Trump called Republican candidate Marco Rubio "Little Marco" during a televised primary debate, participants scouring Google images for meme fodder stumbled upon an image – taken the previous August in a furniture store – of Rubio sitting in a comically oversized chair, his face beaming with childlike glee. Merciless photoshops, unsurprisingly, followed. Finally, while still vying for the Democratic Presidential nomination, Clinton's perceived out-of-touch persona was mocked in a series of annotated images that cast her as painfully inauthentic compared to Democratic rival Bernie Sander's inescapable, effortless cool.

The affect evidenced by "Ted Cruz Blobfish," "Little Marco," and "Cool Bernie" images, along with all the other playful – if ideologically ambiguous – engagement with the 2016 election, might seem to oppose, or at least hinder, more "serious" political participation. But just because something is silly doesn't mean it can't also forward a serious message – maybe not for the image creator, but for any of the tens or hundreds of thousands, even millions, of audience members who subsequently remix, retweet, or simply save the image to their hard drives for later. And maybe not out of a sense of play; maybe because they feel angry or confused or even frightened (we truly do apologize for that Ted Cruz blobfish). The specific affective response is almost irrelevant. What matters, and what connects all this affective participation of the present with the affective participation of the past, is the fact that people care, for whatever reason, and as a result feel compelled to do or say something in response. This is how all public debate unfolds. Not in opposition to affect, and not in opposition to conflict. As a basic *function* of them, just as public debate is also a basic function of unity and rationality. Not taken separately. Not taken as a binary. But taken, instead, as an ambivalent tangle. Same as it ever was.

Trumping the play frame

The previous section illustrated the significant through line between public discourse past and present. It established this connection, in part, via a discussion of Donald Trump of all people, who is often framed as nothing the American electorate has ever seen before. In this section, we will take the somewhat conflicting and somewhat complementary stance that, while there is precedent for the behaviors exhibited by Trump, and precedent for public pushback against Trump, the tools that facilitate this expression and pushback are new, unwieldy, and *profoundly* ambivalent. That ambivalence – ushered in by reduced social risk, the communication imperative, and Poe's Law – changes the conversation, changes the stakes, and changes how we can and should talk about what to do about all these changes.

The double-edged sword of affective attunement

People have long debated the social and cultural issues that matter to them, whether to express support or lob criticism. But the reduced social risk of digitally mediated spaces allows more people to speak more freely about sensitive subjects than would be safe, or even logistically possible, in embodied contexts. Equally integral to this discourse, and setting it further apart from embodied interactions, is the communication imperative. People are, of course, free to express all kinds of affinity in embodied spaces. But unlike embodied affinity – which, as discussed in Chapter 2, may come with bodily or professional risks (or more basically than that, simply be inconvenient) – the process of expressing affiliation online can be as easy as clicking the Like button.

When publics lend their voices to resonant causes, they evidence what Papacharissi (2015) describes as "affective attunement." This attunement facilitates collective unity by connecting counterpublic participants to like-minded others, emboldening them in the process. In response to the harassment directed at Leslie Jones, for example, friends and sympathetic onlookers used the hashtag #LoveforLeslieJ to express support for Jones and try to counterbalance some of her abusers' hatefulness. That said, just as supporters could search for and use this hashtag, so too could Jones' abusers, revealing the flipside of affective attunement; the same affordances of reduced social risk and the communication imperative that engender support can also connect those bent on silencing and antagonizing.

It's not just that people have more opportunities – for better and for worse – to participate in public debate online. They also have the opportunity to directly address those implicated in, impacted by, or precipitating that debate. Whether the person in question is a traditionally public figure or an everyday citizen swept up into an unfolding controversy, the affordances of digital media facilitate a whole lot of talking back. This talk was possible in the pre-internet era, to be sure; letter writing campaigns existed before the internet, as did telephone calls placed to politicians' beleaguered office assistants. But digital media lend unprecedented immediacy, public visibility, and at times outright ferocity to familiar ambivalence. Evidencing this unprecedented influence in the context of the 2016 US Presidential election, *Wired* reporter Issie Lapowsky (2015b) notes that "It's no longer just up to the campaigns to steer the conversation and their opponents to counter it. Now we can all play a role in spinning the new narrative, which dramatically changes the power structure in campaigns."

And not just in campaigns; legislative action is also subject to the distributed imposition of populist commentary. When Indiana Governor and Trump's eventual Vice President Mike Pence signed a restrictive anti-abortion bill into law, for example, frustrated feminists decided to target the Governor directly with a "Periods for Pence" social media campaign (see E. Crockett 2016). In addition to calling and emailing Pence's office with explicit narrative accounts of their latest menstrual cycles (accounts they would then post publicly to their group's Facebook page, à la the *Battletoads* shenanigans highlighted in Chapter 3), participants posted messages about cramps, flow level, number of tampons used, and other exacting, clinical details, directly to Pence's Facebook page – the satirical rationale being that, if Pence is so concerned with his constituents' reproductive cycles, his office would want to be kept abreast of every period in the state at all times. By commandeering the news cycle through satirical interventions, participants were thus able to influence the direction of public debate surrounding the bill.

As always, this distributed commentary cuts both ways. The same basic tactic used on Pence was used in the sustained harassment of Leslie Jones. For months, when people talked about Jones, or when people talked about her *Ghostbusters* reboot more generally, discussions of the abuse she suffered weren't too far behind. And just as Periods for Pence participants were able to speak their truth with minimized fear of negative retribution, Jones' harassers were able to continue their campaign from the relative safety of their own Twitter feeds – a fact that ultimately prompted Twitter to address the controversy. "We know many people believe we have not done enough to curb this type of behavior on Twitter," a spokesperson wrote; "We agree. We are continuing to invest heavily in improving our tools and enforcement systems to better allow us to identify and take faster action on abuse as it's happening and prevent repeat offenders" (Warzel 2016).

The reduced social risk that facilitated both Periods for Pence and Jones' harassment also underscores what Tim Highfield (2016) calls "shaming and callout culture." Public shaming is in no way a new phenomenon, of course, and isn't restricted to digitally mediated spaces. However, it takes on new dimen-

sions when any person across the globe with an internet connection and a minute or two of extra time on their hands can
join the collective chorus. In embodied spaces, there are
physical, logistic, and even legal limits (in terms of room capac-
ity or the need for demonstration permits) to how large a crowd
can grow, how quickly. But not online. With just a few clicks
of a few different buttons, participants can instantaneously
identify a person or behavior that violates an established normative ideal and then, just as instantaneously, rally around
that person, place, or thing, perhaps to demand an apology,
perhaps to demand the person face professional consequences,
perhaps simply to make their displeasure known.

Some examples of shaming and callout claim an explicitly progressive agenda, for example the Twitter account
@YesYoureRacist, which retweets racist posts that contain the
phrase "I'm not racist, but…" in order to call the poster out
for being exactly that. But Jones was also a target of shaming
and callout – though much more nefariously, what she was
being shamed and called out for was being a successful black
woman. One who decided that she'd had enough, and pushed
back against the initial wave of harassment she received. This
stance prompted alt-right apologist Milo Yiannopoulos to
accuse Jones of being, as *Vox*'s Raja Romano (2016) writes,
"unable to handle criticism" – thus catalyzing a second and
even more ferocious wave of harassment. Unity, once again,
built atop conflict, and conflict, once again, built atop unity
– but amplified in whole new ways.

Poe's Law and its (continued) complications
Whether the apparent goal is conflict or unity, whether
the apparent register is affective or rational, digitally mediated
debate is complicated by the difficulty – if not impossibil-
ity – of parsing the ironic from the earnest during public
conversations online. This difficulty stems back to our old
friend Poe's Law, which can thwart even the most earnest
attempts to discern intent during collective conversations –

not just what shades of affect are being communicated, but what argument a person might be trying to make through those shades, if they are arguing anything at all. In the case of Boaty McBoatface, for example, pro-Boaty participants used all the tools in their communicative toolkits to signal their displeasure with NERC, the British Crown, and democracy in general. But that doesn't mean, necessarily, that these participants actually agreed with their own stated opinion. Milner himself walked this line. While he numbered among the staunchly pro-Boaty public, he also numbered among the public who thought the story was kinda just funny, and therefore was engaging, at least in part, because it was making him and his Twitter friends laugh. Just by observing Milner's Boaty-related tweets and retweets, an outsider would have a difficult time knowing to which public – or, more appropriately, which publics – he belonged. Phillips herself was unsure, prompting her to ask Milner if he was sincerely concerned about the trampling of populist will, or if he was playing along because the whole thing was silly. "......... I don't even know anymore," he replied.

In the vast majority of cases, however, one is unable to ask whether an online participant really meant it when they said, for example, that rainbow tie-dye cakes are a stepping stone on the road to fascism, or that they "condemn the cowardly campaigns of moral subjugation and propaganda that seek to instill self-hatred and surrender within European-American youth and justify the continued invasion and degradation of the lands, institutions, and cultural heritage that is rightly ours" ("Union of White NYU Students" 2015, ... eyeroll), or that they think Ted Cruz really is the Zodiac Killer. The same questions persist when assessing visual content, like images of "Little Marco" and his fun little whirlygig hat and lollipop, or images of Ted Cruz likened to literally the world's grossest fish.

Where sincerity ends and Chapter 3's play frame begins is up for grabs in an environment governed by Poe's Law. Maybe the creators and sharers and tweakers of this content were merely signaling silliness – just the play frame, and nothing more. Because a grown-ass person the state of Florida sent to the Senate is wearing a fun little whirlygig hat and holding a lollipop. Or because, come on, that blobfish resemblance is actually pretty uncanny. Then again, maybe these images spoke to something more serious, related to how those creating, sharing, and tweaking the content felt about Marco Rubio and Ted Cruz. Or maybe they were signaling a little bit of both: a serious political or cultural argument approached through the play frame.

In cases of polar research vessel names and tie-dye cakes, these stakes aren't especially high. What someone really means might be a point of curiosity, but is nothing to lose any sleep over. Cases in which a person is variously defamed, from being accused of a serious crime to being accused of being a blobfish, become more muddled. Maybe it's funny and harmless when the person accused is a politician you hate, but you would probably think it was far less funny and far less harmless if it was *you* some amorphous group of anonymous strangers was accusing of being, well, anything. Funny until it stops being funny; there but for the grace of the internet go you. And in cases featuring more explicitly offensive content, from extreme vulgarity to personal insults to broader identity antagonisms, what someone really means can make all the difference. Without knowing whether something is an actual bite or simply looks like a bite or is a satirical combination of both, one can't be sure if the appropriate response is to bite back, walk away, or laugh and join the conversation.

The question is, does that matter? Is "responding appropriately" a behavioral ideal for such a fractured and fracturing space? In an article co-written with Allum Bokhari, fellow contributor to the ultraconservative *Breitbart* blog (Bokhari and Yiannopoulos 2016), Milo Yiannopoulos argues that motives make all the difference, and should therefore determine how a person reacts to posted content. Speaking to the anti-Semitic, racist, and generally antagonistic things members of the alt-right post to social media – i.e. their malignity, bigotry, and intolerance of feeling – he and Bokhari note that "Just as the kids of the 60s shocked their parents with promiscuity, long hair and rock'n'roll, so too do the alt-right's young meme brigades shock older generations with outrageous caricatures." But no worries, they argue. These "young meme brigades" aren't *actually* bigots. At least, Bokhari and Yiannopoulos assert, they're not bigots any more than "death metal devotees in the 80s were actually Satanists." Through this framing, Bokhari and Yiannopoulos suggest that harmful expression isn't really harmful, because it isn't really real. The appropriate reaction is therefore to acknowledge the play frame, stop being so sensitive, and move along. This was precisely Yiannopoulos' critique of Leslie Jones' reaction to the initial onslaught of Twitter harassment. She took it seriously, responded publicly, and was punished accordingly, essentially for refusing to *not* take her harassers' racist words at face value.

Rhetorical somersaults aside ("you should know better than to take us seriously, but make sure you take us seriously because if we are actually joking in the way we say we are, you taking us seriously is, quite literally, the entire punchline of our joke, so please ignore us when we say we're just joking"), this position speaks to the complications unearthed by an environment that so thoroughly facilitates fracture and confusion. Poe's Law is simply what happens when more people, more capable of writing themselves into existence in a variety of ways, are more able to participate in more conversations through vernacular media that are more modifiable, modular, archivable, and accessible than any conversations that have come before. In the face of so much *more*, all participants can do is assess the content itself, and derive, or attempt to derive, conclusions about what has been communicated, not what someone might have meant to communicate.

And this, in our minds, is the appropriate response to arguments like those forwarded by Bokhari and Yiannopoulos. Online, if something appears to signal bigotry, it's bigotry. Because that is, quite literally, the message being communicated. And when only the message is the message, what the creator (original Photoshop artist, tweeter, comment poster, etc.) might really mean in their heart of hearts is moot. For one thing, meaning doesn't exist in the creator's heart; recalling our discussion of Roland Barthes (1977) in Chapter 4, the meaning of a text exists in its destinations, not in its origin. But even if meaning did live in the heart of the creator, the incessant clatter of tangled, multiplicitous, unattributed and unattributable texts would make it next to impossible to connect *this* meaning with *that* heart. We can't know for sure exactly who we're dealing with; consequently, who cares what their heart is like.

More importantly, however, we all have the right to reject someone else's play frame, to shake our heads and say "that's not funny." Something might *look* like a harmless joke to the teller. But if it hurts us, regardless of what the other person might have been trying to accomplish, that's a bite. The basic idea that *you* don't get to tell *me* how I'm feeling is intuitive enough. Online, we all need to remember that that same truth holds for everyone else.

Chapter overview and looking forward

This chapter has illustrated the ambivalent overlap between the evil twins of conflict and unity, along with affect and rationality. While this intertwine of ambivalence spans public debates regardless of media, it is most conspicuous, and most conspicuously vexing, when the voices of *some* silence the voices of *others*, particularly online, when questions of whose voices these are and why they might be participating cannot be satisfactorily answered. In those cases, what can be done?

What should be done? Where do we locate individual and collective responsibility? What rules should apply to whom? Who can say, for sure, who is outright rejecting the established rules and who is fighting over the correct interpretations of what the rules mean?

Our position is simple. We are staunch advocates of the democratic process and think that problematic speech should be countered through more speech. Except actually maybe not, because not all speech, and not all voices, are given equal weight, and that position privileges those whose voices already carry further and louder than others. So okay, we're staunch advocates of the democratic process and think that the only voices that should be silenced are the voices that silence others. Except actually maybe not, because sometimes those silencers are silencing silencers, and that's good, except when it isn't, and anyway even if we silence all hateful expression, that doesn't mean we eradicate it, it means we can no longer hear it. It'll just move elsewhere, to embodied spaces or spaces online that are more difficult to access. And wouldn't it be better to know what upsetting things people are saying, so at least we're not blindsided when something awful happens?

So okay, we're staunch advocates of the democratic process and think it's actually good for things to get a little heated sometimes, because that's how we know that democracy is working. Yes. Except actually maybe not, because underrepresented populations disproportionately bear that burden and are therefore framed as a kind of cultural collateral – you'll still be targeted, hope that's cool, but at least we'll know what we're up against, thanks guys. That burden is one that has been borne too long by too many of the same people. So okay, we are staunch advocates of the democratic process...as our voice trails off and we stare blankly into the distance.

Looking toward the conclusion – and the future more broadly – we don't have the definitive answer here. We have a handful of different answers, but they are all "yes *but*," not "yes *and.*" We maintain, regardless, that we all benefit individually and collectively when there are more voices participating in a conversation. We also maintain that we are grateful to all those who have fought to include more voices in the chorus, and grateful to those who continue that fight. If history has been plagued by lack of voice and lack of representation, maybe the future will be plagued by too many and too much – and that's progress, even if also impossibly ambivalent.

Conclusion

On our time spent digging in the dirt

Like the broader world that subsumes and predates it, the ambivalent internet defies easy explanation. While there is quite a lot – tonally, behaviorally, aesthetically – connecting moments present to moments past (a statement as true now as it was a century ago), the present moment is replete with whole new reasons to throw up one's hands in desperation, exasperation, or bemusement. It is difficult, for instance, to know how best – most effectively, most humanely, most democratically – to respond to online speech that antagonizes, marginalizes, or otherwise silences others. On one level, this is a logistic question about what *can* be done, what available digital tools can be harnessed or created to help mitigate or even prevent online hate and harassment. The deeper and more vexing question is what *should* be done. This question is especially pressing when considering the profound, embodied distress experienced when individuals' identities are deliberately hijacked and spun, without consent, without compassion, intractably out of control by the commentary, critique, and play of others.

But vernacular expression online, just like vernacular expression offline, is a spectrum; not all cases meet the threshold of outright harassment. Much more common are behaviors that aren't pointedly aggressive and silencing as much as they are, well, *strange*. Cookie Monster screaming about sugar in his ass. Garlic bread remix art. A comment apocalypse in response to a rainbow tie-dye cake recipe posted by a radio station. Not that these cases are resoundingly positive; as ambivalent expression, they can tear down one group even as they build up another. Myopic play with the "Bed Intruder" meme, fetishized laughter directed at Tommy Wiseau's earnest cinematic efforts, and the litany of Three Wolf Moon Amazon reviews amplifying classist stereotypes all evidence this potential.

Whether mostly antagonizing, mostly amusing, mostly confounding, or mostly a combination of all three, online expressions that don't fit into any discernable category, which show a different face from every angle, and which are as likely to elicit a furrowed brow as an uncontrollable giggle, are extremely difficult to pin down. There are simply no universalizing theories to apply, and no self-contained textual analyses to conduct. The reasons for this difficulty are every bit as messy as the expressions themselves. First are the complications ushered in by the affordances of digital media, which allow just about anyone to modify, recontextualize, and further amplify just about anything. The communication imperative facilitates this process again and again, as more and more people create and explore and tinker with themselves across a variety of digital platforms. And reduced social risk, often spurred on by anonymity, allows these tinkerings to veer into territory that participants might be inclined to avoid in embodied spaces, for better and for worse.

What emerges from this cacophony isn't a singular, self-contained, easily traceable litany of texts, authors, and meanings. Rather, online spaces are tangled with tissues upon tissues of quotations, multiplicities upon multiplicities of authors, and densely knotted meanings hinging not on who made what thing, or even on the thing itself, but on what memetic motifs resonate with an unknown number of unseen audiences, who can further their own resonant meanings simply by posting a link. Here even classification can be a problem; something might *look* like X behavior (a joke, a sincere argument, evidence of affective attunement), but thanks to Poe's Law prodded along by context collapse, it's not always possible to verify that it is indeed X behavior. And even if it is X behavior *now*, with some people, it may have started out as something else entirely, with the when, or where, or why remaining elusive. Such, such, such are the joys of the ambivalent internet.

As normal sources of meaning – the text itself, the author who created it, and the intended messages of both – are untenable, the most pressing question here is therefore not *can* or *should* we respond, but *how* do we respond, what is there to even say? This conclusion will suggest a way forward, drawing from Mary Douglas' (1966) concept of "dirt work" laid out in the Introduction and seeded throughout each chapter. As Douglas explains, behaviors and values deemed dirty or taboo couldn't exist without a sense of cleanliness and propriety to compare them to. By exploring fringe elements (at least, the elements regarded as fringe within a particular culture or community), one is therefore able to identify traditional norms and values. Applied to online ambivalence, a dirt work approach allows observers to sidestep what can't be known (textual origins, creators' intent, immutable meaning), and instead focus on what *can* be known. Namely, how specific vernacular expressions – however unusual or unintelligible they might appear – illuminate and often complicate broader cultural logics. A process that functions, essentially, to extract norms from that which is not normal.

To illustrate this process, we will turn to one last oddity as we part: a 2016 remix video called "Trump Effect." Essentially a smashcut of each chapter, the video is an exemplar of folkloric expression, identity play, constitutive humor, collective storytelling, and public debate. It is also profoundly ambivalent, making it a perfect candidate for our final dirt work analysis.

Ambivalence all the way down

On March 30, 2016, Twitter user @immigrant4trump tweeted a dizzying 2-minute 30-second YouTube video at then-Republican Presidential candidate Donald J. Trump. The video, entitled "Trump Effect," opens with Trump making a barking sound. "What was that?" he asks. "Is that a dog?" He laughs. "It's Hillary!" Jump cut to several scenes of chaos at political demonstrations. A gun fires three shots in quick succession. A police officer appears on-screen, blood dripping down his forehead. A voiceover begins; it's the villainous, xenophobic, fascist Illusive Man from the videogame *Mass Effect 2*. The Illusive Man's in-game monologue, performed by American actor Martin Sheen, is repurposed for Trump's cause. "We're at war," the Illusive Man begins. Jump cut to shots of anti-Trump protesters blocking the road at a Trump rally in Arizona, then shots of a white man walking alongside several black people at what appears to be a Black Lives Matter demonstration. "Humanity is under attack," the Illusive Man continues. Two American flags are lying on the ground, one slightly rumpled, in front of the apparent Black Lives Matter protesters; the lone white man stands front and center. Dubbed over shots of Trump Tower, Trump ascending on an escalator, and Trump's helicopter, the Illusive Man asserts that Trump is humanity's last hope against "the greatest threat of our brief existence." Jump cut to Trump's "Trump Ice" branded water; Trump laughs, daintily sipping water from one of the tiny bottles.

Another jump cut, this one to Trump's daughter Ivanka as she sings her father's praises. A title card flashes on screen and lists three quotes: "Donald Trump is simply awe-inspiring" – all who gaze upon him; "I wrote The Art of the Deal" – Donald Trump; "No more oreos" – Donald Trump. Back to Ivanka explaining what a dire situation the country is in, as footage labeled "FILE" in the top left corner shows a group of individuals scurrying across a road. "Border Patrol Zero Tolerance," the bottom ticker reads. Quick cut to US soldiers, apparently being held hostage, on their knees with their hands raised to their heads. Another quick cut to CalTrans workers at the scene of a freeway overpass collapse. The music picks up tempo. Hillary Clinton is shown laughing as footage of

Democratic party financier George Soros is shabbily dubbed with a raspy Sith Lord voice. "I will show you true power," Soros says. Clinton's image shifts to stark red/black contrast; she continues shrilly laughing.

Jump cut to Trump at a podium; he raises his right hand. "We need a leader," the Illusive Man states, one surrounded by "the brightest, the toughest, the deadliest allies we can find." In a series of quick cuts, those allies appear: former Republican Presidential candidate Ben Carson simpers beside Trump at a podium, Trump makes a clown face standing beside New Jersey Governor Chris Christie at another podium, and Alabama Senator Jeff Sessions gesticulates wildly in front of a third podium. Blank screen, replaced by news footage announcing the move of an Indianapolis factory to Mexico: 1,400 workers are expected to lose their jobs. Ben Carson reappears, apparently half-asleep. He mumbles that it's not about political party, it's about the people of America. His eyes flutter shut. The image of a tattered American flag flies in the background, followed by a black man in an Army combat uniform splayed out, eyes closed, on the sidewalk next to a cane.

Jump cut to an image of US President Barack Obama addressing Congress. Trump speaks, as footage of Congress, abandoned houses, and Obama grinning as he awkwardly lifts small hand weights rattle by: "Too many mistakes are being made by the politicians! Too many mistakes are being made by people that truly DON'T know what they're doing! We can't have it anymore!" A poorly lit shot of Trump smiling and laughing appears on screen. "We're gonna turn it around!" he continues, as a close-up of a raindrop falls onto a leaf. The music swells; the clouds part; Trump's voice grows more emphatic. "We are gonna become *rich* again! We're gonna become *great* again! We're gonna turn it around *fast!*" he shouts, backdropped by a series of quick cuts: time-lapsed city streets, a cable modem bathed in green light, Trump Tower from street level, more freeways, the milliseconds flying past on a digital clock, and Trump, backlit at a campaign rally, as a young man standing in the audience wears a sweatshirt that reads, in hand-drawn lettering, "KKK Endorses."

"Nobody's gonna tell us what to do, we're not gonna take it," Trump bellows as an American flag flies proud. "I'm working for you folks!" Now there is an astronaut on the moon. "We're gonna win at every. Single. *Level*," he promises, offset by images of more astronauts and a jumbo jet that appears to have been shot in front of a green screen. "We're gonna win so much you're gonna get sick and tired of it!" Jump cut to a shot of Trump scowling as he lumbers away from his helicopter, the rotors still spinning. "And I'm gonna say, I don't care! We're gonna keep winning!" Cuts to a bald eagle's face; fireworks over the Jefferson Memorial; a bald eagle soaring. Back to the American flag. "Because we're gonna make America great again, we're gonna make it greater. Than EVERRR. Before!!!" Shot of a bald eagle in profile; two shots of fireworks; three shots of the Statue of Liberty, each taken at different times of day.

Fade to black. A title card repurposing *Mass Effect 2*'s cyberpunk logo reads "Trump Effect." A quick cut to "Coming Fall 2016." Hillary Clinton appears after the tagline dissolves; she barks like a dog. "BEWARE OF DOG," another title card flashes. A third appears: "The American people are DONE with career politicians." Jump cut to an image collage of racially diverse Trump supporters, racially diverse Trump rallies, and Trump kissing black babies. "GO OUT & Vote For Trump," the final title card reads. "MAKE AMERICA GREAT AGAIN."

Like so many examples featured in this book, "Trump Effect" generates more questions than it answers. It is unclear, first of all, how or when Twitter user @immigrant4trump first encountered "Trump Effect"; perhaps he (at least he presents on Twitter as male) made the video himself, perhaps not. Whether or not the video was "his," a week after he tweeted the video at Trump, Trump retweeted the link, captioned with the message "MAKE AMERICA GREAT AGAIN!" to his millions of followers. Why Trump chose to do so is also a mystery. Maybe he was taken in by the hyper-patriotic message, and was retweeting the video as an affirmative "USA! USA!" fistpump. Maybe he realized that the video was satirical, or realized that it could have been satirical, but also realized that by retweeting it, he would dominate that day's news cycle (which he did). Maybe it wasn't even Trump retweeting, but instead a member of his staff operating under any number of inscrutable motivations.

Regardless of who actually clicked the button, the retweet was an…intriguing…choice, especially given Trump's uneasy symbiosis with white nationalist groups; the video is, after all, explicitly racist in its framing of Mexican immigrants and Black Lives Matter protesters, footage of whom is synced with the proclamation that "humanity is under attack." But even if Trump was using "Trump Effect" to wave hello to America's racists, his apparent endorsement of its underlying message was still confusing, as the video is not – at least to many didn't *seem* to be – resoundingly complimentary. Beyond its apparent hyperbole, beyond its absurdity, is the incongruity of using a megalomaniacal xenophobic videogame villain to endorse a Presidential candidate. Even *Mass Effect* developers were baffled. As noted in an April 4 response tweet by *Mass Effect* developer Manveer Heir, the Illusive Man is "verifiably the bad guy in the game," making Trump's retweet, essentially, an admission of that villainy. At least an affirmation of his imperial ambitions. And so, whether or not "Trump Effect" was a joke, it sure made a lot of people laugh. And then pause, because what in the hell did they just watch?

While "Trump Effect" offers little in the way of concrete certainty, the ambivalence dirt work present in each chapter provides the tools needed to start digging. First, Chapter 1's focus on the overlap between then and now calls attention to the historical continuities and divergences between politics pre- and post-internet. Trump sure seems like a new breed of politician triggering a new form of political discourse, and digital affordances unquestionably amplify his message and overall persona in ways never before possible. But the historical record reveals that, actually, Trump is but one in a long line of populist demagogues dog whistling, or outright shouting from a bullhorn, their racist ideologies. Folkloric dirt work also reveals the hybrid intertwine between vernacular creativity and corporate output, as the "Trump Effect" video stitches together its folkloric narrative using a dramatic musical score, appropriated news footage, and the voiceover of a popular actor ripped from EA Games' intellectual property – ultimately prompting the company to file a copyright claim on the grounds that use of "game assets" for "campaign propaganda" was "#gross" (Orland 2016).

Building on these emphases, Chapter 2's discussion of the interpenetration of online and offline spaces illustrates the video's dizzying mediated ping-pong. "Trump Effect" is a digital video featuring clips of digitally rendered and embodied footage tweeted to and retweeted by an all-too-real Republican Presidential candidate, a story instantly picked up by online, hybrid, and traditional media and subsequently engaged, spread, and debated by participants across social media and the dinner table alike. Further, the chapter's focus on the breakdown between individuals and the collectives they navigate highlights the mask alignment between those who chose to create and further amplify the video, and the audiences these individuals were performing for. Whatever their reasons for doing so, from earnest solidarity to chortling irony, each participant in the "Trump Effect" story was posing for someone else's camera; the *me* predicated on an affectively attuned *us*.

And in so doing, participants were evidencing the dirt work outlined in Chapter 3, which challenges the demarcation between world-building and world-destroying – or at least world-restricting – laughter. No matter who was included in any of the "Trump Effect" play frames, whether progressive rubberneckers or alt-right instigators or white nationalist foot soldiers, a line was drawn between an *us* who laughed and an othered *them*, which could run the gamut from Trump's supporters, Trump himself, Black Lives Matter activists, *Mass Effect* game developers, and who knows who or what else. Where any of these play frames began and ended was unknown and unknowable, resulting in countless indeterminate bites. Maybe some participants were just being silly. Maybe some were sincerely excited about the prospect of a Trump presidency. Maybe some were sincerely horrified that this was even a possibility. Whoever ended up laughing at whom, and whatever kind of laughter this might have been, the social and anti-social, the generative and destructive, were interchangeable.

Building on the constitutive underpinnings of vernacular expression online, Chapter 4's dismantling of the presumed singularity of authors, texts, and meanings underscores the heteroglossic multiplicity of "Trump Effect." The video may have been created by one person, but even in this ostensibly singular act of creation, the creator was channeling a chorus of Trump supporters and detractors, and providing this chorus further materials for further expression. But "Trump Effect" isn't just a remix of a panoply of texts. It's also a remix of a panoply of narrative motifs. More narrowly, the video draws from and celebrates the American cultural imaginary – essentially, the stories about America that Americans tell themselves, from myths of American exceptionalism to myths of America as a shining city on a hill to myths about kickin yer ass when times get tough. More broadly, "Trump Effect" centers on the hero-savior motif. Trump is the last hope for a dying civilization, the video darkly warns. Good (Trump) *must* triumph over evil (Hillary Clinton and the dark Democratic regime of progressive activism), or we're all doomed – in the process echoing every epic ever told, from Gilgamesh to the story of Jesus to the wizarding world of Harry Potter. Countless voices, working in concert and in conflict, across era, across media, are channeled through resonant motifs that persist regardless of whether they're employed to satirize, celebrate, or something in between.

Chapter 5's analysis of the evil, overlapping twins of conflict and unity and affect and rationality constitutes one last site of dirt work. "Trump Effect" evidences each intertwined impulse, representing for each participant, regardless of political orientation, a constitutive *us* to align oneself with, and by extension, a *them* to clash against. This alignment (and clashing) bespeaks connection and affinity and, in many cases, deep aversion – all animating the impulse to participate in public discourse, whether the underlying argument is one of support ("Trump 2016!") or denouncement ("Anyone but Trump 2016!") or even apathy ("It doesn't matter, we're screwed either way!"). There would be no reason to talk, to clash, to rally around a particular cause and rally against those in disagreement, if one didn't feel something strongly first.

All these twists and turns culminate in our final point of ambivalence. Because of the tissues and remixes and modified masks and Poe's Law explosions, we can't know much about "Trump Effect." *And*, we can learn a great deal from "Trump Effect." Not by focusing on the obvious entry points, i.e. the text itself or its creator or what they hoped to accomplish by posting, but how this video – how all the case studies we've explored in this book – complicate so many of our most basic assumptions. For example, that now is not then. That you are not us. That socializing is positive. That texts and authors and meanings have borders. That fighting is the opposite of togetherness, and emotion is the opposite of argument. What "Trump Effect" does, if approached just so, is show that none of these assumptions is as obvious or as clear or even as helpful as we might expect or prefer them to be.

This is not a conclusion that can be reached by starting at the center. This is a conclusion that can only be reached by starting at the margins, with behaviors that don't clearly fit anywhere. Considering why these expressions don't fit, and what strictures are in place to ensure that they can't, teaches us what actually composes that center. And further, how much fracture the center obscures. Through dirt work, ambivalent expression that seems like just a ghost story, just a gorilla meme, just a political remix, is thus revealed to be so much bigger, so much messier, and so much more intertwined with everything else. A jumble that is, appropriately enough, both the ultimate source of and ultimate hindrance to meaningful cultural insight. Ambivalence all the way down. ¯_(ツ)_/¯

Notes

1 While we have chosen not to use the term *trolling* as a behavioral catch-all, the book does assess *subcultural* trolling, the bounded community of self-identifying trolls partaking in established linguistic and behavioral markers. Subcultural trolling coalesced on and around 4chan's /b/ board in the early–mid 2000s, and peaked in pop cultural visibility around 2011 (see Phillips 2015). This subset of trolling has directly influenced many of the participatory behaviors and memetic traditions explored in this book, and thus remains salient as a historical, if not broadly behavioral, touchstone.

2 For many twentieth-century folklorists, any entanglement with the commercial sphere was anathema to "real" folklore. This perspective echoes prominent folklorist Richard M. Dorson's (1976) foundational critique of so-called "fakelore": behaviors, texts, and traditions that emerge from or enter into capitalist culture. And abhorrence of the commercial sphere is hardly the only bone of contention more traditional folklorists might levy against our blithe collapsing of the commercial and the folk. Some might maintain that orality, a longstanding disciplinary criterion for folkloric inclusion, is still paramount, and on those grounds question "fixed" (i.e. written down or archived) online expression. This is to say nothing of those folklorists still resistant to the idea that folklore is even possible on the internet, a group whose ranks have diminished significantly over the years, but whose persistent concerns highlight the fact that folklore, like all academic disciplines, is large and contains multitudes.

3 Our use of scare quotes around "fake" here is to indicate that, regardless of their origins, all profiles are real; the question is whether or not the information a profile contains accurately reflects the embodied identity of the person whose profile it is.

4 The axiom "Poe's Law" traces back to 2005, when a poster on a Christianity forum going by the name of Poe said that,

without an obvious signal of satire or irony, it's impossible to tell an authentic young earth Creationist from a parody of a young earth Creationist.

5 A mid-twentieth-century story out of Loleta, California (not far from where Phillips attended college and later taught at Humboldt State University), evidences this point. In archived notes chronicling Humboldt County place names of Indian origin, linguist Karl Teeter (1958) recounts a story – brought to our attention by Lynnika Butler, Language Program Coordinator of the Humboldt Bay area Wiyot Tribe, whose ancestral lands encompassed Loleta and the surrounding area – of one Mrs. Herrick, a wealthy white woman from what was then known as Swauger Station. She wanted to change the name of the town to its original Indian name, so approached a Wiyot elder and asked him what the town's name was. Instead of answering "Guduwalha't," the actual name of the town, he said "Hash, wiwiduk!" which in colloquial Wiyot translates as "Fuck off, lady!" Like many white people at the time, Mrs. Herrick thought Indian languages were akin to baby talk, and furthermore that Indian people couldn't pronounce their own words properly; presuming the Wiyot elder was a simpleton with a speech impediment, she recorded "wiwiduk" as "liliduk." That she subsequently added an "o" and dropped the "k" is a function, Teeter suspects, of her not listening very carefully to begin with (Butler 2016).

6 Adrienne Massanari introduced us to 2014's Rainbow Tie-Dye Cake Comment Apocalypse during a conversation at the 2015 Association of Internet Researchers Conference. We thank her for sharing the love.

7 #YesAllWomen because, when the male pronoun is used as a stand-in for "human beings," it signals to cis and transgendered women that being female is an aberration from some universal male norm.

8 Thank you to Caroline Sinders for directing Phillips' attention to the various public slights afforded by social media, which she frames as "light emotional abuse."

9 Although, of course, millennials didn't invent sexting. Sexual experimentation online has been prevalent as long as there has been an online to sexually experiment on. By the early 1990s, sex writer Susie Bright (1992) was chronicling the various "computer age erotic technologies" enjoyed by online participants, and "tinysex," text-based sexual play, was common on MUDs ("multiuser dungeons") and MOOs ("multiuser dungeons, object-oriented"), virtual

worlds that flourished throughout the 1990s. Julian Dibbell (1998) provides a particularly detailed account of his own experiences with tinysex in LambdaMOO, a text-based virtual world that became ground zero for conversations about sexual violence in digital spaces.

10 We recognize here that *collective* has different connotations within different scholarly lineages. In particular, scholarship of public discourse (Bennett & Segerberg 2012; Papacharissi 2015) uses *collectivism* to signal the organized, directed actions of members of strongly coherent social groups (labor unions, for instance). We instead employ the term to highlight the fact that all listeners and all hearers of a story are brought into a broad constellation of participants, together responsible for the fate of that story and its constitutive narrative elements. These ties may not be individual and interpersonal enough to merit use of the term *connective*, may not be interdependent enough to merit use of the term *communal*, and may not be goal-oriented enough to merit the use of the term *collaborative*, but they remain fundamentally participatory, and fundamentally social in that participation. Our use of *collective* thus mirrors the *collectivism* outlined by Milner (2016) as central to memetic participation.

11 We drafted this chapter over the course of several months during the 2016 Presidential election, adding updates as needed. The most significant of these updates was also the most last-second; as mentioned in the main text, our final manuscript was due the day after Trump's, let's say, *stunning* victory over Democratic rival Hillary Clinton. We have therefore acknowledged his status as President-Elect, because we had to, but have not engaged with his victory speech or any events subsequent to November 8, 2016. Which is lucky, in a way, as we wouldn't have had time enough to pick our jaws up off the floor.

12 Conspicuously missing from NERC's published list were precisely the kinds of offensive, vulgar, or scatalogical names readers of this book might have come to expect, suggesting that either participants uniformly decided to behave themselves, or that NERC was preemptively selective about what submissions it would allow, and later chose to publicize. Our vote is for the latter, but of course this suspicion can't be proven.

13 "Arlington Cemetery" here refers to Arlington National Cemetery in Arlington County, Virginia – across the Potomac River from Washington DC – where US military personnel killed in conflict have been buried since the American Civil War.

14 See Allegra Kirkland (2016) for a profile of white nationalist Trump supporters, and Stephen Piggott (2016) for a discussion of Trump's ongoing problem with love from hate groups.

15 This quote is often misattributed to the French Enlightenment philosopher Voltaire, whose political philosophies Hall was herself summarizing.

References

"50 Shades of Bic" (2012). Awesome, but... *Amazon Product Review Page*, September 11. www.amazon.com/review/R2XS62A35EFRBA.

Allen, Danielle S. (2004). *Talking to Strangers: Anxieties of Citizenship since Brown v. Board of Education*. The University of Chicago Press, Chicago.

"Amazon Customer" (2008). Dual function design. *Amazon Product Review Page*, November 10. www.amazon.com/review/R2 XKMDXZHQ26YX.

Applebome, Peter (2009). Think a t-shirt can't change your life? A skeptic thinks again. *The New York Times*, May 24. www.nytimes .com/2009/05/25/nyregion/25towns.html.

Apte, Mahadev (1985). *Humor and Laughter: An Anthropological Approach*. Cornell University Press, Ithaca, NY.

Arendt, Hannah (1963). *Eichmann in Jerusalem: A Report on the Banality of Evil*. Penguin Books, New York.

Arthur, Kate (2014). The Bill Cosby #CosbyMeme hashtag backfired immediately. *BuzzFeed*, November 10. https://www.buzzfeed.com/ kateaurthur/the-bill-cosby-cosbymeme-hashtag-backfired-immediately?utm_term=.guwrE2Kom#.qunDv5ewR.

Asen, Robert and Brouwer, Daniel C. (2001). Introduction: Reconfigurations of the public sphere. In Robert Asen and Daniel C. Brouwer (eds.) *Counterpublics and the State*. SUNY Press, Albany, NY. 1–32.

Baker, Richard A. (2006). *200 Notable Days: Senate Stories, 1787 to 2002*. Senate Historical Office, Washington, DC.

Bakhtin, Mikhail M. ([1935] 1981). Discourse in the novel. In Michael Holquist (ed.) *The Dialogic Imagination: Four Essays*. University of Texas Press, Austin, TX. 259–422.

"Banana Slicer Reviews" (2015). *Know Your Meme*, November 10. http:// knowyourmeme.com/memes/banana-slicer-reviews.

Barthes, Roland (1977). *Image, Music, Text*. Hill and Wang, New York.

Basso, Keith H. and Hymes, Dell (1979). *Portraits of "The Whiteman": Linguistic Play and Cultural Symbols among the Western Apache*. Cambridge University Press, Cambridge.

Bateson, Gregory (1972). *Steps to an Ecology of Mind*. University of Chicago Press, Chicago.

Baym, Nancy K. (1995). The performance of humor in computer-mediated communication. *Journal of Computer-Mediated Communication* 1(2). doi: 10.1111/j.1083-6101.1995.tb00327.x.

Baym, Nancy K. (2015). *Personal Connections in the Digital Age*, 2nd edn. Polity, Cambridge.

BBC News (2016). Fury as Trump mocks Muslim soldier's mother Ghazala Khan, July 31. www.bbc.com/news/election-us-2016-36935175.

Bennett, W. Lance and Segerberg, Alexandra (2012). The logic of connective action: Digital media and the personalization of contentious politics. *Information, Communication & Society* 5(15), 739–68.

Blank, Trevor J. (2009). Introduction. In Trevor Blank (ed.) *Folklore and the Internet: Vernacular Expression in a Digital World*. Utah State University Press, Logan, UT. 1–20.

Blank, Trevor J. (2013). *The Last Laugh: Folk Humor, Celebrity Culture, and Mass-Mediated Disasters in the Digital Age*. The University of Wisconsin Press, Madison, WI.

Bogost, Ian (2016). Things you can't talk about in a Coca-Cola ad. *The Atlantic*, January 28. www.theatlantic.com/technology/archive/2016/01/things-you-cant-talk-about-in-a-coca-cola-ad/431628.

Bokhari, Allum (2015). The media is wrong, white student unions are not "hoaxes" created by racists. *Breitbart*, November 24. www.breitbart.com/tech/2015/11/24/exclusive-the-media-is-wrong-white-student-unions-are-not-hoaxes-created-by-racists.

Bokhari, Allum and Yiannopoulos, Milo (2016). An establishment conservative's guide to the alt-right. *Breitbart*, March 29. www.breitbart.com/tech/2016/03/29/an-establishment-conservatives-guide-to-the-alt-right.

boyd, danah (2014). *It's Complicated: The Social Lives of Networked Teens*. Yale University Press, New Haven, CT.

Bright, Susie (1992). *Susie Bright's Sexual Reality: A Virtual Sex World Reader*. Cleis Press, Berkeley, CA.

Broderick, Ryan (2012). A guide to the dark world of James Holmes internet fandom. *BuzzFeed*, July 31. www.buzzfeed.com/ryanhatesthis/a-guide-to-the-dark-world-of-the-james-holmes-inte#.ctQdXWXMx.

Brunvand, Jan Harold (1981). *The Vanishing Hitchhiker: Urban Legends and Their Meanings*. W.W. Norton & Company, New York.

Brunvand, Jan Harold (2001). *Encyclopedia of Urban Legends*. W.W. Norton & Company, New York.

Burgess, Jean (2007). Vernacular creativity and new media. Ph.D. dissertation: Queensland University of Technology. Brisbane, Queensland, Australia.

Burke, Timothy and Dickey, Jack (2013). Manti Te'o's dead girlfriend, the most heartbreaking and inspirational story of the college football season, is a hoax. *Deadspin*, January 16. http://deadspin .com/manti-teos-dead-girlfriend-the-most-heartbreaking-an -5976517.

Burneko, Albert (2014). Rainbow-cake recipe inspires comment apocalypse. *Deadspin*, June 18. http://theconcourse.deadspin.com/ rainbow-cake-recipe-inspires-comment-apocalypse-1592575661.

Burroughs, William (1963). The cut up method. In Leroi Jones (ed.) *The Moderns: An Anthology of New Writing in America*. Corinth Books, New York. 345–9.

Butler, Lynnika (2016). Interviewed by Whitney Phillips via Skype, April 22.

Carvin, Andy (2010). "Bed Intruder" meme: A perfect storm of race, music, comedy, and celebrity. *NPR*, August 5. www.npr.org/ sections/alltechconsidered/2010/08/05/129005122/youtube-bed -intruder-meme.

Cassell, Justine and Cramer, Meg (2008). High tech or high risk: Moral panics about girls online. In Tara McPherson (ed.) *Digital Youth, Innovation and the Unexpected*. The MIT Press, Cambridge, MA. 53–76.

Chappell, Bill (2016). Boaty by another name: "Sir David Attenborough" is chosen for British research ship. *NPR*, May 6. www.npr.org/ sections/thetwo-way/2016/05/06/477010650/boaty-by-another -name-sir-david-attenborough-is-chosen-for-british-research-ship.

Chayka, Kyle. (2014). The life and times of ¯_(ツ)_/¯. *The Awl*, May 20. https://theawl.com/the-life-and-times-of-%E3%83%84- 39697541e6ac#.m27vlxbs8.

Chess, Shira and Newsom, Eric (2014). *Folklore, Horror Stories, and the Slender Man: The Development of an Internet Mythology*. Palgrave, New York.

Citron, Danielle (2014). *Hate Crimes in Cyberspace*. Harvard University Press, Cambridge, MA.

Coleman, E. Gabriella (2013). *Coding Freedom: The Ethics and Aesthetics of Hacking*. Princeton University Press, Princeton, NJ.

Coleman, E. Gabriella (2014). *Hacker, Hoaxer, Whistleblower, Spy: The Many Faces of Anonymous*. Verso Press, London.

Cosco, Joey (2016). Just about every Chris Christie Vine gag. *Digg*, March 2. http://digg.com/2016/chris-christie-vine-roundup.

Crockett, Emily (2016). Why women are calling Indiana's governor to talk about their periods. *Vox*, April 7. www.vox.com/2016/4/7/11384324/women-calling-indiana-governor-periods-abortion-pence.

Crockett, Zachary (2015). How Esurance lost its mascot to the internet. *Priceonomics*, December 18. http://priceonomics.com/how-esurance-lost-its-mascot-to-the-internet.

Crockett, Zachary. (2016). What I learned by analyzing 7 months of Donald Trump's tweets. *Vox*, May 16. www.vox.com/2016/5/16/11603854/donald-trump-twitter.

Curtis, Pavel (1997). Mudding: social phenomena in text-based virtual realities. In Sara Kiesler (ed.) *Culture of the Internet*. Erlbaum, Mahwah, NJ. 121–42.

Dağtas, Mahiye Seçil (2016). "Down with some things!": The politics of humor and humor as politics in Turkey's Gezi protests. *Etnofoor* 28(1), 11–34.

Dahlgren, Peter (2013). Tracking the civic subject in the media landscape: Versions of the democratic ideal. *Television & New Media* 14(1), 71–88.

Dawkins, Richard (1976). *The Selfish Gene*. Oxford University Press, Oxford.

Davies, Christie (2008). Undertaking the comparative study of humor. In Victor Raskin (ed.) *Humor Research*. Mouton de Gruyter, Berlin. 157–82.

DelReal, Jose A. (2016). Trump mocks sexual assault accuser: "She would not be my first choice." *The Washington Post*, October 14. https://www.washingtonpost.com/news/post-politics/wp/2016/10/14/trump-mocks-sexual-assault-accuser-she-would-not-be-my-first-choice.

Dibbell, Julian (1998). *My Tiny Life: Crime and Passion in a Virtual World*. Henry Holt, New York.

Doctorow, Cory (2016). Petition: David Attenborough to change his name to "Boaty McBoatface." *BoingBoing*, May 7. http://boingboing.net/2016/05/07/petition-david-attenborough-t.html.

Donath, Judith (1999). Identity and deception in the virtual world. In Mark A. Smith and Peter Kollock (eds.) *Communities in Cyberspace*. Routledge, New York. 29–60.

Dorson, Richard M. (1976). *Folklore and Fakelore: Essays toward a Discipline of Folk Studies*. Harvard University Press, Cambridge, MA.

Douglas, Mary (1966). *Purity and Danger: An Analysis of the Concepts of Pollution and Taboo*. Routledge, New York.

Douglas, Nick (2014). It's supposed to look like shit: The internet ugly aesthetic. *Journal of Visual Culture* 13(3), 314–39.

Dundes, Alan (1965). Here I sit: A study of American latrinalia. *Kroeber Anthropological Society Papers* 34, 91–105.

Dundes, Alan (1971). On the psychology of legend. In Wayland Hand (ed.) *American Folk Legend: A Symposium.* University of California Press, Berkeley and Los Angeles. 26–9.

Dundes, Alan (1980). *Interpreting Folklore.* Indiana University Press, Bloomington, IN.

Dundes, Alan (1987). *Cracking Jokes: Studies of Sick Humor Cycles and Stereotypes.* Ten Speed Press, Berkeley, CA.

Dundes, Alan and Linke, Uli (1987). Postscript: More Auschwitz Jokes. In *Cracking Jokes: Studies of Sick Humor Cycles and Stereotypes.* Ten Speed Press, Berkeley, CA. 29–40.

Dundes, Alan and Pagter, Carl R. (1975). *Work Hard and You Shall Be Rewarded: Urban Folklore from the Paperwork Empire.* Wayne State University Press, Detroit, MI.

Easton, Nina (2015). The history of Donald Trump's insults to women. *Fortune*, August 9. http://fortune.com/2015/08/09/trump-insult-women-history.

Ellis, Bill (2003). Making a big apple crumble: The role of humor in constructing a global response to disaster. In Peter Narváez (ed.) *Of Corpse: Death and Humor in Folklore and Popular Culture.* Utah State University Press, Logan, UT. 35–79.

"Fake Customer Reviews" (2015). *Know Your Meme*, November 10. http://knowyourmeme.com/memes/fake-customer-reviews.

Flavia (2012). Meet the 17-year-old girl who runs a fan site for European mass murderer Anders Breivik. *XOJane*, April 20. www.xojane.com/issues/Anders-Breivik-European-Resistance-fan-tumblr.

Fox, William S. (1983). Computerized creation and diffusion of folkloric materials. *Folklore Forum* 16(1), 5–20.

Fraser, Nancy (1993). Rethinking the public sphere: A contribution to the critique of actually existing democracy. In Craig Calhoun (ed.) *Habermas and the Public Sphere.* The MIT Press, Cambridge, MA. 109–142.

Friedersdorf, Conor (2015). The new intolerance of student activism. *The Atlantic*, November 9. www.theatlantic.com/politics/archive/2015/11/the-new-intolerance-of-student-activism-at-yale/414810.

"Garlic Bread" (2016). *Know Your Meme*, June 8. http://knowyourmeme.com/memes/garlic-bread.

Gaver, William W. (1991). Technology affordances. In *CHI '91 Proceedings of the SIGCHI Conference on Human Factors in Computing Systems*, 79–84. http://dl.acm.org/citation.cfm?id=108856.

Gilbert, Sophie (2014). Robin Thicke's *Paula* is one of the creepiest albums ever made. *The Atlantic*, July 2. www.theatlantic.com/entertainment/archive/2014/07/robin-thickes-terrifying-new-album/373794.

Goffman, Erving (1959). *The Presentation of Self in Everyday Life*. Doubleday, New York.

Goldberg, Michelle (2016). How the "Hipster Nazis" of the Alt Right got big enough for Hillary Clinton to denounce them. *Slate*, August 25. www.slate.com/articles/news_and_politics/politics/2016/08/why_hillary_clinton_is_talking_about_donald_trump_and_the_alt_right.html.

Gordon, Mclean (2012). You're as evil as your social network. *Motherboard*, December 11. http://motherboard.vice.com/blog/you-are-as-evil-as-your-social-network-alexander-haslam-on-what-the-prison-experiment-got-wrong.

Graham, Todd and Wright, Scott (2014). Discursive equality and everyday talk online: The impact of "superparticipants." *Journal of Computer-Mediated Communication* 19(3), 625–42.

Gray, Mary (2009). *Out in the Country: Youth, Media, and Queer Visibility in Rural America*. NYU Press, New York.

Greenhill, Pauline, and Matrix, Sidney Eve (2010). *Fairy Tale Films: Visions of Ambiguity*. Utah State University, Logan, UT.

GuyGoald (2016). The garlic awakens. *Imgur*, April 12. http://imgur.com/gallery/hjfv6#kIfJSWO.

Hall, Evelyn Beatrice (1906). *The Friends of Voltaire*. Smith, Elder and Company, London.

Haney, Craig, Banks, Curtis and Zimbardo, Philip (1973). A study of prisoners and guards in a simulated prison. *Naval Research Review*, 1–17.

Harrison, Lily (2014). *Fox & Friends'* #OverIt2014 Twitter chat completely backfires – see some of the best reactions! *E! News*, December 31. www.eonline.com/news/610370/fox-friends-overit2014-twitter-chat-completely-backfires-see-some-of-the-best-reactions.

Haslam, Alex and Reicher, Stephen (2012). Contesting the "nature" of conformity: What Milgram and Zimbardo's studies really show. *PLoS Biology* 10(11). http://dx.doi.org/10.1371/journal.pbio.1001426.

Helmy, Mohamed M. and Frerichs, Sabine (2013). Stripping the boss: The powerful role of humor in the Egyptian Revolution 2011. *Integrative Psychological and Behavioral Science* 47(4), 450–81.

Heritage, Stuart (2016). Boaty McBoatface: Tyrants have crushed the people's will. *The Guardian*, April 19. www.theguardian.com/commentisfree/2016/apr/19/boaty-mcboatface-tyrants-have-crushed-the-peoples-will.

Highfield, Tim (2015). Tweeted joke life spans and appropriated punch lines: Practices around topical humor on social media. *International Journal of Communication* 9, 2713–34.

Highfield, Tim (2016). *Social Media and Everyday Politics*. Polity Press, Cambridge.

House of Qwesi (2009). A viewer's guide to *The Room. The AV Club*, March 11. www.avclub.com/article/a-viewers-guide-to-the-room-25721.

Howard, Robert Glenn (2008). The vernacular web of participatory media. *Critical Studies of Media Communication* 25(5), 490–513.

Hubler, Mike and Bell, Diana (2003). Computer-mediated humor and ethos: Exploring threads of constitutive humor in online communities." *Computers and Composition* 20(3), 277–82.

@immigrant4trump (2016). Trump effect: go out and vote for Trump. *Twitter*, March 30. https://twitter.com/immigrant4trump/status/715428456759033856.

Jackson, Sarah J. and Foucault Welles, Brooke (2015). Hijacking #myNYPD: Social media, dissent, and networked counterpublics. *Journal of Communication* 65(6), 932–52.

Jefferson, Whitney (2013). Robin Thicke throws Miley under the bus in interview with Oprah. *BuzzFeed*, October 11. www.buzzfeed.com/whitneyjefferson/robin-thicke-blames-miley-for-vma-controversy-in-interview-w#.eoBDlRlBW.

Jenkins, Henry (2006). *Convergence Culture: Where Old and New Media Collide*. New York University Press, New York.

Jenkins, Henry (2009). What happened before YouTube. In Jean Burgess and Joshua Green (eds.) *YouTube: Online Video and Participatory Culture*. Polity, New York. 109–26.

Kaleem, Jaweed (2016). "Black lives matter!" chants erupt as Mothers of the Movement take the stage at the DNC. *The Los Angeles Times*, July 26. www.latimes.com/politics/la-na-dnc-mothers-of-the-movement-20160726-snap-story.html.

Kelty, Chris (2008). *Two Bits: The Cultural Significance of Free Software*. Duke University Press, Durham, NC.

Kendall, Lori (2002). *Hanging Out in the Virtual Pub: Masculinities and Relationships Online*. University of California Press, Berkeley, CA.

Keohane, Joe (2016). The cry-bully: The sad mind and evil media genius behind @realDonaldTrump. *Politico*, May/June. www.politico.com/magazine/story/2016/04/2016-donald-trump-politics-campaign-twitter-social-media-213827.

King, Darryn (2015). Ermahgerddon: The untold story of the Ermahgerd Girl. *Vanity Fair*, October 15. www.vanityfair.com/culture/2015/10/ermahgerd-girl-true-story.

Kirkland, Allegra (2016). Great white hope: Trump unites generations of white nationalists. *Talking Points Memo*, May 24. http://talkingpointsmemo.com/muckraker/trump-american -renaissance-2016-conference.

Koebler, Jason (2016). Leslie Jones and the ethics of amplifying online harassment. *Motherboard*, August 26. http://motherboard.vice.com/ read/leslie-jones-hack-the-ethics-of-amplifying-online-harassment.

Kolko, Beth E., Nakamura, Lisa and Rodman, Gilbert E. (2000). Race in cyberspace: An introduction. In Beth E. Kolko, Lisa Nakamura, and Gilbert E. Rodman (eds.) *Race in Cyberspace*. Routledge, New York. 1–14.

Krahulik, Mike and Holkins, Jerry (2004). Green blackboards (and other anomalies). *Penny Arcade*. https://www.penny-arcade.com /comic/2004/03/19/green-blackboards-and-other-anomalies.

Krieg, Gregory (2016). Donald Trump defends the size of his penis. *CNN*, March 4. www.cnn.com/2016/03/03/politics/donald-trump -small-hands-marco-rubio.

Kuipers, Giselinde (2005). "Where was King Kong when we needed him?" Public discourse, digital disaster jokes, and the functions of laughter after 9/11. *The Journal of American Culture* 28(1), 7–84.

Kuipers, Giselinde (2015). *Good Humor, Bad Taste: A Sociology of the Joke*. Mouton De Gruyter, Berlin.

"Kumamon" (2016). *Know Your Meme*, March 22. http://knowyourmeme .com/memes/kumamon.

Lapowsky, Issie (2015a). Yep, #Asktrump backfired. *Wired*, September 21. www.wired.com/2015/09/asktrump-backfire.

Lapowsky, Issie (2015b). Jeb Bush's new campaign hashtag is backfiring big time. *Wired*, November 2. www.wired.com/2015/11/ bushs-new-campaign-hashtag-is-backfiring-big-time.

Lethem, Jonathan (2008). The ecstasy of influence: A plagiarism mosaic. In Paul D. Miller (ed.) *Sound Unbound: Sampling Digital Music and Culture*. The MIT Press, Cambridge, MA. 25–51.

Lewis, Jen and Zarrell, Rachel (2016). I photoshopped Kanye kissing himself and a famous artist reportedly made $100,000 off it. *BuzzFeed*, April 18. https://www.buzzfeed.com/jenlewis/ the-life-of-kanye-kissing-kanye.

Limer, Eric (2013). 11 of the weirdest sites on the internet. *Gizmodo*, October 9. http://gizmodo.com/11-of-the-weirdest-sites-on-the -internet-1442601946.

Lopez, German (2016). There are huge racial disparities in how US police use force. *Vox*, August 26. www.vox.com/cards/police-brutality-shootings-us/us-police-racism.

Manovich, Lev (2001). *The Language of New Media*. The MIT Press, Cambridge, MA.

Mansbridge, Jane J. (1983). *Beyond Adversary Democracy*. University of Chicago Press, Chicago.

Marwick, Alice E. and boyd, danah (2010). I tweet honestly, I tweet passionately: Twitter users, context collapse, and the imagined audience. *New Media and Society* 13(1), 114–33.

Marx, Karl (1867). *Capital*. Penguin, New York.

Massanari, Adrienne L. (2015). *Participatory Culture, Community, and Play: Learning from Reddit*. Peter Lang, Bern.

Matthews, Dylan (2016). The alt-right is more than warmed-over white supremacy. It's that, but way way weirder. *Vox*, August 25. www.vox.com/2016/4/18/11434098/alt-right-explained.

McCormick, Rich (2014). Hack leaks hundreds of nude celebrity photos. *The Verge*, September 1. www.theverge.com/2014/9/1/6092089/nude-celebrity-hack.

McCulloch, Richard (2011). "Most people bring their own spoons": *The Room*'s participatory audiences as comedy mediators. *Participations* 8(2), 189–218.

McIntosh, Jonathan (2012). A history of subversive remix video before YouTube: Thirty political video mashups made between World War II and 2005. *Transformative Works and Cultures* 9. doi:10.3983/twc.2012.0371.

McPherson, James M. 2003. *The Illustrated Battle Cry of Freedom: The Civil War Era*. Oxford University Press, Oxford.

Mikkelson, David (2008). You've got to be kidneying. *Snopes*, March 12. www.snopes.com/horrors/robbery/kidney.asp.

Milgram, Stanley (1963). Behavioral study of obedience. *Journal of Abnormal Social Psychology* 67(4), 371–8.

Milioni, Dimitra L. (2009). Probing the online counterpublic sphere: The case of Indymedia Athens. *Media, Culture & Society* 31(3), 409–31.

Mill, John Stuart ([1859] 2009). On liberty. In Stefan Collini (ed.) *J. S. Mill: On Liberty and Other Writings*. Cambridge University Press, Cambridge. 1–115.

Milner, Ryan M. (2016). *The World Made Meme: Public Conversations and Participatory Media*. The MIT Press, Cambridge, MA.

Mizuiro, Metkuratsu (2013). SLENDER MAN visits the Krusty Krab. *YouTube*, October 19. https://www.youtube.com/watch?v=kxiuaqDjOLw.

Morreall, John (1989). Enjoying incongruity. *Humor* 2(1), 1–18.

Morris, Meaghan ([1988] 2007). Banality in cultural studies. In Simon During (ed.) *The Cultural Studies Reader*, 3rd edn. Routledge, London. 119–44.

Mouffe, Chantal (2005). *On the Political*. Routledge, London.

Narváez, Peter (2003). Tricks and fun: Subversive pleasures at Newfoundland wakes. In Peter Narváez (ed.) *Of Corpse: Death and Humor in Folklore and Popular Culture*. Utah State University Press, Logan, UT. 113–40.

Natesw (2014). My dead girlfriend keeps messaging me on Facebook. *Reddit*, July 1. https://www.reddit.com/r/nosleep/comments/29kdıx/my_dead_girlfriend_keeps_messaging_me_on_facebook.

Newman, Jason (2010). *The Room* viewing guides for newbies: How to watch the worst movie ever made. *Movie Fone*, December 9. http://news.moviefone.com/2010/12/09/the-room-movie-schedule-viewing-guide.

Nissenbaum, Asaf and Shifman, Limor (2015). Internet memes as contested cultural capital: The case of 4chan's /b/ board. *New Media and Society*. doi:10.1177/1461444815609313.

"NYC Cardstand Earthcam Trolling" (2016). *Know Your Meme*, March 23. http://knowyourmeme.com/memes/events/nyc-cardstand-earthcam-trolling-i-ll-be-there-in-30-minutes.

O'Connor, Brendan (2015). Who's behind the fake "Union of White NYU Students?" *Gawker*, November 23. http://gawker.com/who-s-behind-the-fake-union-of-white-nyu-students-1744300282.

Oring, Elliot (1987). Jokes and the discourse on disaster. *The Journal of American Folklore* 100(397), 276–86.

Oring, Elliott (1992). *Jokes and Their Relations*. The University Press of Kentucky, Lexington, KY.

Oring, Elliott (2003). *Engaging Humor*. University of Chicago Press, Chicago.

Oring, Elliot (2008). Humor in anthropology and folklore. In Victor Raskin (ed.) *The Primer of Humor Research*. Mouton de Gruyter, Berlin. 183–210.

Orland, Kyle (2016). EA trumps Trump ad, takes down supporter's retweeted Mass Effect video. *Ars Technica*, April 4. http://arstechnica.com/gaming/2016/04/ea-trumps-trump-ad-takes-down-supporters-retweeted-mass-effect-video.

Owens, Trevor (2013). Born digital folklore and the vernacular web: An interview with Robert Glenn Howard. *Digital Preservation*, February 22. http://blogs.loc.gov/digitalpreservation/2013/02/born-digital-folklore-and-the-vernacular-web-an-interview-with-robert-glenn-howard.

Pan, Joann (2012). James Holmes Tumblr "Holmies" shock internet. *Mashable*, July 31. http://mashable.com/2012/07/31/holmies
-tumblr/#k7D96tx7haqJ.

Papacharissi, Zizi (2004). Democracy online: Civility, politeness, and
the democratic potential of online political discussion. *New Media
& Society* 6(2), 259–83.

Papacharissi, Zizi (2010). *A Private Sphere: Democracy in the Digital
Age*. Polity, Malden, MA.

Papacharissi, Zizi (2015). *Affective Publics: Sentiment, Technology, and
Politics*. Oxford University Press, Oxford.

Parkinson, Hannah Jane (2014). What rhymes with disaster? Robin
Thicke trolled hard in Twitter Q&A. *The Guardian*, July 1.
www.theguardian.com/music/2014/jul/01/robin-thicke-trolled-
twitter-qa-misogynist-ask-anything-pr-fail.

Pasternack, Alex (2010). After lawsuits and therapy, *Star Wars* Kid Is
back. *Motherboard*, June 01. http://motherboard.vice.com/blog/
after-lawsuits-and-therapy-star-wars-kid-is-back.

Pearce, Katy, and Hajizada, Adnan (2014). No laughing matter: Humor
as a means of dissent in the digital era: The case of authoritarian
Azerbaijan. *Demokratizatsiya* 22, 67–85.

Penny, Laurie (2014). Laurie Penny on misogynist extremism:
Let's call the Isla Vista killings what they were. *The New
Statesman*, May 25. www.newstatesman.com/lifestyle/2014/05/
lets-call-isla-vista-killings-what-they-were-misogynist-extremism.

Phillips, Whitney (2012). On feeding the Holmies. *Billions and
Billions*, July 31. https://billions-and-billions.com/2012/07/31/on
-feeding-the-holmies.

Phillips, Whitney (2013). So bad it's good: The kuso aesthetic in *Troll
2*. *Transformative Works and Cultures* 14. http://dx.doi.org/10.3983/
twc.2013.0480.

Phillips, Whitney (2015). *This Is Why We Can't Have Nice Things:
Mapping the Relationship between Online Trolling and Mainstream
Culture*. The MIT Press, Cambridge, MA.

Phillips, Whitney and Milner, Ryan M. (2017, forthcoming). Decoding
memes: Barthes' punctum, feminist standpoint theory, and the
political significance of #YesAllWomen. In Steven Harrington
and Tanya Nitins (eds.) *Entertainment Values: How Do We Assess
Entertainment and Why Does it Matter?* Palgrave Macmillan,
London.

Phillips, Whitney and Miltner, Kate (2012). The meme election: click-
tivism, the *BuzzFeed* effect and corporate meme-jacking. *The Awl*,
November 2. www.theawl.com/2012/11/the-meme-election.

Piggott, Stephen (2016). Donald Trump's continuing white nationalist problem. *The Southern Poverty Law Center*, May 11. https://www.splcenter.org/hatewatch/2016/05/11/donald-trump %E2%80%99s-continuing-white-nationalist-problem.

Plunkett, John (2016). David Attenborough says Boaty McBoatface should be sunk. *The Guardian*, April 2. www.theguardian.com/media/2016/ apr/21/david-attenborough-says-boaty-mcboatface-should-be-sunk.

Postmes, Tom and Spears, Russell (1998). Deindividuation and anti-normative behavior: A meta-analysis. *Psychological Bulletin* 123(3), 238–59.

Radner, Joan N. (1993). *Feminist Messages: Coding in Women's Folk Culture*. University of Illinois Press, Chicago.

Rappeport, Alan (2016a). Hillary Clinton denounces the "alt-right," and the alt right is thrilled. *The New York Times*, August 26. http:// www.nytimes.com/2016/08/27/us/politics/alt-right-reaction.

Rappeport, Alan (2016b). Donald Trump threatens to sue the *Times* over an article about unwanted advances. *The New York Times*, October 13. www.nytimes.com/2016/10/14/us/politics/donald-trump-lawsuit-threat.html.

Raskin, Victor (1985). *Semantic Mechanisms of Humor*. D. Reidel, Dordrecht.

Read, Max (2013). #FreeJahar: When conspiracy theorists and One Direction fans collide. *Gawker*, April 25. http://gawker.com/ freejahar-when-conspiracy-theorists-and-one-direction-478152664.

Rico, Andrew Ryan (2015). Fans of Columbine shooters Eric Harris and Dylan Klebold. *Transformative Works and Cultures* 20. http:// dx.doi.org/10.3983/twc.2015.0671.

RoboKy (2012). 12 Minutes. *Creepypasta Wikia*, January 27. http:// creepypasta.wikia.com/wiki/12_Minutes.

Rogers, Katie (2016). The complicated appeal of the Harambe meme. *The New York Times*, August 24. www.nytimes.com/2016/08/25/ us/the-complicated-appeal-of-the-harambe-meme.html.

Rogers, Katie and Bromwich, Jonah Engel (2016). Hackers publish nude pictures on Leslie Jones' website. *The New York Times*, August 24. www.nytimes.com/2016/08/25/movies/leslie-jones-website-hacked.html.

Romano, Raja (2016). The Leslie Jones hack is the flashpoint of the alt-right's escalating culture war. *Vox*, August 26. www.vox .com/2016/8/26/12653474/leslie-jones-hack-alt-right-culture -war.

Ronson, Jon (2015). *So You've Been Publicly Shamed*. Riverhead Books, New York.

Ruiz, Carlos, Domingo, David, Micó, Josep Lluís, et al. (2011). Public sphere 2.0? The democratic qualities of citizen debates in online newspapers. *International Journal of Press/Politics* 16(4), 463–87.

Schulzke, Marcus (2012). Fan action and political participation on *The Colbert Report*. *Transformative Works and Cultures* 10. doi:10.3983/twc.2012.0316.

Schwartz, Alvin (1981). *Scary Stories to Tell in the Dark*. Harper Collins, New York.

Sestero, Greg and Bissell, Tom (2013). *The Disaster Artist: My Life Inside The Room, the Greatest Bad Movie Ever Made*. Simon & Schuster, New York.

Sherman, Erik (2012). How McDonald's Twitter campaign fell into the fire. *CBS News*, January 27. www.cbsnews.com/news/how-mcdonalds-twitter-campaign-fell-into-the-fire/.

Shifman, Limor (2014). *Memes in Digital Culture*. The MIT Prss, Cambridge, MA.

Shirky, Clay (2008). *Here Comes Everybody: The Power of Organizing Without Organizations*. Penguin, New York.

Sicart, Miguel (2014). *Play Matters*. The MIT Press, Cambridge, MA.

Song, Sandra (2016). Arthur memes have officially taken over the internet. *Paper*, July 28. www.papermag.com/arthur-memes-have-officially-taken-over-the-internet-1948503136.html.

Stuart, Tessa (2016). Donald Trump's meanest Twitter insults. *Rolling Stone*, March 10. www.rollingstone.com/politics/news/donald-trumps-favorite-twitter-insults-20160310.

Suler, John (2004). The online disinhibition effect. *CyberPsychology & Behavior* 7(3), 321–6.

Surge, Victor (2009). Original Slenderman post. *Something Awful*, June 25. http://forums.somethingawful.com/showthread.php?threadid=3150591&userid=0&perpage=40&pagenumber=3#post361861415.

Swint, Kerwin (2006). *Mudslingers: The Twenty-Five Dirtiest Political Campaigns of All Time*. Union Square Press, New York.

Swint, Kerwin (2008). The election of 1800: The birth of negative campaigning in the U.S. *MentalFloss*, September 23. http://mentalfloss.com/article/19668/election-1800-birth-negative-campaigning-us.

Tangherlini, Timothy (1998). *Talking Trauma*. University Press of Mississippi, Oxford, MS.

Tannen, Deborah (1989 [2007]). *Talking Voices: Repetition, Dialogue, and Imagery in Conversational Discourse*, 2nd edn. Cambridge University Press, Cambridge.

Taylor, T. L. (2006). *Play Between Worlds: Exploring Online Game Culture*. The MIT Press, Cambridge, MA.

Teeter, Karl (1958). *Notes on Humboldt County, California, Place Names of Indian Origin*. Names 6.55–56.

"The Room Reviews" (2009). Amazon review page. https://www.amazon.com/Room-Tommy-Wiseau/dp/B000CFYAMC.

Toelken, Barre (1996). *The Dynamics of Folklore*. Utah State University Press, Logan, UT.

Tracy, Karen (2010). *Challenges of Ordinary Democracy: A Case Study in Deliberation and Dissent*. The Pennsylvania University Press, University Park, PA.

"Transcript: Donald Trump's taped comments about women" (2016). *The New York Times*, October 8. www.nytimes.com/2016/10/08/us/donald-trump-tape-transcript.html.

"Union of White NYU Students" (2015). *Facebook*. https://www.facebook.com/nyuwhitestudents/info/?tab=page_info.

Uther, Hans-Jörg (2004). *The Types of International Folktales: A Classification and Bibliography*, vols. I–III. Suomalainen Tiedeakatemia, Helsinki.

Van Gelder, Lindsy (1985). The strange case of the electronic lover. *Ms. Magazine*, October 1985. http://lindsyvangelder.com/sites/default/files/Plinkers.org%20-%20Electronic%20Lover.htm_.pdf.

Vitak, Jessica (2012). The impact of context collapse and privacy on social network site disclosures. *Journal of Broadcasting & Electronic Media* 56(4), 451–40.

Wagner, Laura (2016). U.K. Science Minister torpedoes "Boaty McBoatface" as ship name. *NPR*, April 19. www.npr.org/sections/thetwo-way/2016/04/19/474805391/u-k-science-minister-torpedoes-boaty-mcboatface-as-ship-name.

Walker, Peter (2016). RSS Boaty McBoatface leads in poll to name polar research vessel. *The Guardian*, March 20. www.theguardian.com/environment/2016/mar/20/eccentric-choices-surface-in-quest-to-name-polar-research-vessel.

Walther, Joseph B. (1994). Anticipated ongoing interaction versus channel effects on relational communication in computer-mediated interaction. *Human Communication Research* 20(4), 473–501.

Warren, Lydia (2012). "Holmies for life": Shocking pictures reveal sick online fans of *Dark Knight* Massacre gunman James Holmes who wear his favourite clothes. *The Daily Mail*, July 31. www.dailymail.co.uk/news/article-2181721/James-Holmes-fans-The-sick-online-fans-wear-plaid-drink-slurpees-support.html.

Warzel, Charlie (2016). Twitter permanently suspends conservative writer Milo Yiannopoulos. *BuzzFeed*, July 20. https://www.buzzfeed.com/charliewarzel/twitter-just-permanently-suspended-conservative-writer-milo?bftwnews&utm_term=.cf4Je9ynb#.bsB9BmKD8.

Weill, Kelly (2015). Racist trolls are behind NYU's "White Student Union" hoax. *The Daily Beast*, November 23. www.thedailybeast.com/articles/2015/11/23/racist-trolls-are-behind-nyu-s-white-student-union-hoax.html.

Weiss, Sasha (2014). The Power of #YesAllWomen. *The New Yorker*, May 26. www.newyorker.com/culture/culture-desk/the-power-of-yesallwomen.

Wheaton, Wil (2016). fuck you, you stupid goddamn science minister. *Wil WHEATON dot TUMBLR*, April 19. https://wilwheaton.tumblr.com/post/143083686879/kwmurphy-boaty-mcboatface-unsuitable-name-for.

Wittkower, D. E. (2014). Facebook and dramauthentic identity: A post-Goffmanian model of performance on SNS. *First Monday* 19(4). http://firstmonday.org/ojs/index.php/fm/article/view/4858/3875.

Zafar, Aylin (2012). BIC creates pens "for her": Amazon reviewers turn on the snark. *Time*, August 31. http://newsfeed.time.com/2012/08/31/bic-creates-pens-for-her-amazon-reviewers-turn-on-the-snark.

Zeller, Tom (2006). On Amazon, all of a sudden everyone's a milk critic. *The New York Times*, August 9. www.nytimes.com/2006/08/09/technology/09milk.html.

Zuckerman, Ethan (2013). From weird to wide. In *Spreadable Media: Web Exclusive Essays*. http://spreadablemedia.org/essays/zuckerman/#.VVucnxfDEbI.

Index